Y. VARGA

POLITICO-ECONOMIC PROBLEMS OF CAPITALISM

PROGRESS PUBLISHERS ■ MOSCOW

TRANSLATED FROM THE RUSSIAN BY Don. DANEMANIS

CONTENTS

Е. Варга. ОЧЕРКИ ПО ПРОБЛЕМАМ
ПОЛИТЭКОНОМИИ КАПИТАЛИЗМА

На английском языке

First Printing 1968

Printed in the Union of Soviet Socialist Republics

INTRODUCTION

"Communism is not a doctrine, but a *movement*. It proceeds not from principles but from *facts*."[1] This was said by Engels, who passionately fought all attempts to turn the revolutionary teaching of the proletariat into a lifeless dogma. Such attempts were made even when Marxism was only beginning to spread. The latest book by Academician Varga, the outstanding Marxist economist, is written in defence of the "living soul" of Marxism, for it throws light upon the discussions taking place between Soviet scholars who are striving for a deeper understanding of the processes at work in the capitalist countries.

This massive work summarises the author's many years of research and revives some of the problems discussed in the past which are no less relevant today than they were at that time. Furthermore, it poses a number of topical theoretical problems demanding an early solution.

Being a genuine scholar himself, the author declares that genuine science has no ready-made answers to new problems, that it must search and investigate and thus find new solutions. Varga even criticises some of the conclusions he drew in the past and which subsequent events have proved wrong. He also develops some of his earlier views, and attempts to answer many of the burning questions being discussed by economists today. His analysis of the crucial problems of political economy gives much food for thought, criticism and discussion. The book is worth reading for this alone.

---

[1] Marx/Engels, *Werke*, Bd. 4, Berlin, 1959, S. 321.—F. Engels, "Die Kommunisten und Karl Heinzen".

The principal aim of the book is to revive some of the theoretical aspects of political economy that dogmatists and revisionists had succeeded in paralysing. Thoughtless dogmatism which, Varga declares, until recently pervaded the works on capitalist economy and policy, has been dealt a heavy blow. Varga states that the best way of fighting dogmatists is to make "concrete analyses of concrete situations", and gives examples to show how these should be made, how new facts which refuse to fit into the old mould should be evaluated, and what approach should be adopted in the study of modern capitalism's new phenomena.

The book also deals a blow at revisionists who repudiate or attempt to revise Marx's basic theoretical propositions often simply throwing Marxist theory completely overboard. Varga's book shows that only a Marxist-Leninist approach can enable us to understand the processes of social development.

Many foreign readers are already acquainted with Academician Varga's books on political economy and will welcome his major study of the crucial problems of modern capitalism.

The book analyses many problems of state-monopoly capitalism. A scientific analysis of the processes at work in modern capitalism and their correct appraisal are essential for the successful outcome of the struggle waged by the progressive forces against the ideology of monopoly capital. This struggle includes the exposure of revisionism, which now as before is a means by which the hostile classes try to influence the proletariat. It also includes the destruction of dogmas which prevent a creative analysis of concrete historical processes and of changes in the modern world.

The spearhead of the author's attacks is directed against the vulgar dogmatic conception which asserts that under modern capitalism there is a simple and one-sided "subjugation" of the state by monopoly capital. Dogmatists assert that state-monopoly capitalism is not a new phenomenon, that all states intervened in the economy, and that this has been the eternal policy of the bourgeoisie. But they ignore that under modern capitalism, state intervention in the economy has a fundamentally different nature and that capitalist reproduction would be impossible without it.

Revisionists, on the other hand, maintain that increased state intervention in the economy has changed the nature of capitalism itself. They believe that capitalism has stopped being capitalism. This leads them to say that in the process of capitalist society's development the state acquires an independent role, becomes more and more independent of private capital and stands above capital. Arguing against a dogmatic approach to this question, and against its revisionist interpretation, Varga rightly considers state-monopoly capitalism a merger of two forces: the monopolies and the state.

The book refers back to a problem that was widely discussed in the Soviet Union in 1947, namely, whether under monopoly capitalism the state pursues a policy in the interests of the whole bourgeoisie (this point of view was then supported by the author) or exclusively in favour of the monopoly bourgeoisie, the finance oligarchy. Varga considered it necessary to revise some of the ideas he had formerly expressed on this problem. In this book he says that, depending on concrete historical conditions, either of these views may be correct or incorrect. He maintains that in "normal" conditions, i.e., when the capitalist system is not subjected to any real danger, the state is a tool of the monopoly bourgeoisie. But when the existence of the capitalist social system is directly threatened (in what may be called "extraordinary" circumstances) the state defends the interests of the bourgeoisie as a whole.

This point of view, though beautiful in its simplicity, does not answer the following question: how does this metamorphosis take place? The author himself emphasises the "dual" ("ambiguous") manner in which the question is posed, saying that with the aggravation of the general crisis of capitalism the danger to the existence of the capitalist state becomes permanent and that the function of defending the capitalist system becomes increasingly important to the monopoly capitalist state.

Then again, if we accept Varga's views, the contradiction between the monopoly and non-monopoly bourgeoisie should automatically be discounted, whereas in reality it becomes particularly acute in "extraordinary" circumstances, i.e., thereby weakening the positions of monopoly capital. We think that the whole controversy on this question is based on a false premise. State-monopoly capitalism both in "normal" and in "extraordinary" conditions does not change its nature, the state remains the same bourgeois state as before, the whole difference being that it is *dominated* by the monopoly bourgeoisie. In this context we could also say that the state in the imperialist countries is concentrated and organised coercion on the part of the monopoly oligarchy. Those sections of the bourgeoisie which dominate the economy, dominate also politics.

We could overlook the schematic nature in which Varga treats this question, were it not for the fact that an anti-monopoly coalition is forming in the West. This is a bloc of various classes, including the non-monopoly bourgeoisie, which if victorious will bring to an end the economic and political rule of the monopolies.

In spite of these inaccuracies, Varga's essay on state-monopoly capitalism contains a number of very interesting ideas. For example, he writes that there is complete unanimity between the monopoly bourgeoisie on some questions and sharp contradictions on others. Varga demonstrates the main contradiction between the monopoly bourgeoisie's two basic aims—that of safeguarding the capitalist social system and of redistributing the national income, with the assistance of the state, in favour of monopoly capital.

The author also looks into the problem of imperialist contradictions and of wars between imperialist countries. He says that as long as there are imperialist contradictions the danger of inter-imperialist wars cannot be discounted, but that there is little chance that one will be allowed to come to a head. Varga's argument could be supplemented by the following: the Soviet Union's foreign policy aimed at safeguarding international peace ties the hands of the imperialists and prevents the contradictions between them from reaching their logical conclusion, an inter-imperialist war.

In his essay dealing with the national liberation struggle the author rightly concludes that the main problem of the newly free countries is whether to follow the socialist or the capitalist path of development. The difficulties arising from this problem are often interlinked with the foreign political orientation of these countries. But their orientation towards socialism or capitalism is far more important than their foreign political orientation, as most of them retain positive neutrality and do not enter military or political blocs.

Varga criticises the definitions of the basic economic law often found in Marxist economic writings and formulates his own definition of that law (or to be more accurate, two laws—the *basic law of capitalism as a whole* and the *law of imperialism*). This definition of the basic economic law of capitalism briefly describes the essence of the capitalist mode of production and of its imperialist stage. But the reader may well be interested why this description has been called a "basic law".

The reader may also ask whether such a concept as a "basic law of the capitalist, class-antagonistic formation" exists at all, especially since Varga himself says that "basic laws should be rational abstractions which single out the typical features of any given formation and that this singling out is expedient and useful only insofar as it obviates repetitions and no further! Basic economic laws cannot and must not state anything new."

The problem of absolute impoverishment under capitalism was correctly reflected in Marxist writings published after the 20th Congress of the C.P.S.U., and former views have been revised in the light of Marxist-Leninist theory on this problem. Even so, Varga's sharp censure of those who continue to assert that this absolute impoverishment is a continuous process is of great value. It is precisely this type of dogmatism that has inflicted great harm on the international communist movement and has distorted Marxist theory.

The struggle against a vulgar approach to the problem of the absolute impoverishment of the proletariat is of long standing. In 1891 Engels criticised the thesis of the Erfurt Programme of the German Social-Democratic Party, which stated that "the *poverty* of the proletariat is for ever increasing". Engels wrote that "this is wrong in the absolute form in which it has been stated here. The organisation of the workers and their constantly growing resistance will form a certain obstacle to the *growth of poverty*. But what *definitely* does grow is the *insecurity of their existence*."[1]

In reviewing Karl Kautsky's book *Bernstein and the Social-Democratic Programme. A Counter-Critique*, Lenin criticised the "theory of impoverishment". He wrote, "He [Marx—*Ed.*] spoke of the growth of poverty, degradation, etc., indicating at the same time the counteracting tendency and the real social forces that alone could give rise to this tendency."[2]

We agree with Varga that the labour aristocracy, its composition and the sources ensuring its privileged position have changed considerably in the course of capitalist development and especially after the Second World War. The data in the book show that the position of the labour aristocracy is weakening because: 1) the share of skilled workers is decreasing, and 2) the difference in pay is diminishing.

But it is not quite clear whether or not a new labour aristocracy is forming, the privileged section consisting not of highly skilled manual workers but of workers with high technical qualifications. This problem calls for special study. In this book Varga stresses his previous view that the function of the labour aristocracy—to safeguard the capitalist system, to disseminate bourgeois ideology among the working class, to sidetrack the workers from revolutionary activities—is to an ever increasing extent being taken over by the workers' bureaucracy, which, in his opinion, includes the bureaucracy of the Social-Democratic parties, the trade union bureaucracy and the co-operative bureaucracy.

There are many different views among Marxists on the problem of the cyclical course of reproduction after the Second World War. Varga holds the following view: 1) the period of the World War should not be included in the cycle; 2) 1947 should be considered the beginning of the post-war cycle; 3) the first post-war cycle continued to the 1957-58 crisis of overproduction; 4) the second post-war cycle began after that crisis. Varga believes that sooner or later a single cycle will establish itself for capitalism as a

---

[1] Marx/Engels, *Werke*, Bd. 22, Berlin, 1963, S. 231.—F. Engels, "Zur Kritik des sozialdemokratischen Programmentwurfs 1891".
[2] V. I. Lenin, *Collected Works*, Vol. 4, p. 201.

whole and that it will be similar to the post-war cycle in the U.S.A. and Britain, i.e., will be shorter than it was before the Second World War.

Varga is right in warning against an overestimation of the "anti-crisis" measures taken by the capitalist state. But even though the idea of crises-free capitalist reproduction is ridiculous, it is undeniable that state activities can influence the factors determining the intensity and duration of the upward phase and the depth and duration of the crisis phase in future cycles.

Much has been written about the nature of capitalist development since the war. Even though the problem has been widely discussed it still remains on the agenda, especially so because anti-Marxists, in their attempts to "refute" Marxism, try to capitalise on the specific features of the post-war cycle. Varga advances many interesting arguments on the causes of these features and much of what Varga has written about crises will be indispensable to any thorough study of modern capitalism and will focus attention on the question of the nature of reproduction and the movements of the cycle in the modern stage.

The author also touches upon the "eternal" controversial question about the nature of the agrarian crisis in the 20th century. Some economists believe that the agrarian crisis is a cyclical and transient process, others (including Varga) regard it as a chronic process, as part of the general crisis of capitalism. The chapter dealing with the agrarian crisis abounds in exhaustive and convincing arguments and can be rightly considered as one of the most interesting in the book.

The author also analyses the problem of the Common Market although, as he himself admits, he deals with it in an abstract and theoretical manner. His analysis arrives at the following conclusion: "A complete economic union would mean a single currency, a single budget, a single state, i.e., complete political integration, the rejection of all individual sovereignty by the countries in question."

The Common Market crisis bears out Varga's views on the contradictions resulting from this attempt at integration.

The book also clarifies the reason for the popularity of Keynes's theories in bourgeois and Social-Democratic circles. The author believes that Keynes's theories are popular not for their defence of capitalism but for the supraclass pseudo-scientific guise in which he clothes his arguments, and for the feeble criticism of capitalism.

The essay on Keynes is one of the best in the book, but we think that a complete denial of the role played by Keynes in working out recommendations for capitalism, and his view that Keynes has done no more than to place the actual policy of monopoly capitalism on a pseudo-scientific basis, are an oversimplification of the relations now existing between bourgeois policy and bourgeois science.

The book ends with an essay on the Asiatic mode of production. Varga argues in favour of Marx's and Engels's views that an Asiatic mode of production did exist, and objects to the fact that the term "Asiatic mode of production" has disappeared from Marxist literature. This question is interesting today as it is from a purely historical point of view, since it helps uncover the influence exerted by the remnants of that mode on the processes now at work in a number of Eastern countries. His proposal to discuss the problem of the Asiatic mode of production should, therefore, be given serious consideration.

A number of events that have taken place since the appearance of the book necessitate a reappraisal of some theoretical and practical propositions and make some of the views expressed in the book obsolete. Recent events show us things in a new light. We cannot, for example, agree with the author's statement that only broad masses of the petty bourgeoisie in town and country can form the class basis of the U.A.R.

———

Varga's book has achieved wide success in the Soviet Union. Two editions have been sold out in record time and many of his views have become the subject of wide discussion.

Varga's *Politico-Economic Problems of Capitalism* is a major contribution to modern economic thought. Although many of the problems raised in the book are still awaiting a final solution, it is successfully breaking the chains in which dogmatists and revisionists had fettered Soviet economic thought.

V. A. Cheprakov, D. Sc. (Econ.)

This book is intended for readers who wish to make a serious study of problems of Marxist-Leninist political economy of capitalism. It presumes that the reader is familiar with the general theory of Marxism-Leninism.

The essays in this book, upon which I have worked for many years, deal in the majority of cases with controversial issues of Marxism. I hope that they will clarify some of the issues or, at least, give the reader food for thought, criticism and discussion.

The book, written polemically, is directed against thoughtless dogmatism, which until recently was widespread in works on the economy and politics of capitalism.

What, in this case, do I mean by dogmatism?

I mean, first and foremost, a denial of the essence of Marxism—the concrete scientific analysis of historical facts, a denial of what Lenin called the "living soul" of Marxism. Dogmatism substitutes ready conclusions which Marx drew as a result of his studies in definite historical conditions for the Marxist method of research. It also means that dogmatists proceed from the assumption that not only are Marx's general laws governing capitalist development valid to this very day, but that all the facts must be identical to those obtained during Marx's or Lenin's lifetime. From here dogmatists are but a step away from adjusting facts to individual conclusions of Marxism, ignoring new facts which fit badly in their schemes instead of analysing new phenomena typical of modern capitalism. Dogmatists attempt to prove the immutability of all of Marx's propositions using *isolated and untypical facts.* Lenin aptly remarked that considering the complexity of capitalist society it is always possible to find *isolated facts* to prove any theory.

The dogmatist considers himself an "orthodox" Marxist. In reality, however, he is a "Marxist" who, as Marx once jokingly described himself, is "no longer a Marxist".

This book is not directed against revisionism of questions of the political economy of capitalism for there is no open revisionism among us. Repercussions of revisionist ideas are sometimes encountered in a concealed form only among the champions of econometrics.

The term "political economy" is used in this book in its broad sense, that is, without a distinct division between politics and economics. For this reason it sometimes deals not so much with economic as with political problems. This is in keeping with the spirit of Lenin's works who, as we know, characterised politics as "a concentrated expression of economics".

The problems of the political economy of capitalism demanding a new critical study are given no exhaustive discussion in this book. A whole series of other problems could be pointed out, for example, the problem of the strategy of the proletarian revolution in the highly developed capitalist countries, the need for detailed Marxist analysis and criticism of econometrics, the definition of the extent to which mathematics can be applied to a research of the anarchically developing capitalist mode of production, the problem of whether the reasoning and behaviour of the individual is decided only by his social being or also by other factors (biological, genetic, etc.). In other words, whether Marx's theory of the dependence of human consciousness on social being refers to classes or to every individual.

Unfortunately, it is beyond my powers to attempt to analyse these problems too. I hope that this will be undertaken by younger scholars.

In conclusion I wish to express my gratitude to E. L. Khmelnitskaya who read the manuscript and offered valuable suggestions and also to S. A. Drabkina for her assistance in preparing the Russian edition of the book.

Y. Varga

Moscow, 1963

MARXISM AND THE PROBLEM
OF THE BASIC ECONOMIC LAW
OF CAPITALISM

Ever since the publication of Stalin's *Economic Problems of Socialism in the U.S.S.R.*, the term *basic economic law* has been extensively used in Soviet economic writings and textbooks. Recently, however, it has been debated whether this term should be abolished. In this essay we shall try to determine the role of the basic economic law in Marxism and in this connection we shall remind the reader of Marxist views on laws in general, and on the difference between natural and social laws in particular.

What is a law?

We find no definition of this concept in Marx's writings. Unlike the bourgeois economists, he preferred to analyse concrete facts and establish laws on the basis of his analysis.

Engels rightly declared that laws are a reflection of the objective processes at work in nature and society. This recognition of the objective nature of laws sharply distinguishes dialectical materialism from idealistic systems which generally proceed from the assumption that laws are only hypotheses invented by scientists to bring a semblance of order into the chaotic processes of nature, and to make it easier for man to comprehend them. "The fact that our subjective thought and the objective world are subject to the same laws, and hence, too, that in the final analysis they cannot contradict each other in their results, but must coincide, governs absolutely our whole theoretical thought. It is the unconscious and unconditional premise for theoretical thought."[1] Laws are objective because they reflect real processes and therefore: 1) exist independently of the *will* of people, 2) exist no matter whether they are *understood* by people or not. The first part of this proposition is common knowledge, the second has received little attention. It is quite obvious that natural laws existed before they were discovered by man and that many natural laws now operating have not yet been discovered,[2] otherwise there would be no progress in the natural sciences.

Great bourgeois natural scientists have always rejected idealism and pragmatism. Max Planck, although a conservative and religious person, said in his *Wissenschaftliche Selbstbiographie* (Scientific Autobiography) that "the external world is not dependent on us, it is a thing absolute in itself, a thing we must face, and the discovery of the laws governing this absolute has always seemed to me the most wonderful task in a scientist's life".[3] Albert Einstein supported this view when he said: "The belief in an external world independent of the perceiving subject is the basis of all natural science."[4]

Economic laws are similarly independent of whether they are understood by people or not. The laws of the appropriation of surplus value, its transformation into profit, into entrepreneur's income, interest and rent, existed long before they were studied and formulated by Marx.

Engels added two important qualifications to his initial definition of law as a reflection of the objective processes in nature and society:

a) only a reflection of the processes at work in the intrinsic essence of things can become a law;

b) a mere reflection of *individual* processes is not a law; only an *adequate* reflection of *regularly recurring* processes in nature and society becomes a law.

A law is not the reflection of a movement per se, but of the essence of a process at work in nature and society.

---

[1] Engels, *Dialectics of Nature*, Moscow, 1966, p. 266.

[2] This was understood by Bernard Bolzano (1781-1848), who called undiscovered laws "truths in themselves".

[3] Max Planck, *Wissenschaftliche Selbstbiographie*, Leipzig, 1948, S. 7.

[4] Albert Einstein, *Ideas and Opinions*, New York, 1954, p. 266.

This is a very important point. The phenomenon and its essence coincide neither in nature nor in capitalist society.[1] Marx said: "It is a work of science to resolve the visible, merely external movement into the true intrinsic movement. . . ."[2]

If the form of phenomena and their essence always coincided, Marx said, there would be no need for science. We see the sun rise and set every day, but in reality it is the Earth that revolves around its own axis. It might seem that the worker exists thanks to the capitalist who provides him with "his daily bread". But in reality the capitalist exists thanks to the workers and their surplus labour. It is the appropriation of this surplus value that makes the capitalist.

Laws are, therefore, based on processes reflecting the essence of nature and society.

Though laws reflect real processes they are not simple mechanical copies of these processes. Laws are not based on single processes but only on those recurring regularly under identical conditions. A great deal of mental effort is needed to formulate a law: it calls for the analysis of a multitude of processes, for the rejection of the incidental and the singular and for the abstraction of the primary from the secondary.

Engels says: "The form of development of natural science, in so far as it thinks, is the *hypothesis*. A new fact is observed which makes impossible the previous method of explaining the facts belonging to the same group. From this moment onwards new methods of explanation are required—at first based on only a limited number of facts and observations. Further observational material weeds out these hypotheses, doing away with some and correcting others, until finally the law is established in a pure form. If one should wait until the material for a law was *in a pure form*, it would mean suspending the process of thought

---

[1] In the ancient world based on slave labour, and also in feudal society, exploitation was obvious and *the phenomenon and its essence coincided*. Only in exceptional cases when commodities were produced for the market was there a certain deviation of the actual from the obvious. This makes the political economy of those formations differ radically from that of capitalism.

[2] Karl Marx, *Capital*, Vol. III, Moscow, 1966, p. 313.

in investigation until then and, if only for this reason, the law would never come into being."[1]

In political economy, as distinct from the natural sciences, hypotheses play only a minor role. It is only in exceptional cases that new facts emerging within the same mode of production cannot be explained by former methods. The transition of capitalism from the stage of free competition to imperialism, for example, introduced changes which *modified* the economic laws of that system.

The same could be said of the general crisis of capitalism.

No hypotheses are needed to discover modifications to capitalist laws. (It is only in the comparatively narrow field concerned with the study of the cyclical movement of capitalist reproduction that hypotheses are required.) The facts of the capitalist economy are known, it is up to science to single out its essential, general manifestations, i.e., its laws. Under capitalism, for example, millions of business transactions take place every day. Money changes hands incessantly. The laws of money circulation, discovered by Marx, reflect the recurring essence of every single transaction, the thing typical of all individual purchases and sales.

Various natural and social laws have different spheres of operation. There is a sort of hierarchical division of laws, depending on how general is their nature and on how large are the natural and social spheres they embrace. *Most general are the basic laws of dialectics.*

Engels wrote: "It is, therefore, from the history of nature and human society that the laws of dialectics are abstracted. For they are nothing but the most general laws of these two aspects of historical development, as well as of thought itself. And indeed they can be reduced in the main to three:

"The law of the transformation of quantity into quality and vice versa;

"The law of the interpenetration of opposites;

"The law of the negation of the negation."[2]

In this connection it is necessary to speak of the vague-

---

[1] Engels, *Dialectics of Nature*, Moscow, 1966, p. 240.
[2] Ibid., p. 62.

ness in which the dialectical method has been described in Stalin's *On Dialectical and Historical Materialism*.

The classics of Marxism have always proceeded from the assumption that our subjective reasoning and the objective world are governed by identical dialectical laws. We are able to reason dialectically only because we are part of an objective dialectical world. We apprehend, comprehend and reflect that world. This explains why the rudiments of dialectics are contained in the works of the ancient philosophers (i.e., Heraclitus), and dialectics (although not materialistic) in the works of Georg Wilhelm Hegel and even some of the prominent contemporary natural scientists who are self-declared opponents of Marxism. The dialectics of nature force them to reason dialectically.

The discovery of dialectical materialism by the founders of Marxism evolved a system of reasoning which greatly advanced natural and notably social studies. However, in this context, it should be remembered that the dialectical approach to natural and social studies is correct only because the development of nature and society itself is a dialectical process.

In defining dialectical materialism Stalin paid far too little attention to this aspect. He overemphasised the subjective aspect, the dialectical approach of man to natural and social phenomena, and left the objective aspect, i.e., the fact that dialectics are a part of nature and society, completely in the shade. Stalin said: "Dialectical materialism is the world outlook of the Marxist-Leninist party. It is called dialectical materialism because its approach to the phenomena of nature, its method of studying and apprehending them, is *dialectical*."[1]

This is undeniably correct, but the omission of the objective aspect may create the mistaken impression that we are reasoning dialectically not because nature itself, and hence also our reasoning as a part of nature is such, but that we see nature as dialectical because our "approach", i.e., the method we are using to study natural phenomena, is dialectical.

Far be it from us to belittle the importance of the dia-

---

[1] *History of the Communist Party of the Soviet Union*, Moscow, 1951, p. 165.

lectical method; for without it the progress of science would be seriously impeded. We are only trying to emphasise that the dialectics of nature and society and the dialectical method form an entity.

As distinct from Stalin, Lenin stresses the objective nature of dialectics: "Dialectics in the proper sense is the study of contradiction *in the very essence of objects*."[1]

It would be wrong to accuse the author of pedantry. Lenin always insisted that the propositions of dialectical materialism, as distinct from subjectivism, be formulated with absolute clearness so as to obviate ambiguity and misinterpretation. The one-sided subjective explanation given by Stalin opens the door to ideological mistakes and misunderstandings.

Even though both the laws of nature and society develop along dialectical lines, there is an essential difference between them. Stalin considered that the major difference lay in the fact that social laws were for the most part "short-lived", and operated only during the existence of one social formation. In our opinion this is not the main distinction. The economic laws of production are as long-lived as mankind itself (after it had evolved from the primitive stage when man gathered the food he found growing wild with his own hands). We shall give some examples of these long-lived economic laws below. Transient economic laws are those operating in various class societies. World communism, too, will have its economic laws. Since communism is the highest form of human society, its laws are eternal and will operate as long as there are people on earth.

In our opinion the major differences between natural and social laws are the following: the operation of natural laws can be observed in its pure form in scientific experiments and abstractions can be made on the basis of controlled experiments. Marx declares: "The physicist either observes physical phenomena where they occur in their most typical form and most free from disturbing influence, or, wherever possible, he makes experiments under conditions that assure the occurrence of the phenomenon in its normality."[2]

---

[1] V. I. Lenin, *Collected Works*, Vol. 38, pp. 253-54.
[2] Karl Marx, *Capital*, Vol. I, Moscow, 1965, p. 8.

Since natural phenomena always occur under identical conditions (if the conditions differ, these changes are easily established) their laws, too, are simple.[1]

This is not true of economic laws. They operate in a constantly changing environment and political economy is, therefore, a historical science, for "it deals with material which is historical, that is, constantly changing."[2]

This applies to all social sciences. *Social laws are therefore no more than tendencies*, the development of which is constantly interfered with, changed and modified by the action of counter-tendencies. In fact, there is no difference between a law and a tendency: the dominant tendency becomes a law. In his preface to the first volume of *Capital* Marx wrote: "It is a question of these *laws themselves*, of these *tendencies* working with iron necessity towards inevitable results."[3]

In his analysis of capitalist laws Marx repeatedly stresses this fact. He says: "The rise in the rate of surplus-value is a factor which determines the mass of surplus-value, and hence also the rate of profit. . . . This factor does not abolish the general law. But it causes that law to act *rather as a tendency*, i.e., *as a law* whose absolute action is checked, retarded, and weakened, by counteracting circumstances",[4] and "thus, the *law* [of the decline in the rate of profit.— Y. V.] *acts only as a tendency*. And it is only under certain circumstances and only after long periods that its effects become strikingly pronounced."[5]

Speaking about the concentration of capital Marx says: "This process would soon bring about the collapse of capitalist production if it were not for counteracting tendencies, which have a continuous decentralising effect alongside the centripetal one."[6]

Even in those rare cases when Marx singles out some law and pronounces it absolute and basic, he always em-

---

[1] In the "microworld", i.e., in nuclear physics, the term "accuracy" has certain limits. But this does not stop us from utilising nuclear power. This inaccuracy may disappear with the development of science.
[2] Engels, *Anti-Dühring*, Moscow, 1962, p. 204.
[3] Karl Marx, *Capital*, Vol. I, p. 8 (italics mine.—Y. V.).
[4] Karl Marx, *Capital*, Vol. III, pp. 234-35 (italics mine.—Y. V.).
[5] Ibid., p. 239.
[6] Ibid., p. 246.

phasises the counter-tendency. Summing up his research on the law of capital accumulation and the emergence of the industrial reserve army he says: "The greater the social wealth ... the greater is the industrial reserve army,[1] ... the greater this reserve army ... the greater is the mass of a consolidated surplus-population. ... The more extensive, finally, the lazarus-layers of the working-class, and the industrial reserve army, the greater is official pauperism. *This is the absolute general law of capitalist accumulation.* Like all other laws it is modified in its working by many circumstances, the analysis of which does not concern us here."[2]

There is a basic difference between natural and social processes which favours the natural sciences. With the exception of astronomy and geology this advantage lies in the fact that natural laws can be observed in a purer form and experimentally verified, while the social sciences are unable to reproduce the phenomena they study and cannot verify social laws in the same way.

What is an experiment? An experiment is the reproduction of a phenomenon, process, or movement under precise and previously determined conditions. Under identical conditions a given movement remains constant and always acts in conformity with certain laws. The whole process can be computed in advance, and thereby prove or disprove the validity of the law or change our conception of it.

Some pedagogical experiments are being conducted in schools. Sometimes, the development of advanced technology is the result of experiments in production. Formulas for natural phenomena can be checked by experiment and this facilitates the discovery of new laws by the natural sciences.[3] In the social sciences there are no such opportunities or if there are, they are exceedingly rare.

---

[1] The accuracy of these words, written 100 years ago, can be seen particularly clearly from the present state of chronic mass unemployment in the U.S.A., the richest capitalist country in the world.

[2] Karl Marx, *Capital*, Vol. I, p. 644.

[3] The discovery of a new planet according to Le Verrier's computations. Proponents of subjectivist idealism attempted to utilise this as proof that new facts and laws can be discovered in this manner. But all their arguments are based on wrong premises: mathematics are senseless if they are not backed by practical experience.

In his *Dialectics of Nature* Engels says that at a given stage in

The term "experiment" is also used in economics. The capitalist is "experimenting" when he makes a study of the market to see if there is an adequate demand for a new brand of soap or motor car, or whether it is advisable to continue production.

In the Soviet Union small pivot plants are built to discover all possible defects in new production methods. But such experiments differ radically from experiments in the natural sciences. These experiments pursue purely practical and not scientific or theoretical aims and could not be adapted for the social sciences because society is constantly changing.

Let us take two examples to illustrate the difference between natural and social laws. Soviet scientists and engineers succeeded in sending a satellite to the Moon and photographing its dark side. This involved intricate computations of the Moon's movements, the velocity of the rocket and the influence exerted on it by the Earth's gravity, and outside of it—of the influence exerted by the forces of friction, the atmosphere, temperature, etc. It was necessary not only to compute the rocket accurately but also to build it with absolute precision, to provide it with intricate and highly accurate equipment. Every operation had to be computed in advance and every possible event foreseen. This could be done only because all the laws of physical motion were thoroughly understood by scientists.

Let us compare this with an ordinary event in the capitalist world. When a trade union calls a strike in an attempt to secure an increase in wages, it naturally hopes that it will be able to achieve its aim. Even though the calling of a strike is simple in comparison with the orbiting of a lunar satellite, and the trade union is able to base its actions on the experience of tens of thousands of former strikes, its outcome cannot be accurately foreseen. Nobody knows whether the capitalists will be able to enlist the services of strikebreakers, or how many of them will be available; whether the mass of the strikers will be willing to suffer the material losses involved in a strike, to what

their development, some natural laws lose touch with reality and become abstractions to which disciples of religion, agnosticism and philosophical idealism ascribe supernatural origin and environmental independence, demanding that the world adjust itself to these laws.

extent the capitalists will be willing to sustain the losses accruing from the stoppage of the factory, how the capitalists and workers in other, and especially allied, branches will react, what will be the reaction of "public opinion", what steps will be taken by the government and its various departments, etc. As distinct from the factors governing the flight of a rocket round the Moon, the factors influencing the outcome of a strike cannot be foretold with any degree of accuracy.

The causes for the difference are obvious. We know that the class struggle is the universal law of all class-antagonistic societies. We also know that the class struggle will inevitably end in the overthrow of the power of the capitalists and the final victory of the proletariat. But the class struggle within capitalist society takes place in constantly changing conditions, differing in every single case. These changes cannot be accurately predicted.

We cannot formulate social laws (and particularly the laws of capitalism) as accurately as natural laws for the following reasons:

Man is undoubtedly the most complex product of natural development, at least on our planet. (We do not yet know what other intelligent beings may inhabit other planets.) At the same time modern man is the product of long historical development, is, in fact, history's most differentiated product: differentiated according to his cultural level, to his environment, colour, past history, social class allegiance, individual education, experience, etc.

Any social movement, and hence also all social laws, are a result of human activity, and humans are the most complex and differentiated products of nature and society. This does not contradict the fundamental thesis of dialectical materialism, i.e., that all social laws are of an objective nature and are independent of the will of people. Obviously, if there were no people, if they did not develop groups and classes, if there was no class struggle, there could be neither history nor social laws. *Social laws are the result of human activity, but they are not deeds of conscious volition.* Striving for large profits, the capitalist expands production, but, in conformity with the objective laws of capitalism, he often gets more than he bargained for—overproduction and a temporary halt in profits.

It is important to have a clear understanding of the following two propositions: 1) social laws are the result of the *activity* of man, and 2) they are not determined by the will of man, but operate objectively and independently of his will. Stalin's expression, "the economic law that the relations of production must necessarily conform with the character of the productive forces has long been forcing its way to the forefront in capitalist countries", should be regarded as no more than a figurative expression, for in reality the class struggle of the proletariat in its endeavours to overthrow capitalism is the guiding force of history. No law "forces its way" (this contradicts the fundamental tenet of dialectical materialism that laws are a reflection of movement), it is the fighting proletariat that breaks its way through and it will be able to win only in the presence of the essential historical prerequisites. The waging of an intensive and purposeful class struggle by the proletariat and the existence of a revolutionary Marxist-Leninist party are among the main prerequisites for this victory.

We can now summarise all that has been said above: natural laws (especially those of an inanimate nature) are clear and definite, and can be expressed by mathematical formulas, because the processes reflected by them always unfold identically, no matter how often they recur (under identical conditions). Social laws are the result of human activity in constantly changing historical conditions; therefore they cannot be expressed in precise mathematical formulas and the development of events cannot be accurately predicted in every case.

* * *

We shall now attempt to unify and generalise the views expressed by Marx and Engels in their various works on the classification of politico-economical laws. Engels's definition of political economy can be taken as the starting point: "Political economy, in the widest sense, is the science of the laws governing the production and exchange of the material means of subsistence in human society."[1]

Political economy is the science of laws concerned with

---

[1] Engels, *Anti-Dühring*, p. 203.

production and exchange which differ as regards the span of their effectiveness. We make a distinction between:

a) *General laws, which are common to all modes of production.* They concern production in general and are therefore unable to explain any concrete historical stage. Marx said that "there are definitions, common to all stages of production, which we consider as universally applicable, but these so-called *universal conditions*, applicable to any mode of production, are essentially nothing more than abstract points, which do not help us understand any actual historical stage of production".[1]

It is precisely for this reason that these laws are given so much prominence in the "works" of bourgeois economists. We mention them here because some people declare that under capitalism "everything" differs from socialism. In his Preface to *A Contribution to the Critique of Political Economy*, and in various places of *Capital* Marx speaks of the numerous laws common to all modes of production. Below we mention some of these laws which have remained important to this day.

Labour as an essential condition for the existence of the human race: "So far therefore as labour is a creator of use-value, is useful labour, it is a necessary condition, independent of all forms of society, for the existence of the human race; it is an eternal nature-imposed necessity, without which there can be no material exchanges between man and Nature, and therefore no life."[2]

The product of labour is always a use-value: "Every product of labour is, in all states of society, a use-value; but it is only at a definite historical epoch in a society's development that such a product becomes a commodity...."[3]

The law of the division of labour: "...division of labour in society at large, whether such division be brought about or not by exchange of commodities, is common to economic formations of society...."[4]

The fund providing the necessaries of life is always produced by the workers: "Variable capital is therefore only

---

[1] K. Marx, *Grundrisse der Kritik der Politischen Ökonomie (Rohentwurf.) 1857-1858,* Berlin, 1953, S. 10 (italics mine.—Y. V.).

[2] Karl Marx, *Capital,* Vol. I, pp. 42-43.

[3] Ibid., p. 61.

[4] Ibid., p. 359.

a particular historical form of appearance of the fund for providing the necessaries of life, or the labour-fund which the labourer requires for the maintenance of himself and family, and which, whatever be the system of social production, he must himself produce and reproduce."[1]

Production must be directed: "All combined labour on a large scale requires, more or less, a directing authority, in order to secure the harmonious working of the individual activities...."[2]

We shall point out only two more of the multitude of laws common to all formations.

The law of the more rapid growth of the production of means of production as compared with that of articles of consumption.

Under any social system the production of the means of production must grow quicker than the production of the articles of consumption, if society is not in a state of stagnation, i.e., if the population is growing. It is obvious that under any social system the instruments of production (no matter how primitive) that will be used by the younger generation must first be manufactured by the older generation. In summing up we may say: in any social system further expansion of the production of articles of consumption is possible only if the production of the means of production has been previously expanded.

Marx says: "In economic forms of society of the most different kinds, there occurs, not only simple reproduction, but, in varying degrees, reproduction on a progressively increasing scale."[3]

There is a law according to which the *volume of consumption can never exceed the volume of production for any length of time*. On the face of it this law may seem tautological and senseless. Yet, in the initial stage of the dictatorship of the proletariat, it is of great political importance.

The proletariat expects the state to improve its material conditions substantially and immediately. The dictatorship of the proletariat naturally takes immediate steps towards a radical redistribution of the national income in *money*

---

[1] Karl Marx, *Capital*, Vol. I, p. 568.
[2] Ibid., p. 330.
[3] Ibid., p. 598.

in favour of the workers and to the detriment of the bourgeoisie and landowners. It can place stocks of food, cloth-
ing, etc., belonging to the ruling class at the disposal of
the workers. It can move the workers from squalid slums
to the castles of the rich. But it is unable to give all the
workers all the articles they need immediately.

Following the establishment of the dictatorship of the
proletariat, during the period of revolutionary reforms,
there is generally a drop in the output of existing enterprises: the best workers join the revolutionary army and
other organs of the new socialist state; the old labour discipline in production, founded on the class domination of
the bourgeoisie, falls to pieces and it takes time for the
new socialist labour discipline to assert itself. As a result
there can be a temporary recession instead of the steep
rise in production, which is essential for a growth in the
real incomes of the working people. Besides, the productive
apparatus, inherited by the proletarian dictatorship from
the bourgeoisie is adapted for the distribution of the incomes of bourgeois society. It cannot, therefore, immediately produce the additional consumer goods necessary to
raise the living standard of the workers. Production
must be switched from consumer goods needed by the
bourgeoisie to those needed by the proletariat. In many
cases it is necessary to build new enterprises to fulfil the
increased requirements of the proletariat. All this takes
time.

A number of additional factors apply to agriculture, the
source of the population's food supply. The establishment
of the dictatorship of proletariat is attended by an agrarian
revolution—the confiscation of land held by the landowners
and its distribution among farm labourers, poor and middle
peasants. This means that ground rent which before the
revolution was appropriated by the landowners is now kept
by the toilers in the countryside. They begin to eat better
than before, but the towns temporarily get less provisions.
Thus the urban population suffers and continues to do so
until the output of foodstuffs is increased.[1]

Enemies of the working class, in particular Right-wing
trade union leaders, utilise this initial temporary deteriora-

---

[1] In exceptional cases, in countries where there is a chronic overproduction of farm produce, such worsening may not set in.

tion in the urban workers' conditions to sow the seeds of discontent with the dictatorship of the proletariat amongst them.

b) *The law of the revolutionary transition from one social system to the other*. Stalin formulated this Marxist law in a new way: "...The economic law that the relations of production *must necessarily conform* with the character of the productive forces."[1]

It is in this form that the law appears in subsequently published textbooks. Some flatterers even called it a major theoretical contribution to Marxist theory. In our opinion, Stalin's formula is nothing but a poorer version of Marx's original formula, for it slurs over the historical and revolutionary content of the law formulated by Marx.

The definition itself is not sufficiently clear and precise. It does not show whether a conformity always exists or not.[2] If not, when and under what circumstances does this conformity arise? Compare it with Marx's concrete revolutionary formula: "At a certain stage of development society's material productive forces come into contradiction with the existing relations of production ... within which they developed until then. They stop being a form of development of the productive forces and become a fetter instead. This is when the epoch of the social revolution sets in."[3]

Thus, it is not a question of "necessary conformity" but of "an epoch of social revolution". Moreover Marx assumes that the "epoch of social revolution" does not necessarily always end in the establishment of a "conformity of the relations of production with the character of the productive forces". This is illustrated by the numerous revolutionary attempts which ended in defeat. The battle can also end with the extinction of the fighting classes.

The first page of the *Communist Manifesto* says: "...Oppressor and oppressed stood in constant opposition to one

---

[1] J. Stalin, *Economic Problems of Socialism in the U.S.S.R.*, Moscow, 1953, p. 10.

[2] J. Stalin also speaks of the "resistance by the moribund forces of society". In his *Dialectical and Historical Materialism* he formulates it more correctly, saying that "...relations of production cannot for too long a time lag behind the growth of the productive forces".

[3] Marx/Engels, *Werke*, Bd. 13, Berlin, 1964, S. 9.—K. Marx, "Zur Kritik der Politischen Ökonomie. Vorwort".

another, carried on an uninterrupted, now hidden, now open fight, a fight that each time ended, either in a revolutionary reconstitution of society at large, or in the *common ruin of the contending classes*."[1] History, and particularly archaeology, tells of the downfall of civilisations and hundreds of states. We do not know what role was played in their decline by class conflicts, although it is quite obvious that in the fall of the Roman Empire, for example, a major role was played by the constant uprisings of the slaves, even though these did not end in victory.

c) *Laws common to several social formations*. The law of the *free appropriation of surplus labour*, created by the exploited classes is common to all class-antagonistic societies. Marx said: "Capital has not invented surplus-labour. Wherever a part of society possesses the monopoly of the means of production, the labourer, free or not free, must add to the working-time necessary for his own maintenance an extra working-time in order to produce the means of subsistence for the owners of the means of production...."[2]

The form of appropriation changes—there is direct appropriation of the surplus labour in slave-owning society, appropriation of the surplus product under feudalism, and appropriation of surplus value under capitalism. Of the last form Marx said: "Production of surplus-value *is the absolute* law of this mode of production."[3]

d) *Laws effective during the existence of only one social formation*. There are many laws which operate only under capitalism: the law of the average rate of profit, the law of capitalist ground rent, etc. A great many of the socialist economic laws are effective only in socialist society.

* * *

Let us en passant stop to consider those "laws", which are not objective laws of social development at all.

1. *Laws promulgated by the state*. These laws are not objective, are not independent of the will of people. They are reglamentations of the ruling class, demanding that the

---

[1] Marx and Engels, *Selected Works*, Vol. I, Moscow, 1958, p. 34 (italics mine.—*Y. V.*).

[2] Karl Marx, *Capital*, Vol. I, p. 235.

[3] Ibid., p. 618 (italics mine.—*Y. V.*).

population under threat of punishment (including the death sentence) conform to definite standards of behaviour. (Objective laws do not "demand", they just operate.) In exploiting societies they form a hypocritical "judicial system", which is claimed to rest on moral principles.

"...Your jurisprudence," the *Communist Manifesto* says, "is but the will of your class made into a law for all, a will whose essential character and direction are determined by the economical conditions of existence of your class."[1]

The hypocritical character of the laws enforced by the capitalist state can be seen from the following: the robbery by individuals, committed for the sake of personal enrichment, is punishable and may even incur the supreme penalty; but mass plunder by the colonial troops of the imperialist countries which serves to enrich the capitalists is not condemned as a crime but praised as a deed of glory.

State laws can be imposed on the population by the ruling class until they do not come into sharp conflict with economic relations. Marx said: "Laws can perpetuate some means of production, the land, for example, in the possession of definite families. But these laws acquire economic meaning when the large land property is in harmony with social production, as for example in England. In France there was petty farming in spite of large land owning, and for that reason the latter was smashed by the revolution."[2]

In the final, historical analysis, economic laws are stronger than the laws promulgated by the ruling class.

2. *"Common law"*. In all socio-economic formations there are laws regulating important dealings between people on the basis of custom (for example, the use of forests and pastures, roads and wells). At a certain stage in their development they either take the form of state laws or are abolished as a result of the struggle between the landowners and peasants. Vestiges of ancient common law are still with us today, even in the highly developed capitalist countries. If a landowner in England has, for example,

---

[1] Marx and Engels, *Selected Works*, Vol. I, Moscow, 1962, p. 49.
[2] K. Marx, *Grundrisse der Kritik der Politischen Ökonomie (Rohentwurf). 1857-1858*, S. 19.

allowed people to pass over his land for a certain number of years, he no longer retains the right to forbid them right of way.

3. *Church laws*, like state laws, demand a definite code of behaviour from the faithful, otherwise the church applies sanctions against the "sinners" breaking its "laws".

The church is nearly always closely linked with the ruling classes. In the name of god it sanctions class society and is protected by it.

These "laws" should be distinguished from objective, natural and social laws. State and church laws demand a certain behaviour from the population. This presupposes that people can act in a different way.

When Stalin declared that the basic economic law "demands" certain things, he committed a strange error for a Marxist. An objective law is a reflection of events comprising the essence of things: a reflection cannot "demand".[1] Objective laws exist, operate, and are valid independently of the will of people, and by their very nature have no need to demand.

* * *

Having dealt with the question of the essence of economic laws in general we can now pass on to the problem of the nature and significance of basic economic laws.

If we remember correctly, Marx twice used the expression "basic economic law" in his *Capital* to emphasise the importance of the laws in question. But he did not single out the "basic law" as possessing special significance distinct from other laws. He also used the term "absolute law". But he never made any attempt to reduce all the laws of capitalism to a single law. Neither did Lenin formulate a basic law of imperialism, instead he enumerated the decisive symptoms of imperialism, one after

---

[1] Natural scientists often use the expression "the law demands". But in that case this is said only for the sake of brevity, for what is actually meant is that for the law to operate accurately it is necessary that, for example, the temperature or barometric pressure remain constant, since a change in barometric pressure would modify the phenomenon under observation.

another. But Stalin brought this problem sharply to the fore. After the publication of his *Economic Problems of Socialism in the U.S.S.R.* our economists took to working out basic economic laws for all social formations and made attempts to deduce from the "basic" other less important laws, which was an entirely wrong approach.

Should we then consider any attempt to single out basic laws for the different social formations, even though this was not done by the classics of Marxism, an anti-Marxist approach? No, we should not. Even though Marx made no direct statements about basic laws, we are able to deduce his opinion on this question from his writings. "*Production in general* is an abstraction, but it is a reasonable one, for it really singles out the general, stresses it and obviates repetitions."[1]

This shows that the basic economic law should be a rational abstraction which contains the most decisive general economic laws of a given social formation and which therefore can be useful for didactic purposes.

At the same time no basic law can embrace all the processes and phenomena of a mode of production.

1. The "basic law" of capitalism naturally cannot contain anything new, anything in addition to what has already been described.

2. No basic law can embrace all, or even the most important laws of capitalism. It is obviously impossible to generalise all the laws analysed in *Capital*—the laws of simple and extended reproduction, the cyclical course of capitalist reproduction, the laws of the appropriation of surplus value and its transformation into profit and its distribution, the laws of the movement of loan capital and ground rent, the laws of the labour market and of the formation of wages, etc. Stalin's statement that his fundamental law determines *all* the principal aspects and processes of capitalism is completely without foundation.

Any attempt to deduce less general laws from a basic law as has been done by some of our economists, *contradicts Marxism.* These attempts are contrary to the spirit of Marxism, which demands that an analysis of concrete

---

[1] K. Marx, *Grundrisse der Kritik der Politischen Ökonomie (Rohentwurf). 1857-1858,* S. 7.

historical facts be made and that laws be established only through a generalisation of these facts.

Marx wrote of research that "the latter has to appropriate the material in detail, to analyse its different forms of development, to trace out their inner connexion. Only after this work is done, can the actual movement be adequately described. If this is done successfully, if the life of the subject-matter is ideally reflected as in a mirror, then it may appear as if we had before us a mere a priori construction."[1] Any attempt to deduce more concrete laws from the basic law is anti-Marxist.

Let us now try to establish whether the law Stalin formulated as the basic economic law of *modern* capitalism expresses a) the most important processes of that social system, and b) the processes symptomatic only of that system, thereby distinguishing it from all other systems.

The basic economic law formulated by Stalin does not satisfy these demands. *It makes no mention of the ultimate result of all the processes under capitalism: the creation of the prerequisites for the inevitable overthrow of the capitalist system by the proletarian revolution.*

Stalin's basic economic law of capitalism speaks only of the "exploitation, ruin and impoverishment ... of the population", but does not mention the revolutionisation of the masses by capitalism, which has always been the essence of all statements of Marxist-Leninist classics on this subject.

His formulation is extremely inaccurate. The term "modern capitalism" applies to modern industrial capitalism, i.e., capitalism after the industrial revolution, as distinct from the manufactory period; the term also implies monopoly capitalism, as distinct from capitalism of the period of free competition; or capitalism in the period of its general crisis, or even the capitalism of today, of the postwar period. In fact throughout Stalin's work it would seem that by the term "modern capitalism" he meant imperialism. But this is no more than a surmise.

Besides, all the features given by Stalin in his fundamental law refer to capitalism in general and not only to the capitalism of today. Stalin's personal contribution,

---

[1] Karl Marx, *Capital*, Vol. I, p. 19.

his teaching about maximum profit, is obscure and inaccurate.

The *striving* for maximum profits has always been the characteristic of the capitalist. Everybody knows Marx's vivid expression in the *Capital*: "A certain 10 per cent will ensure its employment anywhere; 20 per cent certain will produce eagerness; 50 per cent, positive audacity; 100 per cent will make it ready to trample on all human laws; 300 per cent, and there is not a crime at which it will scruple, nor a risk it will not run, even to the chance of its owner being hanged."[1]

From a *social* point of view the maximum profit is the sum of all the surplus value produced by capitalist society. In that sense capitalists as a body have always derived the maximum profit. If it is supposed to mean that monopoly capital, or *one* all-embracing monopoly, is appropriating all the surplus value, this, as will be seen from the statistics of any capitalist country, is entirely incorrect: about half the surplus value or profit is even now being appropriated by non-monopoly capital. Lenin emphasised that there was no such thing as "pure" monopoly capitalism, and never could be. No matter how hard various authors try they are unable to give a satisfactory explanation for the term "maximum" profit of monopoly capital.

Stalin's statement about the "exploitation, ruin and impoverishment of the majority of the population" of the capitalist countries is correct but the works of Marx and Engels convincingly prove that this occurred commonly even a hundred or more years ago, and hence is not a feature typical only of modern capitalism.

Let us now turn to "war and militarisation" as a special method of appropriating profits in the epoch of modern capitalism. This proposition is also incorrect. Even in the pre-monopoly stage, capitalists made huge profits on wars. Naturally, the sums that were allotted to militarisation over 100 years ago now seem negligible, but we should remember that the purchasing power of the money unit was many times higher than it is now, that there was a smaller population and, finally, that the labour productivity, and hence the amount of the surplus value produced within

---

[1] Karl Marx, *Capital*, Vol. I, p. 760.

the year, were also much lower than today. The burden of war expenditure, even though it may seem negligible in modern times, was extremely heavy then. Engels who is an authority on military matters wrote over 80 years ago: "The army has become the main purpose of the state, and an end in itself; the peoples are there only to provide soldiers and feed them. Militarism dominates and is swallowing Europe."[1] Military deliveries were a source of huge profits at the time Engels wrote these words and even as far back as the Roman Empire.

The basic economic law formulated by Stalin does not refer to the specific laws of modern monopoly capitalism noted by Lenin in his work on imperialism—the law of progressive concentration, the law of uneven development, etc.

In conclusion we can say that the basic economic law of modern capitalism as formulated by Stalin by no means satisfies the inherent requirements of such a law.

We also consider incorrect the definition of the basic economic law of capitalism given in the textbook *Political Economy*, namely, that ". . . the production of surplus value is the basic economic law of capitalism".

Naturally the production of surplus value is one of the most important processes under capitalism, without it there would be no capitalism. That is why Marx calls the production of surplus value the absolute law of capitalism. But he does not call it the basic law. Surplus value is not only produced but also *appropriated by the bourgeoisie*. This process is also very important, in fact, no less important than the production of surplus value.

If the definition mentions only the production of surplus value and fails to mention anything else, it may be taken to imply that the production of surplus value, i.e., capitalism, can exist indefinitely. *Here, as in Stalin's definition, we miss the essence of the aggregate of Marxist economic laws, namely: the operation of the economic laws of capitalism inevitably leads to the downfall of capitalism, creates the prerequisites for the revolutionary overthrow of bourgeois rule.*

Let us now attempt to formulate the basic economic law

---

[1] Engels, *Anti-Dühring*, p. 235.

of capitalism as a whole, including the imperialist stage. This is possible, for although there is a distinction between monopoly capitalism and pre-monopoly capitalism, both are but stages of the same social formation.

Let us remind our reader that according to Marx basic laws should be *rational abstractions which single out the typical features* of any given formation, and that this singling out is expedient and useful only insofar as it obviates repetitions and no further! Basic economic laws cannot and must not state anything new.

The basic economic law of capitalism, in keeping with the revolutionary spirit of Marxism, may be roughly expressed in the following words:

In appropriating the surplus value produced by the workers, capital concentrates and socialises production through accumulation and centralisation, creates the material prerequisites for socialism, exacerbates the contradiction between the social character of production and private appropriation. This contradiction, which is only temporarily resolved by the periodic crises of overproduction, makes the rule of capital ever more unbearable for working people throughout the world and, by means of a proletarian revolution, steers capitalism towards its inevitable downfall.

We think that this definition of the basic economic law of capitalism describes the most important processes operating under all stages of capitalism, and corresponds to the revolutionary essence of Marxist theory.[1]

As regards the special law for imperialism, its definition should be based on the properties established by Lenin which distinguish it from capitalism in general.

The specific law of imperialism—presupposing a knowledge of the basic law of capitalism in general—could be formulated roughly as follows:

By abolishing free competition, dividing up markets and coalescing with the state, monopoly capital secures superprofits, subjects the whole capitalist world to its power and deepens the rift between the rich imperialist and the

---

[1] True, we could add a number of other important processes, such as the commodity nature of production, or abstain from including the periodic crises, but the latter would make the definition inadequate. But this is a matter of didactics, rather than principle.

economically underdeveloped countries, between the finance oligarchy and the working masses, transforms an ever greater slice of the population into hired workers and capitalism into moribund capitalism, pushing it inevitably towards a proletarian revolution.

The main difference between the formula for the basic economic law of capitalism given by Stalin and the one given above is that the former is static and fails to express the dynamics of capitalism, while the latter is dynamic and shows that capitalism is doomed.

THE QUESTION
OF THE BOURGEOIS STATE

The Marxist-Leninist teaching on the state, summarised by Lenin in his *State and Revolution,* is known throughout the world. Essentially, it amounts to the following:

The state exists only in a class society. It is a tool of the ruling class and serves to consolidate (or expand) its power. In a class-antagonistic society this is effected mainly by the state machine of coercion—the army, police, gendarmerie, courts, prisons. A major role is also played by historico-conditioned ideology—religion, chauvinism, social demagogy. In a communist society, which does away with class domination, the state becomes superfluous and gradually fades away.

The accuracy of the Marxist-Leninist teaching about the state is so obvious that only demagogues can argue against it. Their assertion that the state stands above classes is absurd. In applying the Marxist-Leninist teaching on the state to a *concrete-historical analysis of the role played by the state in various countries over definite periods of time*, we must remember that like all Marxist propositions the Marxist-Leninist theory on the state is a scientific abstraction: it shows what all states in class societies have in common, but does not and could not possibly reflect all the concrete aspects of a reality which is richer and more diverse than could be expressed in any single formula. We must remember the essence of the Marxist-Leninist teaching but also bear in mind that constant repetitions of that teaching is no substitute for a concrete analysis.

That Marx himself held this point of view is convincingly demonstrated by his splendid analysis of the events in France in *The Eighteenth Brumaire of Louis Bonaparte.*

Marx shows that even though the events were unfolding at a time of bourgeois domination, their fear of the proletariat and the petty bourgeoisie and their uncertainty about the outcome of the class struggle, cleared the path for the seizure of state power by an adventurer backed by a corrupt army: "The struggle seems to be settled in such a way that all classes, equally impotent and equally mute, fall on their knees before the rifle butt."[1]

"Thus the industrial bourgeoisie applauds with servile bravos the *coup d'état* of December 2, the annihilation of parliament, the downfall of its own rule, the dictatorship of Bonaparte."[2]

But every state must have a class basis. Marx said: "And yet the state power is not suspended in mid air. Bonaparte represents a class, and the most numerous class of French society at that, the *small-holding (Parzellen) peasants*."[3]

Marx developed this idea in his analysis: "The Bonaparte dynasty represents not the revolutionary, but the conservative peasant; not the peasant that strikes out beyond the condition of his social existence, the small holding, but rather the peasant who wants to consolidate this holding, not the country folk who, linked up with the towns, want to overthrow the old order through their own energies, but on the contrary those who, in stupefied seclusion within this old order, want to see themselves and their small holdings saved and favoured by the ghost of the empire."[4]

This example shows how Marx's concrete historical analysis developed and enriched the theory on the state. The rule of Napoleon III, who in addition to the state apparatus and the armed forces relied heavily on the French peasantry, lasted for close on 20 years. Only after the defeat of the Paris Commune could the French big bourgeoisie helped by the Prussian troops re-establish the direct, open class domination that had existed up to 1848 under the "bourgeois-king".

Though more than a century has passed since *The Eighteenth Brumaire of Louis Bonaparte* was written and

---

[1] Marx and Engels, *Selected Works*, Vol. I, p. 332.
[2] Ibid., p. 327.
[3] Ibid., p. 333.
[4] Ibid., p. 335.

although the present historical situation differs substantially from that of 100 years ago, this work is still extremely topical.

* * *

The diversity of forces fighting for state power mentioned by Marx in his *Eighteenth Brumaire of Louis Bonaparte* is explained by the fact that in real life there are no "pure" modes of production (cf. the essay "The Asiatic Mode of Production"). Though the financial oligarchy is undoubtedly the dominant force in the modern capitalist world, there is no "pure" mode of production even in the highly developed countries. Nor is it found in those regions where feudalism still dominates, nor in regions still living under primitive state organisations without central government, such as in the remote parts of South America and Africa. Besides, the modes of production undergo constant changes, which are either slow or of a revolutionary nature. In addition to the dominant mode of production there are remnants of the preceding and shoots of future modes of production. The only exception is the socialist mode of production, for only the *prerequisites* of socialism can mature in capitalist society.

This is even true of individual countries. Italy, for instance, is a monopoly capitalist country, a country ruled by the big bourgeoisie. But elements of medieval feudalism continue to exist in the South—latifundias, receiving rent in kind from the peasants, etc. In the South of the United States, the strongest imperialist power in the world, there are also many remnants of pre-capitalist modes of production.

But although these remnants do not affect the country's nature and do not interfere with the domination of the financial oligarchy, no detailed historical analysis should ignore them. A noteworthy fact in this connection is that in 1961-62 the United States Government had to move several contingents of its armed forces into some of the Southern states to restrain local police from forcibly preventing the implementation of the law allowing integrated classes of whites and Negroes.

At the present time, when the forces of socialism are growing and capitalism is gripped by a deep crisis, when the political rule of imperialism is collapsing in the colonies and each year sees the emergence of new, politically independent states, many of which are undecided as to their future road of development, our incomplete knowledge of all the relevant facts obtaining in those countries sometimes makes it difficult to understand which classes are dominant.

* * *

The nature and role of the state in imperialist countries may change substantially even though capitalist development remains at the same stage, that of imperialism. Twentieth century Germany is a case in point.

There were substantial changes in the German state even though the rule of the big bourgeoisie continued right through the 20th century. During the Kaiser period which lasted up to 1918, the big bourgeoisie was economically the ruling class, but historical reasons forced it to leave political power to the Kaiser and the Junkers. Its domination in the economic sphere did not make it strong enough to wrest political power from the landed aristocracy. The army, navy and government remained under the personal control of the Kaiser—the Council of Ministers was responsible only to him—and thus a vote of no confidence by parliament could not topple a government favoured by the Kaiser. The state apparatus was controlled by the aristocracy—the Junkers—and all the ministers, diplomats and generals were aristocrats. The appointment by Wilhelm II of Bernhard von Dernburg, who was not an aristocrat, as Colonial Minister caused a major sensation.

But the economic policy of the state was conducted in the interests of the big bourgeoisie, and the social and political privileges of the nobility hurt the pride of the big bourgeoisie but not its purse.[1]

The German revolution at the end of the First World War destroyed both the power of the Kaiser and the privileges of the aristocracy, dealt a harsh blow to the domination of the German bourgeoisie and temporarily (Soviet power in Bavaria, the creation of the Red Army in the Ruhr) shook

---

[1] Only high protective duties and licences on imports of agricultural products were established in the interests of the Junkers.

its foundations. With the help of Right-wing trade union leaders and the Social-Democrats and in alliance with the generals and bourgeois hirelings, the bourgeoisie succeeded in suppressing the revolution and re-establishing its rule.

Although bourgeois rule continued even under the Weimar Republic, the latter differed in many respects from the Kaiser Germany. To mask this rule at a time when it was threatened by real danger, Right-wing Social-Democrats—Noske and Co.—were placed at the head of the government. Socialist reforms were discussed but never got any further. As the rule of the bourgeoisie consolidated, the Social-Democrats at the helm of the state apparatus were gradually replaced by political leaders representing the big bourgeoisie, among them Walther Rathenau, Gustav Stresemann and others who openly assumed state power.

The long drawn-out crisis of 1929-33, the collapse of the "Grossbanken", mass unemployment, universal dissatisfaction and the vast growth of the German Communist Party, shook the foundations of the big German bourgeoisie. In a desperate attempt to safeguard its rule, the German bourgeoisie turned to fascism. In 1933, Hitler came to power.

The fascist state differed in many respects from the Weimar Republic even though the rule of the bourgeoisie continued. Mere adventurers became state leaders, former stool pigeons like Hitler, thieves looting government property like Göring, and shameless demagogues like Goebbels. This clique did what the government of the big bourgeoisie had been unable to do. They used demagogy and violence to subject the working class to their power; consolidated the rule of the big bourgeoisie, appointed capitalists as official "führers" over the factory and office workers employed in their enterprises; increased military expenditure to animate the economy; seized the property of the Jewish bourgeoisie and handed it over to the German bourgeoisie, whipped up such base instincts as anti-Semitism, racism, chauvinism, the lust for murder, etc., and prepared the ground for the Second World War, which was to realise the age-old dream of the German bourgeoisie of a domain stretching from Europe to the Urals.

Hitler's defeat put an end to the fascist state; but the ensuing administration of the Western Powers saved bourgeois rule in West Germany.

At present West Germany is a state dominated by a financial oligarchy even more openly than under nazism, which resorted widely to anti-capitalist demagogy whenever necessary. The present state camouflages itself with a veil of Christianity and Catholicism. Some of the traits of fascism have survived: the Communist Party is prohibited and there is obvious chauvinism and militarism.[1] As under the Weimar Republic, the Social-Democrats are once more entitled to head the government in accordance with the number of seats they hold in parliament, but they fully support the policy of the big bourgeoisie.

This very cursory review shows that a mere reiteration of the basic principles of the Marxist-Leninist teaching on the state—namely that under imperialism it is an instrument of the big bourgeoisie—fails to explain the many changes which state power in capitalist Germany underwent in the twentieth century. Nor is there any need to prove how important these changes were in deciding the fate of the German proletariat and the development of the revolutionary movement.

For the sake of clarity let us repeat that when we say that a mere repetition of the basic principles of the Marxist-Leninist teaching on the state does not enable us to understand concrete historical development, we do not mean to imply that we in any way doubt its correctness. The changes we discussed above had no bearing upon the essence of the state. The big bourgeoisie continued to rule throughout all these periods (exceptions were the short revolutionary crisis at the end of the First World War, and, naturally, in the German Democratic Republic, where the rule of the bourgeoisie has been overthrown). Changes have occurred only in *the methods by which the bourgeoisie ruled, and in the state apparatus and ideology with the help of which it tried to sidetrack the proletariat from the revolutionary road of development.*

---

[1] The following true-sounding story is told in West Germany. When for reasons of ill health the former nazi Foreign Minister Constantin von Neurath was released from the prison for war criminals, he paid a "courtesy call" to Adenauer and to the Ministry for Foreign Affairs. When asked at the Ministry if he had noticed changes in Germany, Neurath answered, "No, nothing much has changed, *only the Führer has aged terribly!*"

A few more words about the state apparatus. In all capitalist countries the state apparatus is growing constantly, but irregularly. It grows most rapidly during world wars when hundreds of thousands of people are enlisted for temporary work in state institutions. Capitalists also hold jobs in these institutions but this is purely to defend the interests of their firms. The state apparatus shrinks when peace is concluded and then gradually begins to expand again. The table below shows the number of people employed in U.S. government institutions.

Employment in Non-Agricultural Establishments, by Industry Division[1]

(millions)

	Total	Government
1955	50.7	6.9
1961	54.1	8.8
1962	55.3	9.2

The above figures show that the state apparatus accounts for one sixth of the population employed in all non-agricultural branches. The number of people employed in the non-agricultural sphere has grown by 10 per cent in seven years, the number of people employed in the state apparatus—by more than 30 per cent. Contrariwise, there has been a decrease in the number of employees in industry, construction and transport during the same period.

The state apparatus is subordinated to the ruling class and is used by it in its own interests. But only the highly paid top executives of that apparatus have fused with the big bourgeoisie and share their interests. The bulk of the medium and small officialdom is a part of the proletariat, even though its conditions differ in many respects from those of hired workers. However, their interests differ from those of the big bourgeoisie, and are in some respects opposed to them. In many countries they have their own trade unions, which fight for higher wages and sometimes even resort to strikes.

---

[1] *Federal Reserve Bulletin*, August 1962, p. 1048; May 1963, p. 700.

Although the bulk of civil servants are hired employees, they are far less united than the industrial proletariat. There is a much greater difference in the pay drawn by the high- and low-ranking civil servants than there is between the workers' aristocracy and unskilled workers. Moreover civil servants often split up into hostile groups.

In Germany there has always been a traditional enmity between Prussians and Western Germans and between Catholics and Protestants. Under the Weimar Republic civil servants of aristocratic origin despised the Social-Democrat "upstarts"; in Hitler's time—the adventurers of all brands, whom the nazi regime appointed their seniors.

While there is no denying that the bourgeois state apparatus is an instrument of the ruling class and is used by it to suppress other classes, in certain historical conditions it may be turned wholly or partly against the ruling class, as has been shown by Marx in his *Eighteenth Brumaire of Louis Bonaparte*. Usually this happens after a defeat in war.

At the same time this does not signify that the bourgeois state apparatus should not be destroyed after the proletarian victory. We are only trying to show the possibility of its partial disintegration with the help of well-organised propaganda even before state power is conquered by the proletariat. This can be used to prepare and facilitate the break-up of the state apparatus.

When Marx and Lenin spoke of the "break-up of the bourgeois state apparatus", they referred primarily to the coercive, administrative and judicial machinery. It would be senseless to destroy public health and postal services, communications or the educational system, in which only the people at the helm need to be substituted and bourgeois ideology exterminated.

* * *

In this connection I shall refer back to the wide discussion which followed the publication of my book on the role of the bourgeois state in war economy.[1]

Sixteen years have passed since the publication of this

---

[1] See *Discussion about Y. Varga's book "Changes in Capitalist Economy resulting from the Second World War"*, supplement to the *Mirovoye khozyaistvo i mirovaya politika* (World Economy and World Politics) magazine, November 1947.

book, and continued study of the problem has revealed why so few practical results ensued. The principal reason is that little, if any, attention was given to some of the basic principles of Marxist methodology. For this reason the discussion was lacking in concrete historical analysis. It paid no attention to:

a) the fact that the laws of capitalism are tendencies which are always opposed by counter-tendencies;

b) that, as was said above, there are no "pure", "static" social formations or modes of production; that their description is no more than a scientific abstraction; that every social formation is in a state of constant change and that every mode of production (except communism) contains remnants of the past and the shoots of the future mode of production; and

c) that there is no such thing as an immutable "thing in itself", because its meaning is always modified by circumstances, and depends on the vantage point from which it is observed.

The discussion on the question of the state centred around the following points:

1. Whether under monopoly capitalism the state is a state of the whole bourgeoisie, as I stated in my book, or a state solely of the monopoly bourgeoisie (financial oligarchy), as was asserted by my opponents. *I now find that depending on the concrete historical situation either thesis may be correct or incorrect.*

Under "normal" conditions, i.e., when the capitalist social system is not subjected to any immediate danger, the monopoly capitalist state is a state of the monopoly bourgeoisie. Its foreign, economic and taxation policies, and even its social policy serve the interests of monopoly capital, and are aimed at maintaining and perpetuating the continued exploitation of the working class in accordance with the requirements of modern technology.

Even those laws which at first glance seem to serve the interests of the working class (for example, the expansion of obligatory education) in reality serve the interests of the capitalists, who need more skilled labour now than they did before. This is self-evident and requires no further explanation.

The state acts on behalf of the interests of the whole

bourgeoisie at times when *the existence of the capitalist social system is in direct danger*.

As the general crisis of capitalism aggravates the threat to its existence, and assumes a permanent character, the safeguarding of the capitalist system becomes a more and more important function of the monopoly capitalist state.

Let us put the problem in another way: in defending the capitalist system (the private ownership of the means of production, exploitation, etc.) does the U.S. state act *only* in the interests of the monopoly bourgeoisie? Obviously not.

All classes and strata of the population receiving a direct or indirect income from the exploitation of the working class are interested in the further existence of capitalism. These include the monopoly, non-monopoly and trading bourgeoisie, bankers and speculators, rentiers, and the rural bourgeoisie (big farmers) and also the highly paid civil servants, employees, trade union leaders,[1] lawyers, etc.

The above shows that either thesis may be correct or incorrect, depending on concrete historical conditions. Thus, the propositions that under imperialism the state serves only the interests of the monopoly bourgeoisie, and that it expresses the interests of the whole capitalist class, are both correct.

2. The other problem under discussion was whether, under specific conditions, i.e., total war economy, the monopoly capitalist state will act against the interests of *some monopolies*, as we asserted, or whether that is entirely out of the question, as asserted by some of our opponents. This problem is analysed in the essay on the problems of state-monopoly capitalism. We shall not dwell on the problem here, but confine ourselves to saying that in this case too the actions of the state depend on concrete historical conditions. The greater the danger to the further existence of the capitalist system in a country, and the more intense

---

[1] Some American trade union leaders have an annual income of $100,000, which is equivalent to a 5 per cent income on a capital of $2,000,000. Naturally they are confirmed defenders of capitalism. George Meany's articles in the central mouthpiece of the American trade unions are a perfect illustration of the above. It is also typical that the newspaper of the American International Trade Union of Dockers called upon its members to boycott ships sailing for Cuba on October 9, 1962, two weeks before the Kennedy administration officially announced the blockade of Cuba.

must be the mobilisation of the whole economy to ensure the fulfilment of war orders, the stronger *the action taken by the monopoly capitalist state against those monopolies, who in pursuit of their personal interests try to harm the war effort. These actions by the state serve to safeguard the common interests of all monopolies.*

In the U.S.A. there was much less need to subordinate the personal interests of separate monopolies to the common interests of monopoly capital than in the warring European capitalist countries, because the U.S.A. had surplus productive capacities and participated in the war for a shorter time and with fewer forces than its allies. If all monopoly enterprises were allowed to do as they pleased and no restrictions were placed on them, prices would soar (as can be observed on the black market) and unrestrained inflation would follow. They could build cars and villas for war profiteers, since these offer profits which are even higher than those ensured by the production of war materials.

3. In my book I said that "the state has become the decisive factor in the war economy".

Many facts endorse this statement. To wage war the state bought up close on 50 per cent of the country's total industrial output, distributed raw materials and the labour force, fixed prices, etc. True, these state measures were often circumvented, there was a black market on which prices were much higher, etc. But this does not alter the essence of our problem.

The objection was that "it is not the state but the monopolies who are the decisive force in the war economy". This objection is a simple logical mistake, "a confusion of conceptions". The class character of the state and its economic role are entirely different things and must not be confused. The proletarian class state always plays the leading role in the economy whereas the bourgeois state plays this role mainly in the war economy. The monopoly capitalist state is a class state of the finance oligarchy and not one standing above classes. The fact that monopoly capital assumes a decisive role only with the introduction of a war economy proves that state power belongs to the monopolies in corpore also under war economy conditions. The decisive role belongs not to individual monopolies but to their state.

47

Our colleagues who consider the monopolies omnipotent in the sense of Stalin's formula on the "complete and final subordination" of the modern bourgeois state by the monopolies, thereby deny that a creation of an anti-monopoly popular front (as outlined in the new Programme of the C.P.S.U.) is possible, and that the containment or elimination of the monopolies can be achieved by political action of the masses before the capitalist system is overthrown.

4. Finally, let us turn to the problem of economic planning by the capitalist state. The discussion of this problem too was marked by a dogmatic approach and a lack of concrete historical analysis. Only extremes were discussed—planned economy and full anarchy of production.

It is self-evident that under capitalism there can be no planned economy in the Marxist sense of the word. Since, under socialism, the basic means of production are public property, the state *determines* directly what should be produced, at what prices the output should be sold, etc. This opens up the possibility for the planned guidance of the national economy as a whole. Under capitalism, where the means of production are the private property of the capitalists, the state can only promulgate laws and ordinances, directing the capitalist what to produce, etc. To what measure these laws and ordinances will be observed by the capitalists once again depends on the concrete historical situation.

But this does not imply that under capitalism there can be no "planning" of any sort. We could of course quibble over words, declaring that the measures the capitalist state takes in its attempt to influence the volume and nature of production, the distribution of capital investments, etc., are not planning in the true sense of the word. However, this would make it impossible to continue our concrete analysis.

In a war on such a scale as the Second World War, requiring the all-out mobilisation of all economic resources of the warring countries, it is essential to plan a substantial share of production. The General Staff places with the government orders for materials and resources and the labour force needed for the next war year. If the economic resources of the country were unlimited, the role of the state would be confined to the distribution of war orders among the monopolies and to paying for them.

But even the resources of the U.S.A., the richest capitalist country, were insufficient to satisfy war needs and the effective demand of private consumers, and this meant that if full anarchy of production had been allowed to continue, it would have been impossible to continue the war. The U.S. administration was forced to introduce a certain rationing in the distribution of steel and other raw materials, to prohibit the manufacture of cars and non-essential consumer goods, to distribute manpower resources among the armed forces and the economy, and also among the individual branches of the economy, to set price limits, etc.

In those capitalist countries which had less resources than the U.S. the state played an even greater role in the economy, to the extent that in nazi Germany even broken window panes had to be handed in to government offices and *food rationing* was introduced.

We could call all these activities of the bourgeois state *distribution* instead of planning. This may even be expedient, for it would distinguish between these activities and socialist planning. But it is not the name but the facts that count, and these show that during the Second World War the activities of the bourgeois state produced a situation which differed substantially from *production for an indefinite market*—the main cause of anarchy of production.

Moreover, even now in times of peace, a number of bourgeois states have adopted "five-year plans". India, for example, is now implementing its third five-year plan, While these plans differ fundamentally from Soviet five-year plans, they do exert a certain effect on the economy. To some extent the state succeeds in guiding the development of production and of the productive forces as a whole by planned regulation of direct capital investments into the state sector and by making the taxation policy influence new investments in the private sector, which is not the case under complete anarchy of production.

We emphasise once more that under capitalism there can be no genuine planning. But at the same time it cannot be denied that the six Common Market countries have "planned" their economic policy for a period of twelve years in advance, and are to some extent still fulfilling this plan. The European Coal and Steel Community also operates according to plan.

The above shows that the dogmatic assertion that there can be only two alternatives—*complete anarchy of production or complete planned economy*—is impractical, untrue and hence anti-Marxist.

Though I have not made a special study of Soviet economy, and well realise the narrow limits of my experience in this matter, I should like to point out that even in the Soviet Union, after decades of genuine planned economy, there are still elements of anarchy in production, and planning does not as yet fully embrace all aspects of the economy. There still exists the private production of peasants from their personal plots, which is partly designed for an "indefinite" market; there is a collective farm market, where prices are not set by state bodies, even though they are regulated and affected by prices in state retail trade.

Consumer demand for some goods cannot be predetermined and planned with absolute accuracy. The consumption of bread, salt, sugar and similar goods of "nonflexible" demand can be computed beforehand with a high degree of accuracy, but the planning bodies cannot accurately foresee how many suits or TV sets the consumer will buy in the following year, nor which materials women will prefer. For these reasons there can be no overall planning of consumption.

* * *

In conclusion I should like to remind the reader that at the time of the debate I was compelled to put an end to the discussion by admitting that there were mistakes in my book. This was not because pressure was exerted on me in the Soviet Union, but because the capitalist press, and especially the American papers[1] made a political sensation of the discussion and true to bourgeois form, used it for violent anti-Soviet propaganda, asserting that I was pro-West, was opposing the Communist Party, etc. It therefore became a matter of little importance to me whether my critics or I were right. After almost fifty years of work in the ranks of the international working-class movement, the bourgeois press was trying to make the capitalist world see me as an opponent of my own Party, and this was something that I could not tolerate.

---

[1] See, for example, *The New York Times* of January 25, 1948.

PROBLEMS
OF STATE-MONOPOLY CAPITALISM

Lately considerable progress has been made in the study of state-monopoly capitalism. The new Programme of the C.P.S.U. based on Lenin's teachings gives a clear picture of state-monopoly capitalism. The development of state-monopoly capitalism in the most important countries has been recently described in a number of writings of the Marxist trend.[1] Although there have been profitable discussions on this problem, we still think that some problems remain unsolved.

INTERNAL CONTRADICTIONS
OF STATE-MONOPOLY CAPITALISM

In conformity with Marxist theory a general theoretical analysis of state-monopoly capitalism should regard monopoly capital as a *single force*, and the whole monopoly bourgeoisie as a class or as the leading layer of the capitalist class with common class interests. In his *War and Revolution* Lenin said: "... The old capitalism, the capitalism of the free-competition age [was growing.—Y. V.] into the capitalism of giant trusts, syndicates, and cartels. This group

---

[1] See S. A. Dalin, *Voyenno-gosudarstvenny monopolistichesky kapitalizm* (Military State-Monopoly Capitalism), U.S.S.R. Academy of Sciences Publishing House, Russ. ed., 1961; Y. A. Pevzner, *Gosudarstvenno-monopolistichesky kapitalism v Yaponii* (State-Monopoly Capitalism in Japan), U.S.S.R. Academy of Sciences Publishing House, Russ. ed., 1961; E. L. Khmelnitskaya, *Monopolistichesky kapitalizm v Zapadnoi Germanii* (Monopoly Capitalism in West Germany), IMO Publishing House, Russ. ed., 1959.

introduced the beginnings of state-controlled capitalist production, combining the colossal power of capitalism with the colossal power of the state into a single mechanism and bringing tens of millions of people within the single organisation of state capitalism. Here is economic history, here is diplomatic history, covering several decades, from which no one can get away."[1]

The coalescence of *two forces*—the monopolies and the state—forms the basis of state-monopoly capitalism. This view is further developed in the Programme of the C.P.S.U. which states: "State-monopoly capitalism combines the strength of the monopolies and that of the state into a single mechanism whose purpose is to enrich the monopolies, suppress the working-class movement and the national liberation struggle, save the capitalist system, and launch aggressive wars."

We want to emphasise that both Lenin and the Programme of the C.P.S.U. speak of a fusion of *two forces*. This means that *monopoly capital and the state are independent forces*, which in the epoch of monopoly capitalism unite to achieve definite aims. This is not a simple unilateral "subordination" of the state to monopoly capital, as asserted by Stalin, and as some of our economists dogmatically continue to assert to this day.

We have made an attempt to define the essence of state-monopoly capitalism somewhat more concretely: "The essence of state-monopoly capitalism is a union of the power of the monopolies with that of the bourgeois state for the achievement of two purposes: 1) that of strengthening the capitalist system in the struggle against the revolutionary movement within the country and in the struggle against the socialist camp, and 2) of redistributing the national income through the state to the benefit of monopoly capital."[2]

In this general formula monopoly capital is defined as a single power. But if we analyse monopoly capital more deeply we shall discover that the monopoly bourgeoisie fully agrees on some questions, but sharply disagrees on others.

---

[1] V. I. Lenin, *Collected Works*, Vol. 24, p. 403.
[2] Y. Varga, *Kapitalizm dvadtsatogo veka* (20th Century Capitalism), Gospolitizdat, Russ. ed., 1961, p. 104.

And this is only natural. Marx pointed out that the bourgeoisie is united in its attempts to squeeze out of the working class as much surplus value as possible, but that this unanimity disappears completely when it comes to the distribution of the surplus value which has now become profit. Lenin emphasised that competition remains under monopoly capitalism, and therefore also under state-monopoly capitalism, and that this excludes a complete community of interests among the bourgeoisie.

Thus, in Soviet writings one could encounter the erroneous tenet declaring that in every monopoly capitalist country there exists a centre which represents the interests of the monopoly bourgeoisie and gives directives to the state apparatus (such as the Federation of British Industries or the National Association of Manufacturers in the U.S.A.). But, even though the monopoly bourgeoisie has certain common interests, its individual layers controlling the various economic branches have their own specific interests which contradict those of the monopoly bourgeoisie as a whole. There are even constant contradictions among the various monopolies in a single branch. The monopoly bourgeoisie have the following interests in common:

a) *to safeguard the capitalist social system.* This is an aim shared by the whole monopoly bourgeoisie without exception;

b) *to keep wages at the lowest possible level.* This too is a common interest of the whole monopoly bourgeoisie;[1]

c) *to reduce the taxes paid by the bourgeoisie* and to shift the tax burden to the other classes and social strata.

In other respects the interests of the various strata of the monopoly bourgeoisie differ and contradict each other. Even though the whole monopoly bourgeoisie is interested in establishing high monopoly prices, their interests diverge when it comes to fixing them. The monopolies in the metal industries strive to establish the highest possible prices for their commodities, while the monopolies buying these com-

---

[1] The monopolies in the different branches have their own specific interests. They all want the wages of their workers to be as low as possible. But the monopolies producing non-essential consumer goods (small cars, radios, TVs, etc.) are interested in an increase in the effective demand of the workers of other monopolies.

modities (the motor, engineering and other industries) are interested in acquiring them at the lowest possible price. *All* monopolies are interested in high protective customs tariffs on industrial goods. But the monopolies of every branch try to establish the highest protective tariffs for the goods *they* are producing; and they certainly are not interested in protective tariffs which boost the prices of the goods they use for production.

Many similar examples could be given, but we think that those enumerated above show that there are only a few spheres in which the interests of the *whole* monopoly bourgeoisie coincide, namely, the safeguarding of the capitalist social system, the high degree of exploitation of workers, and the shifting of the tax burden to the other classes. In all other spheres the monopolies in the different branches have some common interests but also a great many *individual* interests.[1]

The monopolies of any single branch have many interests in common but there are also sharp contradictions between them. Competition leads to the ruination of the weaker. All the monopolies in the same branch are interested in receiving government orders which bring in high profits, and, therefore, fight each other tooth and nail to obtain these orders for themselves.

A constant struggle goes on between the monopolies of different branches and frequently between those of a single branch for the share of goods to be placed by each on a limited market or, in other words, for their share in total profits. This struggle (disregarding cyclical fluctuations) tends to aggravate constantly, since the gap between the productive capacities and the capacity of the market widens all the time.

The struggle between the monopolies of a single branch is particularly accentuated when war orders become the bone of contention. In March 1963 U.S. Defence Secretary McNamara wanted to place an order for 6,500 million dollars (the largest order in U.S. history) with the Dynamics Corporation for TFX military aircraft but after bitter

---

[1] The contradictions are smoothed over through the formation of monopolies which combine enterprises of different branches, by the intertwining of finance capital, etc., but they are not removed.

discussion the Senate was forced to hand it over to their rival, the Boeing Corp.[1]

Many of the contradictions between the monopolies of a single branch, or between separate monopoly enterprises and the interests of monopoly capital as a whole, give rise to conflicts between the state and the monopoly capitalists of a particular branch, or between the state and separate monopoly enterprises. Let us remind the reader of the battle between the American steel smelting industry and President Kennedy in 1961, when state pressure forced the monopolies to abandon their plan of raising prices on steel; and of the conflict between Erhard, West German Minister for the Economy and the Volkswagen AG, which refused to comply with Erhard's demand that the firm desist from raising the prices of its cars. In retaliation the government considerably lowered import duties on cars.

Such conflicts are explained by the fact that *under state-monopoly capitalism the state represents the common interests of monopoly capital*, interests which may well contradict those of separate monopolies or monopoly groupings. This shows that the definition of state-monopoly capitalism based on Stalin's conception ("state-monopoly capitalism implies the subordination of the state apparatus to the capitalist monopolies"[2]) is wrong.

There is no one-sided "subordination" but a joining of forces, which, in spite of this merger, still maintain a certain autonomy. There is certainly no subjection of the state apparatus to separate monopolies or the monopolies of a certain branch, for this would exclude conflicts between the state and separate monopolies. The dogmatists once again forget the basic precept of Marxist philosophy, declaring that *all* capitalist laws are no more than tendencies which are *always* opposed by counter-tendencies.

The relations between monopoly capital and the state are complicated by the parliamentary form of government

---

[1] *The Times*, March 15, 1963.

[2] *Politicheskaya ekonomiya* (Political Economy), Textbook, 2nd Russ. edition, Gospolitizdat, 1955, p. 266. The 3rd revised and supplemented edition of the textbook appeared in 1960. The definition on page 250 has been improved. But Stalin's formula about the "subordination of the state apparatus to the monopolies" has not been altered.

in the monopoly capitalist countries (under a bourgeois dictatorship of the fascist type this complication is removed). The state apparatus, in the narrow sense of the word, i.e., the aggregate of civil servants, the coercion machinery, etc., is a permanent body,[1] while the top layer of the state apparatus, the government and the legislative bodies, change periodically[2] in conformity with parliamentary election results. A change in the parliamentary majority and a change of government do not necessarily entail a substantial change in the relations between monopoly capital and the state, even when the government is formed by the Labour Party or, as in Sweden, by Social-Democrats.[3]

But this does not mean that the parliamentary system, the campaigning of the various parties to win the elections is *irrelevant*. If the monopolies had their way there would always be a Conservative government in Britain. But the monopolies cannot always do as they please. What is the reason for this?

The reason is that in the state-monopoly capitalist countries, factory and office workers and civil servants constitute the majority of the population, and hence of the electors. The bourgeois parties and the government must take this into account, and they, therefore, camouflage and deny the existence of monopoly capitalist domination. In some cases this results in a certain change of government policy. John F. Kennedy, the son of a millionaire, and worth hundreds of millions of dollars, was naturally no enemy of monopoly capital. But since the electors of the Democratic Party are composed primarily of factory and office workers,

---

[1] When an opposition party gains victory over the ruling party in the U.S. a large number of civil servants belonging to the old party are dismissed and replaced by adherents of the new ruling party. This is not done in Western Europe.

[2] The permanent state apparatus is often more important than the constantly changing government. The British Prime Minister Lloyd George once said that although people speak all the time about government decisions, 95 per cent of these decisions are taken by the apparatus, the remaining five per cent by the government according to recommendations of that apparatus.

[3] In the U.S.A. the monopolies secure their interests by financing the election campaigns of both parties: one part of the monopoly bourgeoisie belongs to one party, the other to the second. In Johnson's Government the two key posts, that of War Secretary and Finance Secretary, are held by Republicans.

he declined the unanimous demand of the monopoly bourgeoisie of all parties in the summer of 1962 for an immediate cut in taxes on monopoly capital. The tax cut was postponed to 1963 in order not to jeopardise the chances of the Democratic Party in the 1962 elections. This shows that in spite of the fact that the monopoly bourgeoisie and the state join forces, the relations between them are more complicated and contradictory than would seem at first glance.

State-monopoly capitalism embraces a single country (we shall discuss the emergence of supra-national state-monopoly capitalist organisations later in the book). This means that the contradictions between the interests of monopolies of different countries breed contradictions and clashes between the relevant countries. This has always been the case under imperialism. The development of state-monopoly capitalism has changed nothing in this respect.

* * *

We should like to remind the reader of the *radical contradiction* between the two principal aims of the monopoly bourgeoisie: that of safeguarding the capitalist social system and that of utilising the state to redistribute the national income in favour of monopoly capital. In the struggle for the first and principal aim—the safeguarding of the capitalist social system—the monopolies have the support of all those capitalists whose incomes are fully or partly derived from the exploitation of labour—the non-monopoly bourgeoisie, landowners, rich farmers, and petty bourgeoisie and also highly paid employees, civil servants, the corrupt workers' bureaucracy and workers' aristocracy, in short, of all those elements who do not want a socialist transformation of society. In implementing its second major aim, that of redistributing the national income in favour of monopoly capital with state assistance, the monopolies are treading on the toes of those layers of capitalist society which support the monopoly bourgeoisie in the achievement of the first aim. They alienate them and thereby create conditions for the formation of a broad anti-monopoly-capital front embracing the working people and those layers of the bourgeoisie whose interests have been harmed by the monopoly bourgeoisie.

We shall give only one example to demonstrate how the monopoly bourgeoisie resorts to state assistance to infringe upon the interests of the non-monopoly exploiting classes. On May 17, 1962, Osborn, a Conservative M. P., submitted to the British Minister of Trade an interpellation on the high price of ammonium sulphate that the Imperial Chemical Industries (I.C.I.) were charging farmers. I.C.I. have the monopoly on the production of chemical fertilisers in Britain. He quoted the following facts. For the past twenty years importers of ammonium sulphate paid an import duty of four pounds a ton. On May 3, 1962, the duty was raised to seven pounds a ton. This enabled I.C.I. to sell farmers ammonium sulphate at £20 a ton. At the same time I.C.I. exports large amounts of that chemical at £12 a ton and foreign firms are willing to supply Britain at the same price. Osborn asked the Minister to abolish the protective duty on ammonium sulphate. The Minister of Trade did not deny the facts but refused to abolish the tax on the ground that the export at lower prices makes for a better use of productive capacities and thus lowers production costs. This argument has been used time and again to justify the superprofits of monopoly capital.

But it did not stop at that. In the course of the debates it was pointed out that the British Government is paying the farmers a subsidy of £8/15 per ton of superphosphate with the alleged aim of expanding agricultural output through wider use of artificial fertilisers, but that this money is almost fully appropriated by I.C.I. in the form of high monopoly prices. The Minister of Trade defended this state of affairs, to which Labour M. P. Douglas Jay remarked: "Does the Government ever dare to condemn any action of I.C.I.?"[1]

Obviously, even if British landowners and farmers do support monopoly capital in defending the capitalist social system, they oppose it when it comes to the distribution of the national income. The contradictions between them

---

[1] Taken from the Parliamentary Records published by *The Times* on May 18, 1962. It is noteworthy that several months after this debate Hugh Gaitskell, the late leader of the Labour Party, announced that in the event of a Labour victory the Imperial Chemical Industries would *not be nationalised.*

are mitigated by the fact that the richest landowners are closely linked with monopoly capital.

This example also illustrates the devious means by which the national income is redistributed in favour of monopoly capital. The British Government uses the taxpayers' money, including that collected from the workers, to pay the farmers subsidies, which are then appropriated from the farmers by I.C.I. which sells them superphosphate at a price exceeding that quoted on the world market by £7 a ton. Thus, a part of the money earned by British workers (being subjected to direct capitalist exploitation) is syphoned into the money bags of the monopolies. We see that the fusion of state power and monopoly capital proceeds dialectically and contains innumerable contradictions which come to light during a concrete analysis.

Stalin's formula on the "subordination" of the state to the monopolies stops us from seeing things in a true light through a concrete analysis.

THE UNEVEN DEVELOPMENT OF STATE-MONOPOLY CAPITALISM

Like all processes under imperialism, the development of state-monopoly capitalism is irregular both in time and in various countries. Some manifestations of state-monopoly capitalism could be observed even before the First World War. For example, the trade agreement signed between Germany and Japan contained a special clause regulating the supply of dyes to Japanese textile firms by the German chemical industrialists' association. However the final transition to state-monopoly capitalism began only during the First World War.

Lenin said: "World capitalism, which in the sixties and seventies of the last century was an advanced and progressive force of free competition, and which at the beginning of the twentieth century grew into *monopoly* capitalism, i.e., imperialism, took a big step *forward* during the war, not only towards greater concentration of finance capital, but also towards transformation into *state capitalism*."[1]

Since that time state-monopoly capitalism has developed

---

[1] V. I. Lenin, *Collected Works*, Vol. 23, p. 267.

unevenly. It weakened after the end of the First World War, became stronger during the 1929-33 economic crisis, ebbed after the crisis, intensified during the Second World War, weakened slightly after it, and now experiences a *qualitatively new* upswing, expressed in the setting up of supra-national state-monopoly organisations and in the attempts to create a supra-national state-monopoly capitalism.

This undulating development is due to the fact that the tendency towards the strengthening of state-monopoly capitalism is opposed by strong counter-tendencies, which at times gain the upper hand. But their victory is short-lived because the tendency towards the strengthening of state-monopoly capitalism is victorious in the end. If we compare historically similar periods, for example, the first decades after the First and the Second World Wars, we discover that after the Second World War, following the end of the inevitable period of weakening, state-monopoly capitalism rose to a considerably higher level than it had occupied during the corresponding period following the First World War.

This undulating line of development is easily explained. Obviously, the monopoly bourgeoisie as a whole strives for the main aim of state-monopoly capitalism, which is the safeguarding of the capitalist social system, and the redistribution of the national income in its favour. But, on the other hand, it objects to state "interference" in the economy and to social legislation on principle. To this day its ideal is "to be master in its own house". This contradictory attitude of the monopoly bourgeoisie to state-monopoly capitalism explains why it grows unevenly—makes a leap forward when there is a genuine threat to the existence of the capitalist system and recedes a bit when that danger disappears. Lenin said: "War and economic ruin have forced all countries to advance from monopoly capitalism to state-monopoly capitalism. This is the objective state of affairs."[1] The Programme of the C.P.S.U. gives an identical definition: "World wars, economic crises, militarism, and political upheavals have accelerated the development of monopoly capitalism into state-monopoly capitalism."[2]

---

[1] V. I. Lenin, *Collected Works*, Vol. 26, p. 170.
[2] *The Road to Communism*, Moscow, 1961, p. 471.

It is also clear that state-monopoly capitalism must grow stronger *in the historical aspect*. The internal contradictions of capitalism are constantly worsening: socialism is winning the battle, the system of colonial rule is rapidly approaching its final collapse, the former colonial peoples are enemies of imperialism and more and more of them strive to embark on the road to socialism. Socialism is to an ever greater extent becoming the decisive factor in historical development. This signifies that the very existence of the capitalist social system is being subjected to an ever-increasing danger. The monopoly bourgeoisie has but one way out, that of strengthening the capitalist system through state-monopoly capitalism. In our opinion the best definition of the development of state-monopoly capitalism has been given by O. V. Kuusinen, who said:

"Initially it was regarded as a sort of 'emergency measure', resorted to only during wartime or during a grave economic or political crisis and abandoned the moment the 'emergency' had passed. At present, the imperialist bourgeoisie can no longer maintain its domination without state-monopoly capitalism even during relatively normal periods. This is due to the aggravation of the general crisis of the capitalist system, to the growing disintegration of capitalism and weakening of its internal forces—economic, political and ideological."[1]

The monopoly bourgeoisie (finance oligarchy) has taken this historically unavoidable road and to this day continues to travel along it by fits and starts, stopping on the way to limit the state-monopoly capitalist superstructure when it feels that its supremacy has somewhat consolidated. Both in Britain and in West Germany a substantial part of formerly nationalised enterprises have been denationalised and handed over to private capital on favourable conditions. In West Germany not only state enterprises built under Hitler (such as the Volkswagenwerk which was financed by workers' money, collected on the false promise that the workers would be provided with cheap cars) but also state property, which belonged to the Prussian state even in the 19th century, have been handed over to private capital. In Italy, on the other hand, the power industry is

---

[1] *World Marxist Review*, No. 4, Prague, 1960, p. 7.

being nationalised, although naturally, the former owners are paid a lavish compensation. All this is a perfect example of the unevenness of capitalist development. Yet, in spite of the denationalisation of some state enterprises in West Germany, in 1962, 74 industrial companies with a subscribed share capital of 100 million marks each were state property; their total share capital amounted to 20,200 million marks, *22 of them accounting for a total capital of 5,800 million marks were state-monopoly enterprises.*[1] If we add state incomes to that figure we can see that even denationalisation has not wrought substantial changes in the state property's share.

In the United States, where the bourgeoisie considers its rule relatively secure, it constantly fights against state "interference". The demands of the extreme Right-wing of the Republican Party, supporting the fascist Birch Society, are typical in that respect. They supported the candidacy of reactionary Senator Barry Goldwater for the Presidency. Below are some of the demands advanced by this movement:

the repudiation of all social and economic legislation promulgated after 1932;

curtailment of trade union rights;

promulgation of laws on the right to work[2];

abolition of state housing construction;

abolition of income tax;

the refusal to enter into disarmament agreements with or without guarantees.[3]

This fascist gang openly demands what the American monopoly bourgeoisie only dares to dream about, namely, that all taxes be paid by the mass of consumers, that all legislative or trade union restrictions on the exploitation of labour be abolished and that nothing be allowed to hamper the arms race.

Obviously, the monopoly bourgeoisie will not reject the chance of getting war orders, no matter how much it talks about disarmament. War orders yield much higher

---

[1] Deutsches Wirtschafts institut. Bericht N. 14, 1962, S. 290-91.

[2] This includes laws legalising strike-breaking, which give entrepreneurs the right to offer workers worse conditions than are fixed in the collective agreement, etc. In short, it boils down to "being master in one's own house".

[3] *The New Republic*, May 28, 1962, p. 16.

profits than any other investment. Only occasionally is some data on this subject published. An investigation conducted by a committee under Senator McClellan on the deliveries of Nike missiles, for which the Government paid $2,500 million, revealed the following facts. The order was given to the Western Electric Company which handed 40 per cent of the order over to subcontractors. Profits were divided as follows: Consolidated Steel supplied the Douglas Aircraft Company with commodities amounting to $146 million, making on them a profit of $9 million. In order to make a profit, the Douglas Aircraft Company added a further $10 million to the price and sold the output to the Western Electric Company. The latter added another $9.8 million. The cost of production for the government order was $146 million, but it netted the three participants a total of $28.8 million profit, or almost 19 per cent of the total.[1]

No matter how much some monopolies may be against state "interference", against state-monopoly capitalism, no matter how much they may deride state functionaries among themselves, they never reject government orders, which are an important cog in the mechanism of state-monopoly capitalism.

What the big capitalists think of the people holding key government posts can be seen from the following statements:

"In the quiet, high-ceilinged dining rooms of the Detroit Athletic Club, where the movers and shakers of the automotive industry gather, they added a new tooth to an old saw: 'FDR showed that the Presidency can be a lifetime job, *Truman showed that anyone can be President, Ike that we really don't need a President, and Kennedy that it can be dangerous to have a President'*."[2]

But the top-brass of the finance oligarchy who call the tune, or at least some of them, are political realists and cherish no illusions on the situation. They are compelled to reckon with the socialist countries and also with the power of the trade unions. For political reasons they therefore attempt to create the illusion that the state opposes the monopolies. For propaganda reasons the state "strug-

---

[1] *The Economist*, April 21, 1962, p. 250.
[2] *Newsweek*, July 16, 1962, p. 11 (italics mine.—*Y. V.*).

gles" against cartels, which are "prohibited" by law in the U.S.A. In 1961-62 the U.S. Government accused the General Electric Co. and 28 other firms in the electrotechnical industry of having, by mutual agreement, sold the government heavy electrotechnical equipment at excessive prices. Various organs of state power and private firms lodged 1,600 similar complaints.

The clash of the government with G.E.C. was settled out of court: the company had to pay the government $7,470,000 compensation. The government expects all other claims to be settled in the same way, and according to the London *Economist* this will yield the government a further $50 million. This may seem a considerable amount but actually it comprises only 20 per cent of company profits for 1961. However the swindle becomes obvious when we realise that "if the Internal Revenue Service decides that the damages qualify as deductions from taxable income, the Treasury ... may actually be worse off".[1]

The government gives the company with its left hand what it takes back with the right.

The development of state-monopoly capitalism is both complex and contradictory. In the final analysis all the profits are always reaped by the largest monopolies, although the manner in which this is done is by no means simple.

STATE-MONOPOLY CAPITALISM
AND THE PROLETARIAT

The constant development of state-monopoly capitalism is an objective process. Historically it is the final phase of imperialism, the preparatory stage for socialism. In his famous definition Lenin says: "state-monopoly capitalism is a complete *material* preparation for socialism, the *threshold* of socialism, a rung on the ladder of history between which and the rung called socialism *there are no intermediate rungs*."[2]

On the surface this would warrant the conclusion that the Social-Democrats are right in declaring that the proletariat should *indiscriminately* support *all* measures which

---

[1] *The Economist*, August 4, 1962, p. 444.
[2] V. I. Lenin, *Collected Works*, Vol. 25, p. 359.

tend to strengthen state-monopoly capitalism. They even allege that state capitalism already is socialism, which is pure demagogy since the domination of the bourgeoisie continues. As stated above, the relation of the bourgeoisie to state-monopoly capitalism is both contradictory and inconsistent, and changes depending on how stable or unstable their domination is at any given moment.

Should the proletariat adopt a positive attitude to all state-monopoly measures irrespective of their nature?

Of course not! State-monopoly capitalism contains a dialectical contradiction: on the one hand it creates the material and organisational preconditions for socialism; on the other, it becomes responsible for a temporary strengthening of the capitalist system and the more intense exploitation of the proletariat with the assistance of the state. For this reason the proletariat should support or oppose state-monopoly measures, depending on their concrete historical content.

We shall give two examples relating to the same historical period. While the laws adopted in connection with President Roosevelt's "New Deal" were aimed at saving American imperialism from the economic breakdown threatening it as a result of the crippling 1929-33 crisis, *the social legislation* of the "New Deal"—freedom and recognition of trade unions, limitation of the working day, etc.—was undoubtedly in the interests of the American working class, and since the prerequisites for the overthrow of bourgeois rule had not yet matured in the U.S.A. it would have been stupid to oppose Roosevelt's "New Deal", and particularly the socio-political measures.

Quite a different situation developed in connection with the state-monopoly measures taken by Hitler. Any support of his measures would have been a betrayal of the proletariat, and the support given them by the Right-wing Social-Democrats and trade union leaders cannot be regarded in any other light.

In every concrete historical situation the attitude of the proletariat to the state-monopoly measures of any government depends first and foremost on the maturity the preconditions for the socialist revolution have attained. If there is a struggle for power, it would be senseless to support any measures of the government tending to strengthen the capitalist system. But while there is no revolutionary situation in a country and bourgeois rule is still stable, the struggle to curb the arbitrary rule of monopoly capital, and for democratic nationalisation of the key branches may be a good method of mobilising the masses.

Depending on concrete conditions, nationalisation has a different significance for the bourgeoisie and for the proletariat. On principle, the bourgeoisie is against nationalisation. As Lenin once said, the bourgeoisie favours the nationalisation of economic branches running at a loss, only, of course, if they receive ample compensation for their nationalised assets. Under adverse political conditions, they may even consent to the nationalisation of profitable branches, but attempt to regain them as soon as political conditions make this possible.

This can be seen from the nationalisation carried out in Britain when the Labour Party won the election immediately after the Second World War, and the subsequent denationalisation in 1951 when the Conservatives returned to office.

After the Second World War, as after the First, the deep dissatisfaction of the British working class with the capitalist system brought victory to the British Labour Party. Right-wing leaders of the Labour Party recommended extensive nationalisation as a means of pacifying the workers. With the consent of the bourgeoisie the government nationalised many industries, paying the ex-owners ample compensation.

The further fate of the nationalised industries is a case in point. The coal industry, which is in a state of permanent crisis (and not in Britain alone),[1] is state property to this

---

[1] Data showing the development of the British coal industry:

	1938	1951	1960
Coal output (million tons)	227	223	194
Number of miners (thousands)	782	699	602
Coal output per miner/shift (tons). . . .	3.0	3.2	4.0

(*United Kingdom Annual Abstract of Statistics*, 1961, pp. 135, 138.) The number of miners decreased by 100,000 in ten years, the labour productivity rose by 25 per cent!

day. The British bourgeoisie never demanded its denationalisation, not even under the Conservative government. The reason for this is not hard to see. The government pays the former mine owners compensation, and supplies capitalist industry with coal at a loss which is covered by the taxpayer.[1] The surplus value being created by the miners is thus indirectly appropriated by the industrial bourgeoisie as a whole. An identical state of affairs can be observed in the railways.

Conversely, the profitable enterprises which were nationalised by the Labour government—the steel-smelting industry and motor transport—were denationalised by the Tory government on conditions favourable to the monopolies. By the middle of 1962 only a small part remained state property.

Fundamentally, the proletariat favours the nationalisation of monopoly-dominated branches. This is true both of the Communists, who see in nationalisation an important material and organisational step on the road to socialism, and also of non-Party workers whose economic aims it advances.

Even though the monopoly capitalist state defends primarily the interests of monopoly capital, there is a great difference in the conditions under which the workers struggle for wage increases in private monopoly-owned enterprises, and in state-owned enterprises. The struggle for wage increases threatens to cut the monopoly bourgeoisie's profits. The management of every enterprise is directly and materially concerned with the outcome of the struggle. In state-owned enterprises, the workers are opposed by directors, Ministers, etc., who have no direct material interest in the outcome of the struggle. Therefore their resistance to the workers' demands is usually less stiff than that of the monopoly bourgeoisie. Fascist countries, however, are an exception to this rule. In the advanced state-monopoly capitalist countries with a parliamentary form of government, where factory and office workers constitute the bulk of the electors, political motives also play

---

[1] According to the *United Kingdom Annual Abstract of Statistics* (1961, pp. 256-57) state expenditure on the coal-mining industry from 1951 to 1961 exceeded income by £534,000,000. This sum probably does not include all losses.

a major role. For tactical reasons the ruling party does not want to alienate electors by an outright refusal to increase the wages of factory and office workers. Important are also the cold war policy and the existence of the world socialist system, and, as mentioned above, the desire not to alienate the workers by provocations which would induce them to lend a more willing ear to communist ideas.

The revolutionary proletariat *fights for nationalisation* because this helps to enlist into the struggle against the monopolies not only factory and office workers, but also broad layers of the peasantry and the petty urban bourgeoisie, who are similarly oppressed by the monopolies. Moreover, they realise that a democratic management of the nationalised enterprises can alleviate the conditions of the working people.

SUPRA-NATIONAL
STATE-MONOPOLY ORGANISATIONS

An important new phenomenon in the development of state-monopoly capitalism after the Second World War is the rapid growth of state-monopoly organisations embracing several countries. Hundreds of such organisations are now in existence.

Like all other social phenomena, supra-national organisations also had their predecessors before the Second World War. A good example is the Bank for International Settlements in Basle, which was originally set up to deal with Germany's reparations after the First World War. Later it began to conduct transactions on an international scale between central emission banks, all of which are state or semi-state institutions. The Bank also functioned during the Second World War, and, through its board meetings enabled the monopolies of the warring countries to arrange their common business (on international cartels, trusts, payments, etc.) on neutral ground.

With the assistance and participation of the relevant governments international cartels were formed and functioned even before the Second World War. There was a series of inter-state agreements on railway transit traffic, postal and telegraph communications, etc. But before the Second World War they were the *exception*, now they have become the *rule*.

In general, the causes and aims of state-monopoly capitalism on a supra-national scale differ but little from those of state-monopoly capitalism on a national scale. The ever increasing concentration of production in giant enterprises makes the domestic market of a single country too narrow for the requirements of monopoly capital, a state of affairs that has been aggravated by the disintegration of the world market following the Second World War, the creation of arbitrary currency zones, the restriction of imports, state control over the import and export of capital, high duties, etc. Supra-national state capitalist measures were intended to alleviate this situation.

The aims of supra-national organisations are identical to those of state-monopoly capitalism on a national scale —the defence of the capitalist social system and the securing of high monopoly profits.

Both economic and military-political organisations serve to defend the capitalist social system. The difference between them is negligible, for all supra-national economic organisations have a political character. The International Monetary Fund, for example, an economic supra-national organisation commanding many thousands of millions of dollars, is first and foremost concerned with maintaining the stability of the imperialist countries' currencies when their balance of payments shows a deficit. The International Bank for Reconstruction and Development (and the financial institutions associated with it) is expected to direct the development of the emerging countries in a way favourable to the monopoly capital of the imperialist powers, i.e., to perpetuate their dependence on these powers. To this day the United States has the final word in both organisations since it owns the bulk of their capital.

A number of agreements between countries and organisations (international agreements on wheat, coffee, etc.) are aimed at preventing a drop in prices arising from the agrarian crisis of overproduction affecting almost all branches of agriculture. Their other aim is to render economic support to well-to-do farmers who are staunch defenders of private property.

So far only the first shoots of supra-national state-monopoly organisations have sprung up in the sphere of production. These are the powerful coal and steel community of six West European countries (E.C.S.C.),[1] and Euratom. But their number will undoubtedly increase. The closer coalescence of the monopolies of different capitalist countries that is being achieved through mutual capital investments paves the road for this development.

No full picture can be gained of the intertwining of capital since statistical methods in the separate countries vary considerably. The picture is also distorted by the constant migration of short-term capital—bank deposits, funds used for gambling on the stock exchange, etc.

The following example illustrates this interlinking of capital. According to the Department of Trade, U.S. long-term private capital investments abroad in 1961 amounted to $49,000 million, foreign long-term private capital investments in the United States to $21,000 million.

According to data issued by the Federal Statistics Board at the end of 1960, 261 foreign shareholders owned 53 per cent of the share capital in 2,537 West German joint-stock companies, accounting for 17 per cent of the total share capital in the country. British shareholders held 932 million, Dutch—422 million, French—215 million marks' worth of stock. This does not include the capital of the branches of American, British, Belgian and other firms in West Germany whose capital is unknown.

At the beginning of 1961 the private foreign capital investments of West German companies accounted for 2,750 million marks, of which 963 million were invested in Western Europe.

According to data issued by the industrial association IRI, at the close of 1960 long-term foreign capital investments in Italy exceeded $3,000 million; Italian capital investments abroad—$2,000 million.

Other links include participation in international institutions (the International Monetary Fund, the World Bank), the exchange of patents and licences, etc.

But, no matter how important this mutual coalescence of capital, *its significance should not be exaggerated*, for now, as before, *national* monopoly capital continues to be

---

[1] According to the E.C.S.C. new capital investments in the coal-mining and steel-smelting industries comprised $1,500 million in 1961.

the decisive factor in the economy and policy of every highly developed country.

Supra-national organisations, such as NATO, CENTO, etc., serve to defend the capitalist system both militarily and politically. They differ from military-political unions, typical of the former period, by a more rigid organisation, including the joint command over a part of the armed forces, the deployment of NATO forces in foreign countries, especially in those bordering on the socialist countries, joint manoeuvres, standardisation of part of the armaments, etc. They are also more long-lived than those of former periods. In spite of constant internal crises,[1] NATO and the other military-political unions of the highly developed capitalist countries will probably continue to function in one form or another as a means of struggling against the socialist countries right up to the final collapse of capitalism.

The Common Market is a new and important phenomenon in the development of supra-national state-monopoly capitalism. However, since it has been widely discussed by the Soviet press and literature, a detailed study of this question is unnecessary.

Although the Common Market *is something new*, in many respects it is a return to the conditions that existed before the First World War. It is an attempt to overcome the dividedness of the world market by uniting the markets of six countries; to re-establish equal conditions for competition through the universal application of the most favoured nation principle in trade agreements, to ensure the free flow of capital and the stability of the gold content of the currencies of most capitalist countries, etc. Equal conditions for competition are to be promoted through the mutual abolition of duties. These measures serve primarily the interests of the big monopolies.[2] At the same time the

---

[1] The main reason for the discord within NATO is the U.S. nuclear monopoly, giving America the decisive say in problems of war and peace. In spite of the pressure exerted on the U.S.A. by its NATO partners it refuses to relinquish this monopoly.

[2] This is clearly illustrated by the internal struggle in Britain over the question of her entry into the Common Market. Monopoly capital favours this entry; landowners, farmers and the bulk of the workers frown upon it.

Common Market is an attempt on the part of the West European imperialist powers to consolidate their position following the political liberation of the colonial countries, to enable them to conduct a vigorous policy of neocolonialism and to compete with the United States.

Politically, the Common Market is a desperate attempt to resolve imperialism's inevitable internal contradictions and to oppose the socialist world system by a single imperialist front, or at least by an apparent unity. All imperialist statesmen—de Gaulle, Hallstein, Churchill, etc.—admit that in the creation of the Common Market political aims outweigh the economic.[1]

For these political reasons the United States supported the union of the West European countries in the Common Market and exerted pressure on Britain to join the E.E.C., even though this union would accelerate the waning of U.S. economic and political influence.

The Common Market member-countries are trying to conduct an independent economic policy vis-à-vis the United States. The following episode is a case in point. Under pressure from interested monopolies, President Kennedy declared in May 1962 that duties on glass and carpets would be raised. Belgian glass exports to the U.S.A. were the hardest hit. In reply, the Common Market countries raised the duty on a number of synthetic fibres and materials made from them from 20 to 40 per cent[2] as from July 17, 1962.

The Common Market is a house divided against itself. West Germany and France have still been unable to fix common prices on agricultural products. The Italian industrialists are selling France refrigerators at a price that is 25 per cent lower than their price on the French domestic market—in the first half of 1963 alone they sold France 140,000 refrigerators. In reply the French Government issued orders stating that refrigerators imported from Italy

---

[1] During his visit to Western Europe in the summer of 1962 Dwight D. Eisenhower said at a press conference in London that the Common Market was an important question that should be regarded as a union of the free world against "aggressive communist imperialism", i.e., against the socialist community.

[2] *The Times*, June 7, 1962. The squabble between the U.S.A. and the Common Market broke out in 1963.

could be sold only with special permission from the Minister for Industry.

At the Congress of the West German Pig Iron and Steel Union held in Düsseldorf in June 1963, complaints were voiced about the loss inflicted by the Common Market on the West German iron and steel industry. Zol, the Chairman of the Union, said in his report that "while other large steel producing countries enjoy stable prices on the domestic market, protected by duties and taxes, the West German steel market has become an export field for all countries. Owing to the devaluation of the French franc by almost 30 per cent, French steel became in 1957-58 cheaper than domestic steel. Besides, the blocking of steel prices by the French Government has widened the price gap to the detriment of West Germany. Belgian and Luxemburg iron and steel works are exerting a strong pressure on the West German market price."[1] The Congress noted that the reserves created by high domestic prices had made the Belgians particularly successful in expanding their position in the Common Market.

Political contradictions are no less acute. De Gaulle blocked Britain's entry into the Common Market on political grounds, because he considered Britain the instrument of American influence in Western Europe; while Belgium and the Netherlands were for Britain's entry on political grounds, believing that it would offset the threat of West Germany's political domination in Western Europe.

Even politicians in the same country hold contradictory views on the lines along which the Common Market should develop. Hallstein is trying to steer a course of close economic union between the Six and advocates a common economic policy. De Gaulle and Erhard on the other hand were strictly against this course. At a meeting of the Ministers and Ambassadors of the Six, Erhard said that he strove not for a centralised European state but for European federation in which different countries and peoples could live their own lives according to their ideals, although the economic integration of the Six was achieved through political decisions, he continued, the striving for centralisation in economic policies should not predeter-

---

[1] *Neue Zürcher Zeitung*, July 7, 1963.

mine Europe's future political structure. Erhard specifically warned against accepting the recommendation of the Common Market Commission advocating a fusion of the national economic policies of the member-countries.

Inter-imperialist contradictions cannot be resolved. U.S. monopoly capital is rapidly setting up branches of industrial enterprises in Western Europe so as not to be excluded from the domestic market of the united countries. The more countries join the Common Market, the more diverse will become its internal contradictions.

The Programme of the C.P.S.U. says:

"The dialectics of state-monopoly capitalism is such that instead of shoring up the capitalist system, as the bourgeoisie expects, it aggravates the contradictions of capitalism and undermines its foundations."[1]

---

[1] *The Road to Communism*, Moscow, p. 472.

THE PROBLEM
OF INTER-IMPERIALIST
CONTRADICTIONS AND WAR

In the autumn of 1951, when the draft of the textbook on political economy was being discussed, the following question was raised: does Lenin's theory on *the inevitability of wars between imperialist countries* apply in modern conditions, when the world is split into two camps—the socialist and the capitalist—when the cold war is at its height and there is an ever present threat of thermonuclear extinction?

The participants were almost unanimous in the opinion that Lenin's theory was also correct in modern conditions.

Like all other controversial issues, this question was referred to Stalin, the chief arbiter of the conference, whose answer was categorically affirmative. Stalin said that those who were denying the inevitability of wars between imperialist countries saw only the external phenomena and failed to see the abysmal forces which, operating almost unnoticeably, would decide the course of future events.

Twelve years have passed—a long time if we consider how rapidly events develop nowadays—and there is less likelihood of a war between the imperialist powers today than there was in 1951.

There are dogmatists who reiterate that inter-imperialist wars are unavoidable even today. But they are wrong because they disregard the profound changes that have taken place in the world since the time when this theory was formulated.

The 20th Congress of the C.P.S.U. has put an end to this misguided view on the fatal inevitability of wars. The resolution of the Congress reads: "...The Leninist precept that so long as imperialism exists, *the economic basis* giving rise to wars *will also be preserved*, remains in force. That is why it is necessary to display the greatest vigilance.... But war is not fatalistically inevitable."[1]

The problem could be considered solved. And yet there are those who think that the denial of the inevitability of wars refers only to wars between the imperialist and socialist camps and that it does not apply to inter-imperialist wars, even under modern conditions. Some dogmatists therefore continue to reiterate the erroneous arguments advanced by Stalin. For this reason we consider it necessary to take a closer look at Stalin's reasoning.

Stalin admitted that the theoretical contradictions between capitalism and socialism are stronger than those between the capitalist countries. He pointed out that this had been true even before the Second World War, and that, in spite of it, when Hitler attacked the Soviet Union, the Anglo-Franco-American bloc "not only failed to join forces with nazi Germany, but, on the contrary, had to enter into a coalition with the U.S.S.R. against nazi Germany."

This argument lacks what according to Lenin *"constitutes the very gist, the living soul, of Marxism—a concrete analysis of a concrete situation"*.[2]

Both before and during the Second World War the Soviet Union was the only socialist country. A large proportion of the bourgeois world was convinced that the victory of socialism in Russia had been "accidental"—a result of the absence of democracy under tsarism. They considered socialism in the Soviet Union a transient historical phenomenon which would crumble under the impact of an external blow or domestic difficulties.

Today there exists a powerful socialist world system. The capitalists are now particularly afraid that some of the countries which have thrown off the imperialist yoke are embarking on the socialist road of development and that *socialism is spreading even without war*. Today *nobody* in the capitalist world considers socialism in the Soviet Union

---

[1] *Resolutions of the 20th Congress of the C.P.S.U.*, Moscow, 1956, p. 11 (italics mine.—*Y. V.*).

[2] V. I. Lenin, *Collected Works*, Vol. 31, p. 166 (italics mine.—*Y. V.*).

transient, and those who declare that it can spread only through violence are few and far between. Capitalist die-hards now admit that socialism can emerge in under-developed countries but not in the rich advanced capitalist countries.

It goes without saying that the prevailing historical situation today differs radically from that which obtained on the eve of the Second World War. Socialism has become the decisive factor in world historical development. This does not imply that the socialist world is able to dictate to the capitalist world, but it does mean that prior to taking important foreign or even domestic policy measures every imperialist country must carefully balance the effects of these measures on the relations between socialism and capitalism. This makes the present historical situation different from that before and during the Second World War.

Under modern historical conditions the argument that despite the contradictions between socialism and capitalism the Anglo-Franco-American bloc had to enter into a coalition with the Soviet Union against nazi Germany, becomes invalid. The coalition with the Soviet Union was formed *not before but after* the outbreak of the inter-imperialist war. The behaviour of the British and French military missions in Moscow in 1939 proved beyond doubt that before its outbreak, British imperialism had no serious intention to conclude a military alliance with the U.S.S.R. The Western imperialists entered into an alliance with the U.S.S.R. only after Hitler had attacked them, had smashed the French Army and occupied nearly the whole of Western Europe, was threatening to carry the war into British territory and to become the dictator of the whole of Europe. They formed this coalition with the Soviet Union not to defend the latter, but in the hope that they would succeed in weakening both Hitler and the U.S.S.R.[1] It was also for this reason that they delayed the opening of the second front. The memoirs of Churchill and of other Western political leaders relate how they tried to prevent the entry of Soviet troops into Central Europe. In any case it would be wrong to use the events that unfolded in the concrete

----

[1] Harry Truman openly demanded that a policy aimed at weakening both Germany and the U.S.S.R. be conducted.

conditions of the Second World War to assess an entirely different historical situation.

The present historical situation also differs from all other stages of the imperialist epoch in the following respect: *formerly there have always been opposing coalitions of imperialist powers*. Before the First World War there was the Triple Alliance and the Franco-Russian Entente. Before the Second World War there was the Rome-Berlin-Tokyo Axis and the British-French-American group. Now under the impact of socialism's rapid advance *all Western imperialist powers*, in spite of the sharp differences between them, *form a single military bloc*—the North Atlantic Treaty Organisation. This is a radical change as compared with the situation prevailing before the Second World War. Now American, British and French troops are stationed on West German territory; West German troops are holding manoeuvres; there are joint manoeuvres on land, sea and in the air; and all weapons, except thermonuclear ones, are being gradually standardised.

NATO is not a stable military alliance. For all we know it may collapse when faced by a serious military test, as did the Triple Alliance before the First World War. NATO is shaken by one crisis after the other. But these crises are resolved by negotiations and compromises. The Common Market and the plan for an "integration" of Western Europe are aimed at creating an organisation that will smooth out and eventually solve the economic and political contradictions between the continental imperialist powers, and will enable them to resist the U.S.A.'s attempts at world domination. Stalin's assertion that the contradictions between the large NATO member-countries will inevitably lead to military conflict is unscientific.

To avoid ambiguity let us repeat—the existence of NATO, the Common Market and other imperialist alliances, does not result in a political stabilisation of capitalism. Let us remember the events that shook the capitalist world in 1962: the war in Algeria; the terrorist actions of the OAS in Algeria and France; the political crisis in France; the crisis of the Adenauer regime in West Germany; the war between the Yemen and the U.A.R. on the one hand, and Saudi Arabia and Jordan on the other; the war in the Congo, which in reality was a war against the people of the Congo, and at the same time a war under the U.N. flag against Britain and Belgium, who supported Tshombe and defended the interests of the Union Minière de Haut Katanga; the crisis in Rhodesia; the war between Portugal and its African colony of Angola; the smouldering civil war in South Africa; the semi-war between India and Pakistan; the uprisings and military coups in the Latin American countries; the "war" on Cyprus in the beginning of 1964; the "confrontation" between Malasia and Indonesia; the conflict between Panama and the U.S.A. and that between Somalia and Ethiopia. Let us also remember that for many years now the South Vietnamese have fought the aggression of the U.S.A. and its puppets.

There is no political stabilisation of capitalism. But this does not mean that inter-imperialist wars are inevitable.

The historic events of the past twelve years have refuted the concept on which Stalin built his theory on the inevitability of inter-imperialist wars. His conception was based on the view that economically the U.S.A. will always have the edge over Britain, France, West Germany and Japan and that "to think that these countries will not try to get on their feet again, will not try to smash the U.S. 'regime', and force their way to independent development, is to believe in miracles".[1]

But Stalin completely forgot Lenin's law of uneven development under imperialism. The defeated imperialist powers needed no war to free themselves from U.S. economic domination. The uneven development removed this domination by peaceful means. The economy of West Germany, France, Italy and Japan developed rapidly, that of the U.S.A. lagged behind; the share of the U.S. in world industrial output dropped to 40 per cent, its share in foreign trade turnover fell even more substantially; it lost about a third of its gold reserves, which by the end of 1962 were smaller than they had been before the Second World War. The chronic deficit in U.S. balance of payments due to far too extensive foreign expenditure on the defence of the capitalist world created a constant danger to the stability of the dollar. The U.S.A. had to ask West Germany, France

---

[1] Stalin, *Economic Problems of Socialism in the U.S.S.R.*, Moscow, 1953, p. 39.

and Italy to help it maintain the stability of the dollar, not to exchange their dollar reserves for gold, to pay their debts ahead of time, to buy more armaments in the U.S.A. and to assume a larger share in the war expenditure of the capitalist world, etc.

The U.S.A. can no longer dictate in the economic field, as it did in the initial post-war period. It is compelled to ask its Western allies for financial help to maintain the stability of the dollar. And all this has come about without a war. With the creation of the Common Market the position of the continental imperialist powers has grown even stronger.

The other imperialist powers have no need to war with the U.S.A. to further their economic development, in fact, they *are as yet unable to wage such a war.*

The supremacy in this field enjoyed by the U.S.A. in the capitalist camp will be difficult to overcome, not only because of its strategic superiority but also for purely economic reasons. In the 1962/63 fiscal year the U.S.A. earmarked some 60,000 million dollars for military requirements (we are including in this sum also expenditure on atomic energy, on military aid to various countries, etc.). In 1960 the aggregate national income of the principal West European countries was 179,000 million dollars, of which West Germany accounted for 54,000, France for 44,000, Italy for 25,000 and Britain for 56,000 million dollars.[1]

These figures are not accurate. But they do show that neither West Germany nor France could *on their own* compete with the U.S.A. in the field of armaments. Even if all four powers united their forces against the U.S.A., they would have to spend about one-third of their national incomes on armaments even during times of peace, and for internal political reasons this is hardly possible.

* * *

When the problem was discussed in 1951 our main argument against the inevitability of a new inter-imperialist war was that the statesmen of the imperialist powers had

---

[1] *Statistical Yearbook of the United Nations,* 1961, p. 486 (recalculated into dollars according to the official rate of exchange by the author).

learnt a lesson from history. The First World War resulted in the destruction of the bourgeois and landowner rule in Russia; the Second overthrew capitalism in Central and Southeastern Europe, China and North Korea. The statesmen of the imperialist powers must realise that a third world war would have fatal consequences for the capitalist system as a whole.

Stalin refuted this argument too. He wrote that "war with the U.S.S.R., as a socialist land, is more dangerous to capitalism than war between capitalist countries; for whereas war between capitalist countries puts in question only the supremacy of certain capitalist countries over others, war with the U.S.S.R. must certainly put in question the existence of capitalism itself".[1]

We consider Stalin's theory on inter-imperialist war incorrect. It does not take into account the fact that defeat in a large-scale modern war (even if it is waged between the capitalist countries) will also endanger the further existence of capitalism, especially in the defeated countries. Any defeat in war discredits the ruling class, its government and social system, destroys discipline in the army, which in the imperialist countries, in addition to professional officers, consists in the main of factory and office workers, i.e., of people who are not objectively interested in the existence of the capitalist system,[2] and unleashes class forces both within and without the army that result in the overthrow of bourgeois rule. The events of the 20th century show that the overthrow of the capitalist system in developed countries—in Russia, Hungary, etc.—followed in the wake of a military defeat of the bourgeoisie of those countries.

One must not overlook the possibility that the armies of the victorious imperialist countries might completely occupy the vanquished countries in order to defend the capitalist system there. The U.S. and British armies disarmed

---

[1] J. Stalin, *Economic Problems of Socialism in the U.S.S.R.*, pp. 39-41.

[2] In Italy and France the Communist Parties regularly poll 25 per cent of all votes. The share of Communists in the army is probably even higher, since the anti-communist parties gain many votes from among women, old people, and the ruling classes, who do not serve in the army.

the partisans in France and Italy in 1944 purely to defend capitalism. But in the unlikely event of a large inter-imperialist war not involving the socialist world, the historical situation would be different from that in 1944. As a result of such a war the imperialist world as a whole would be considerably weakened, while the socialist world would gain strength. This would enable the socialist world easily to fulfil its internationalist duty and to defend those nations endeavouring to throw off the capitalist yoke.

It is equally obvious that a third world war between the imperialist countries—the socialist world remaining neutral —would be no less dangerous for the capitalist system than a war between capitalism and socialism.

We therefore consider that even though there are economic reasons for inter-imperialist wars, and even though the struggle for raw material sources and markets, and for the export of capital is no less acute between the imperialists today than it was before the Second World War, bourgeois statesmen have learnt a lesson from the First and Second World Wars, which robbed capitalism of its power over one-third of the world's population, and that they therefore see the dangers entailed to their class in a new inter-imperialist war. This alone will stop them from allowing a new war to come to a head.

The likelihood of a large inter-imperialist war is also lessened by the fact that not only have the class and economic risks resulting from such a war become much greater, but the *chances of monopoly capital winning have become much smaller*. The only advantage it stands to gain is an increase in war orders.

Inter-imperialist wars were waged in the past either to gain colonies or recarve them. Speaking about the First World War Lenin said that "the fate of the colonies outside of Europe is being decided on the battlefields of Europe". In spite of all the talk about a "new order in Europe" and "Asia for the Asians", Germany and Japan waged the Second World War to subjugate the European and Asian countries, and to exploit them as colonies.

In modern conditions it is extremely unlikely that an imperialist country will unleash a war against another country to seize colonies. We saw the disintegration of the colonial system of imperialism after the Second World War. Only a few remnants remain of the former large colonial empires, and their future is in no doubt. Monopoly capital has learned to exploit the ex-colonies, which have remained bourgeois, by neo-colonialist methods, without dominating them politically.

Technological progress in general, and that of weapons and equipment in particular, is very important in our time. Military equipment now becomes obsolete in a year or two. Sometimes a new weapon becomes obsolete even before it is produced. This happened to the British thermonuclear weapon Blue Streak, for the development of which Britain spent several hundred million pounds, but which had to be scrapped because it had become obsolete even before it could be produced.

This means that the big monopoly capitalists are obtaining steadily increasing war orders without a war. It is common knowledge that from 1950 on the war budgets of all imperialist countries increased with every passing year. From this point of view too monopoly capital, which determines the foreign policy of the imperialist countries, does not want war.

At the same time the ruling classes in the imperialist countries realise all too well that the Second World War brought *a substantial decrease in the national wealth of the warring countries.* Even in the U.S.A., whose territory was untouched by war, the aggregate volume of private property decreased as a result of the Second World War[1]; the sum total of state property increased but very little. Some big monopolies, the principal suppliers of war materials, and some speculators did get rich on the war, but the ruling classes of Britain, France, West Germany, Italy and Japan undoubtedly incurred considerable losses. Wars for the purpose of enrichment have become senseless.

We shall not attempt to guess what weapons would be used in an inter-imperialist war, if it were to break out. With the crazy tempo at which war equipment is developing these days, this cannot be foreseen. Much depends also on whether it will involve the U.S.A. with its powerful thermonuclear arsenal. But there is no doubt that even if

---

[1] Simon Kuznets, *Capital in the American Economy. Its Formation and Financing,* Princeton, University Press, 1961.

the U.S.A. did not participate, it would be more destructive than the Second World War. Weapons have changed. Many countries have a certain stock of tactical thermonuclear weapons, bombers are more powerful, incendiary bombs more effective, tanks are larger, rifles better, etc. The losses of the warring countries and the destruction wrought would undoubtedly be much larger than during the last war.

Scientists throughout the world, broad circles of the intelligentsia and people in general, irrespective of what class they belong to, are becoming more and more aware of the fatal consequences of a thermonuclear war. Even the very rich will be unable to avoid its consequences, for war, like cancer, does not distinguish the rich from the poor. This awareness of a common danger is a powerful deterrent against war.

Let us now summarise what has been said above: imperialist contradictions exist and therefore the danger of inter-imperialist wars cannot be dismissed. However it is extremely unlikely that a third world war will be sparked off. No single country has anything to gain from such a war. The havoc wrought would undoubtedly be even greater than it was during the Second World War; the downfall of capitalism in the defeated countries is almost inevitable and the consequences of a thermonuclear war would be fatal to humanity. The possibility of a new inter-imperialist war is not excluded. But as long as the decision of war or peace is not left to the discretion of a madman like Hitler, but to bourgeois *statesmen aware of the threat such a war involves for the capitalist system, it will not come to pass.*

THE PROBLEM OF THE BOURGEOISIE'S ROLE IN THE NATIONAL LIBERATION STRUGGLE OF THE COLONIAL PEOPLES

For a long time the bourgeoisie's role in the national liberation struggle of the colonial peoples was interpreted as follows:

a) the colonial bourgeoisie is reactionary; it participates in the liberation movement only under pressure by the masses. It attempts to assume the leadership in the movement to keep it within the framework of the existing social system;

b) it is always ready to compromise with the imperialist bourgeoisie at the expense of the working people in its own country;

c) the national liberation struggle of the colonial peoples can be victorious only if it is headed by the working class led by the Communist Party.

The views expressed in the first and second statements are only relatively correct, insofar as practice has shown that in some historical conditions the bourgeoisie struggles on its own initiative against imperialism, while in others it compromises with the latter. But developments over the past decade have demonstrated that the idea expressed in the third statement is wrong.

Since the Second World War more than fifty colonial and semi-colonial countries have won political independence from the imperialists. Only in four of them—China, North Vietnam, North Korea and Cuba—has the proletariat been in the vanguard of the national liberation struggle, in all others—India, Pakistan, Burma, Indonesia, Ceylon, Egypt, the Sudan, etc.—the movement was headed not by the proletariat but by the bourgeoisie. In the case of the Sudan and Ghana it was headed not by the bourgeoisie, because there was no national bourgeoisie, or hardly any, but by other layers of the population, notably the intelligentsia.[1]

The fate of the country depends to a large extent on what class leads the people to victory in the liberation struggle, i.e., whether it is the proletariat and the Communist Party or the bourgeoisie and its parties. In the event of the former the anti-imperialist revolution achieves the objectives of a bourgeois-democratic revolution (destroys the feudal system, carries out radical land reforms) and launches immediate socialist construction.

In the event of the latter, the new government takes steps to more or less eliminate the feudal system, but refuses to carry out land reforms[2] or take steps to change the country's existing social system. This, however, does not alter the fact that in some countries the struggle for political independence has been waged under the leadership of non-proletarian classes. This happened in Turkey. Facts do not endorse the theory that the anti-imperialist struggle for liberation can be won only under the leadership of the working class and the Communist Party.

* * *

The Second and Sixth congresses of the Comintern advanced the erroneous theory that the bourgeoisie in colonies and dependent countries is always reactionary and that the national liberation struggle cannot be victorious under its leadership. This theory was formulated under the impact of the betrayal of the Chinese liberation movement by the Kuomintang and it was believed that the bourgeoisie in all colonies would act similarly.

In submitting his draft resolution to the Second Congress for discussion, Lenin suggested that it should contain only

---

[1] The view that the liberation of the colonies is possible only under the leadership of the proletariat and the Communist Party had taken such firm roots in our country that even after India became a dominion, one often heard assertions that "essentially nothing had changed" in India and that she remained a British colony.

[2] In Indonesia the peasants still turn 50 per cent of the harvest over to the landowners.

a statement to the effect that Communists are obliged to support all bourgeois-democratic movements in the colonies. He stressed that the national movement in the colonies was bound to be of a bourgeois-democratic nature, since peasants accounted for the bulk of the population in the less advanced countries. At the insistence of a number of delegates, who asserted that the bourgeoisie in the colonial and imperialist countries had already allied against the revolutionary movement in the colonies, Lenin agreed that the words "bourgeois-democratic" be replaced by "national revolutionary".[1] Lenin agreed to this more "radical" wording because the principal aim of the debates and the resolution was to convince representatives of the Communist Parties from imperialist countries, who at that time were greatly influenced by the bourgeois and Social-Democratic views that the colonialists had an "educational" mission as regards the "backward" peoples, that they were obliged to assist the anti-imperialist movement in the colonies being oppressed by "their" bourgeoisie. If Lenin had refused to agree to these "leftist" changes, the anti-colonial resolution would not have received a majority vote.

The Sixth Congress of the Comintern, too, was strongly influenced by the Kuomintang betrayal and a wrong appraisal of the Indian "non-co-operation and non-violence" movement, which did not fail to find its reflection in the Congress resolution on the colonial question. As a result the tendency of the national bourgeoisie to compromise with the imperialists was overemphasised, and the movement headed by them was styled "national reformist".

Post-war events showed that in contemporary historical conditions characterised by a general weakening of the imperialist positions and the formation of a world socialist system, which is advancing at a more rapid pace than capitalism, the bourgeoisie in the colonies and dependent coun-

---

[1] Graziadei, the delegate of the Italian Communist Party, did not vote for the resolution but proposed a number of obviously reformist changes, suggesting, for example, that the statement that "Communists are obliged to help the anti-imperialist movement" be replaced by "show an active interest in"; Serrati also refused to vote for it giving a "leftist" motive—that Communists should not help *any* bourgeois movement. (*Vtoroi kongress Kominterna* [Second Congress of the Comintern], Partizdat, Russ. ed., 1934, pp. 98-161, 490-96.)

tries is often both willing and able to lead the national liberation movement to victory.

Naturally, when victory is won in the liberation struggle under bourgeois leadership, the initial result is the establishment of *political* sovereignty, and no more. *Genuine economic independence* from imperialism can be achieved only along the non-capitalist road of development.

The forms taken by the liberation movement since the Second World War have been so multifarious and have so often changed even within a single country, that it is impossible to give a precise formula that would embrace them all.

* * *

In the colonial and semi-colonial countries the bourgeoisie has a dual nature. Like the *bourgeoisie* of the imperialist countries it is interested in defending the capitalist system; and in this respect plays a *reactionary* role. But its specific colonial interests clash with those of the imperialist bourgeoisie and therefore it is willing to head the struggle of the working people in those countries against imperialism and in this context plays a historically *progressive* role.

The political vacillations of the colonial bourgeoisie spring from this duality. While in general it opposes imperialism, it may under specific conditions strike a bargain with it. But the events of the post-war years show that such compromises are only temporary and that the bourgeoisie soon continues its struggle for full political independence.

The world socialist system (a major place in which is held by former colonial and semi-colonial countries) is of overriding importance to the national liberation movement in the colonies. The colonial peoples, including the bourgeoisie, are proud of the victory the former colonies have won over imperialism and of their economic successes. The example of former colonial countries, now equal nations in the socialist community, gives them faith in their future. The colonial peoples are well disposed to these countries. The equality being enjoyed by the peoples formerly oppressed by tsarism creates a bond of sympathy that unites oppressed peoples throughout the world with the peoples of the Soviet Union. The very existence of the world socialist system strengthens the positions of the colonial peoples in their struggle against imperialism.

The socialist and newly free countries are interested in defending peace and their gains against imperialist attacks and this common interest cements their friendship. All former colonies (except Pakistan, Turkey and a few other countries), and the bourgeoisie leading them, have refused to participate in military blocs with the imperialists and are playing an important and progressive role in the world today. *The existence of the world socialist system strengthens the progressive and weakens the reactionary role of the colonial bourgeoisie.* But the richest sections of the colonial bourgeoisie are economically linked with capitalists in the imperialist countries and for this reason are becoming more and more reactionary. This can be seen from developments in India and Iraq.

An analysis of the bourgeoisie's role in the national liberation struggle of individual countries would involve extensive research, firstly, because of the bourgeoisie's dual nature, and secondly, because it is not homogeneous.

This is no less true of the bourgeoisie in the imperialist countries. In addition to the monopoly bourgeoisie there is a non-monopoly bourgeoisie, a rural bourgeoisie, and so on. But the policy of the bourgeoisie as a whole and hence that of the imperialist state is determined by the monopoly bourgeoisie, by the finance oligarchy. There is no unity in the ranks of the monopoly bourgeoisie—various groupings controlling different branches of economy constantly struggle amongst themselves. But as regards its *social* and economic role, the monopoly bourgeoisie of the imperialist countries acts in concert.

This is not true of the bourgeoisie in the colonies and semi-colonies. It also consists of different, and often interlinked sections, but unlike the finance oligarchy in the imperialist countries, no single section dictates the policy of the whole colonial bourgeoisie.

Changes in the nature and political actions of the various sections are dictated by a number of factors: 1) the level of the colony's economic development, 2) the duration of imperialist rule, 3) whether it was a semi-colony with its own state machinery and army, as China; was ruled directly by the imperialists, as Indonesia; or was ruled partly directly and partly by local rulers, as India. The position of the bourgeoisie also depends on whether the colonialists formed only a thin layer of the bourgeoisie (industrialists, planters) and of the higher civil servants, or constituted a large proportion of the population which appropriated the country's principal wealth—the fertile lands—as in South Africa and Algeria. Even though all colonies and semi-colonies are subjugated by the colonialists and are exploited by them, the position and political actions of the colonial bourgeoisie vary greatly from country to country. It is therefore impossible to give a general appraisal of the colonial bourgeoisie's nature or of its policy.

The following are the principal sections of the bourgeoisie in the colonies and semi-colonies:

The *comprador bourgeoisie* is closely linked with the imperialist bourgeoisie, which it serves by procuring raw materials, distributing its commodities within the country, handling its credit operations among the native population, etc. The comprador bourgeoisie is reactionary, and in political respects usually supports the imperialists against their own people. In China it remained hostile to the new government even after the establishment of the people's democratic government, and, when the socialist reorganisation of the country abolished the compradors' original functions, it finally ceased to exist as a class.

The small but influential industrial bourgeoisie occupies a position in between the comprador and the national industrial bourgeoisie. In India, for example, it co-operated closely with the British bourgeoisie in joint companies, even though it is highly independent in economic and notably in political respects.

In some countries, (India for example) the *industrial national*[1] *bourgeoisie* is a mighty economic and political force.[2]

---

[1] We think that it is not expedient to style only the industrial bourgeoisie of the former colonies "national", for this creates the false impression that all other sections are not national.

[2] Some Soviet economists are of the opinion that there was and still is a "monopoly capitalism" in India. This is wrong: the fact that there are some large enterprises, like TATA, does not mean that there is monopoly capital, let alone monopoly capitalism. If India's economic development proceeds along the capitalist road, it may become a monopoly capitalist country, but even then the state capitalist sector will bulk large in its economy.

Many ex-colonies, most newly free African countries and Burma, do not have a native industrial bourgeoisie.

The industrial bourgeoisie in the former colonies and semi-colonies has always vacillated. Usually it participated in the anti-imperialist national liberation struggle and sometimes even headed it. Competition from the privileged imperialist bourgeoisie made its economic positions precarious. It is common knowledge that unless a newly free country renounces capitalism, foreign capital continues to hold a strong position in its economy even after political liberation. The native industrial bourgeoisie therefore continues to struggle against foreign capital even after liberation.

On the other hand, the colonial and semi-colonial bourgeoisie often betrays the liberation struggle (for instance the betrayal by the Kuomintang in 1927) if it threatens to turn into an agrarian revolution or to dangerously strengthen the proletariat's role in the country's policy. It should be remembered that old agrarian relations are still in force in many of the former colonies and that all bourgeois sections receive a large share, indeed even the bulk of their income, through the exploitation of peasants. Even in the most developed former colonies and semi-colonies there are far less industrial workers than peasants.

This creates a contradiction in the posture and politics of the industrial bourgeoisie in the ex-colonies. As producers of industrial consumer goods (hardly any producer goods are being manufactured in the ex-colonies) they are interested in expanding the domestic market and, hence, in land reform. But a radical land reform would put an end to the concealed agrarian overpopulation, which is responsible for the extremely low wages, and which is extremely profitable for the national and imperialist industrial bourgeoisie. Besides, as we have already mentioned, the bulk of the industrial bourgeoisie receives a large share of its income from the exploitation of the peasants (usury, trade, and sometimes rents). For this reason the bourgeoisie does not support radical land reforms and tends to withdraw from the national liberation struggle if it threatens to turn into an agrarian revolution. On the whole the industrial bourgeoisie played a positive role after the war in most colonies and newly free countries.

The *rural bourgeoisie* consists of kulaks and landowners of the non-feudal type who themselves engage in agricultural production. This is the most numerous but not the most influential section of the bourgeoisie in all the colonies and newly free countries, except the least developed territories of Africa and Latin America, where there is as yet no bourgeoisie since land is not privately owned and the tribal system continues to exist to this day.

On the one hand, the rural bourgeoisie comes up against the colonialists and to a certain degree also the feudalists who try to restrict it, make it dependent and exploit it. But, on the other, the kulaks and landowners are against radical land reforms, indeed they are often against any land reform whatsoever. Sometimes they temporarily participate in the anti-imperialist struggle but withdraw from it the moment there are indications that it is turning into an agrarian movement. On the whole this layer of the bourgeoisie plays a reactionary role.

In this definition of the rural bourgeoisie we have excluded feudalists and all types of large tenants, who let the leased land to sub-tenants. This is a purely parasitical, reactionary section, which was formerly the principal social support of the imperialists. This well-to-do section is not only against any agrarian revolution, but usually against the anti-imperialist movement, since only under imperialist protection can it continue to exist as a class.

Rural merchants and usurers are closely connected with the rural bourgeoisie economically and politically and often form a single front with.

The *intelligentsia* is not a separate class. It plays a considerable and generally positive role in the colonial society's political life. The intelligentsia, especially the students, often become the mouthpiece of the mass of the working people struggling against imperialism.

By analogy with the imperialist countries, we often consider that the intelligentsia in the colonies and newly free countries are descendants only of the well-to-do classes.[1] This is not strictly true. We know, for instance, that a part

---

[1] The theses of the Sixth Congress of the Comintern on the revolutionary movement in the colonies and semi-colonial countries state that the intelligentsia is often the most consistent bearer "of the objective interests of the whole national bourgeoisie.... They are unable to be-

of the student body in the Arab countries are the children of very poor parents and that they actively participate in the anti-imperialist struggle. In pre-revolutionary China whole villages and many poor families collected money to pay for the keep of at least one student from their village. We think that this problem calls for an approach from a concrete historical standpoint.

It goes without saying that the Marxist proposition that social being determines social consciousness is absolutely correct. But this does not mean that it should be turned into a dogma. It always applies to classes and social layers *as a whole*, but not always *to individuals*.

Even in the *Communist Manifesto*, Marx pointed out that during periods of major social upheavals some people descended from the ruling classes or even belonging to them join the revolutionary camp.

The founders of Marxism-Leninism, ardent revolutionaries like Marx, Engels, Lenin, were not of proletarian origin. For many years Engels led the life of an English bourgeois and was a businessman. But the cause of the proletarian revolution became the cause of his life. Fidel Castro belongs to a rich landowning family. At the same time Noske, Bevin, Meany and many other counter-revolutionaries and enemies of the proletarian revolution, were of proletarian descent.

Historical conditions exert an influence on the political behaviour of people. The colonialists were systematically trying to subject the ruling classes and especially the colonial intelligentsia to their ideology and culture, and often with marked success. English became the language of the intelligentsia of every nationality in India. The French language, that of the intelligentsia in all of France's African colonies. The sons of Indian maharajahs and of big bourgeois attended the most aristocratic English schools. British and French colonialists tried to mould the sons of African tribal chiefs into loyal servants of imperialism. But returning home these people often became leaders of their own liberation movement.

---

come the bearers of the interests of peasants because the social layers from which they are descended are connected with land ownership." (*Shestoi kongress Kominterna* [Sixth Congress of the Comintern], Stenographic Report, Russ. ed., Issue 6, 1929, p. 139.)

As the relations between the colonialists and the colonies worsened, many students in the colonies began to look about for an anti-imperialist ideology. They did not find such ideas in the works of bourgeois scholars. Turning to Marxism-Leninism, they severed their ties with their own classes, some temporarily, others for ever.

The events of the past 20-25 years have shown that *full account must be taken not only of economic but also of historical, national, cultural and moral factors, if an understanding of the political actions of the separate colonial strata is to be gained.* All these factors are directed against imperialism, and no less than economic exploitation they make the peoples in the colonial and newly free countries, especially the intelligentsia, hate the imperialists.

The African peoples, irrespective of their economic position, will never forget that the European conquerors sold their ancestors into slavery to America, partitioned the whole of Africa, without any consideration for nationalities and tribes inhabiting the various territories, disregarded their historical background and religion, robbed them of their land, drove them into the desert and left them there to starve. They cannot forget because, in a more disguised form, this is continuing even now. In Kenya, British troops have until recently waged war against the Kikuyu people; in Madagascar, the French colonialists have killed 80,000 people (according to their own data) to suppress "an uprising after the First World War". In 1956, France sent 400,000 soldiers to suppress the Algerian struggle for national liberation and to defend the estates of French landowners. In South Africa the colonialists still treat Africans like semi-slaves, deport them to desert reservations, daily imprison many hundreds of natives and refuse to give them any say in decisions affecting the fate of their country. Even now the wages of white workers in the British possessions of Rhodesia are several times higher than those drawn by natives. Even today American Negroes are restricted in their political rights and work under worse conditions than white Americans. How could an African, whatever his social position, forget and forgive so much?

How could any Indian (be he a bourgeois, peasant or worker) ever forget the many humiliations the British inflicted upon his country when they were masters of India? In his autobiography, Jawaharlal Nehru, who received a first-class education in England, and whom even the English considered a master of the English language, tells of what the Indians had to go through.

How could any Chinese forget how the imperialists attacked his peace-loving country and divided it up into "spheres of influence" or how they established "extraterritorial rights" and, on the gates of public gardens in Chinese towns, hung up signboards reading: "Entrance to Chinese and dogs prohibited", etc.

The history of the relations between the colonial peoples and the colonialists is a powerful non-economic factor driving all strata, including the bourgeoisie, and especially the intelligentsia, into the fight against imperialism.

The defenders of colonialism try to justify colonial oppression by declaring that it was necessary to spread culture, in fact, they go so far as to assert that it was in the interests of the most "backward" peoples. The imperialists consider all the peoples in the colonies and emergent countries, especially the non-whites (two-thirds of humanity) lower races, in need of guidance by the whites—Europeans and Americans.[1]

Colonial peoples of all classes, especially the intelligentsia, consider the imperialist assertion that they are uncultured an insult. And they are right in so doing.

Indian culture is older than European culture and in many fields, notably in the arts, is certainly not inferior to the European. Up to the 19th century Indian textiles (muslin) were luxury articles which were highly valued by the European upper classes.

Arab culture has also surpassed European culture in many respects. In the Middle Ages Spain was the only European country where a deep study was made of the sciences and her Arab universities were the best in Europe. Modern mathematics and physics are inconceivable without the Arabic decimal system. Even the word "algebra" is borrowed from the Arabic.

The Chinese were a highly cultured nation when the white

---

[1] The Japanese imperialists tried to mask their colonial ambitions by advancing the slogan: "Asia for the Asians!"

colonialists were still barbarians. Right up to the 16th century China's science and culture was as high as that of the European colonialists.

Prior to the seizure of the Americas by the Europeans, the Peruvians, Mexicans, and other peoples on that continent also had a highly developed culture, art, and statehood. Two crops which have become an essential part of European food—the potato and maize—were brought to Europe from the Americas, where they had first been cultivated by the Indians.

The peoples of Africa, whom the imperialists always picture as incapable of culture, also had a well-developed culture long before the arrival of the colonialists. Gluckman, a British scholar, wrote: "We ought to remember that when the Europeans first arrived there, there were in the Rhodesias, Transvaal, Orange Free State, across into Angola, and into East Africa, quite big and well-developed civilisations. Right through the continent they were working terraced irrigation; they were mining to a depth of 80 feet for nickel, copper and gold; and they were exporting these metals as far back as A. D. 900 ... to Persia, India, and beyond that to China...."[1]

Modern European culture caught up with Chinese, Indian and Arabic culture only during the Renaissance, and later, the industrial revolution gave Europe the supremacy in material production, technology and the natural sciences.[2]

The economic exploitation of the colonial peoples, their age-long oppression by the colonialists, the lies about their "lack of culture" and inferiority, have roused the indignation of all classes of colonial peoples, in particular that of the intelligentsia, giving birth to a feeling of national unity. This enables the bourgeoisie and the intelligentsia to head the anti-imperialist struggle, and in certain conditions, as we see by the example of India, to lead it to victory.[3]

---

[1] *The New Statesman and Nation*, May 26, 1956, p. 589.

[2] It would be very interesting to make a Marxist study of why the capitalist system and the machine industry developed in Europe and not in other parts of the world, even though the pre-capitalist social system there was identical to that in Europe.

[3] Some of the definitions in the theories promulgated at the Sixth Congress of the Comintern have become obsolete and even incorrect under the new conditions. One of them states: "The national bour-

The national feeling among the colonial peoples created a situation in which even the King of Morocco, who was simultaneously its religious leader, for some time played a progressive role in the national liberation movement of the Moroccan people.

But imperialists, in particular the American imperialists, do not realise the importance of the colonial and former colonial peoples' national feelings. American politicians, magazines and newspapers wonder why the U.S.A. is so unpopular among the Asian, African and Latin American peoples, why they are distrustful of it and despise it even though the U.S.A. pours in thousands of millions of dollars in "aid", while pumping even greater profits out of them. At the same time, the colonial peoples show friendly feelings for the Soviet Union and other socialist countries, even though they are getting less money from them than from the U.S.A.

Imperialists do not understand that dollars alone cannot buy peoples' friendship. They do not understand that the Soviet people regard all colonial peoples, large and small, free or still languishing under the yoke of imperialism, yellow, brown, or black, as their equals; that Soviet assistance has no economic or political strings attached to it, that it is given selflessly, out of friendship between equals. The peoples of the U.A.R. and other countries have long since realised this difference, and are now trying to rid themselves of American aid and to form closer ties with the socialist countries.

Many bourgeois leaders of former colonies studied at universities in imperialist countries. They realise only too well that U.S. monopoly capital is not interested in the development of the productive forces in the former colonies

---

geoisie is unimportant as an anti-imperialist force.... It exerts a restraining influence on the revolutionary movement." (*Shestoi kongress Kominterna* [Sixth Congress of the Comintern], Stenographic Report, Issue 6, Russ. ed., p. 141.)

Developments during the past decade in India, Ceylon, Egypt and North Africa have shown that this is incorrect. They also show that the political conclusion that "the correct tactics in the struggle against the bourgeois parties ... are to unmask their national reformist nature" (ibid., p. 143) is also erroneous. The prediction that the colonial bourgeoisie, like the Kuomintang before it, will gradually join the counter-revolutionary camp, has proved equally false.

nor in their industrialisation, for that would make them economically independent of the imperialists.

The peoples of the economically less developed countries understand that the Soviet Union and the other socialist countries are interested in both an overall development of the productive forces in those countries and in their industrialisation, since this is the quickest way of making them economically strong and independent of the imperialists. No wonder, therefore, that they are friendly towards the Soviet Union and suspicious of the U.S.A.

The bourgeoisie and intelligentsia of the imperialist countries are surprised that the peoples of the former colonies, often even the national bourgeoisie, are well-disposed towards the Soviet Union and the other socialist countries and favour socialist reforms.

From a historical point of view this is easily understandable. In the West European countries capitalism has existed for several centuries. At one time it played a progressive role—abolished feudalism and the obscurantism connected with it, developed the productive forces, and raised the level of education, science and technology. With the exception of the revolutionary workers, all sections of the population were influenced by capitalist ideology.

But the colonial peoples were acquainted primarily with the negative side of capitalism. The capitalist colonialists did not abolish decaying feudalism in the colonies but perpetuated it. Capitalist exploitation was not a substitute for feudal exploitation but supplemented it. Capitalism did not develop the productive forces in the colonies but made them agrarian raw material appendages of their economy and created an enormous concealed agrarian overpopulation and mass unemployment. The native bourgeoisie was not given the elbow room it needed to develop but was cramped by competition from the imperialist bourgeoisie. The intelligentsia was not admitted to government, etc.

Under these conditions capitalist ideology, the view that money is omnipotent, made less of an impact on the minds of the colonial peoples and could not fully replace the old ideology of the pre-capitalist days. For that reason the well-to-do sections in the former colonies, including the bourgeoisie, do not experience the same fear of a transition to socialism often encountered among these layers in the old capitalist countries.

The theory that the colonial bourgeoisie is mainly a reactionary force which will participate in the anti-imperialist struggle only under pressure from the masses and which is always ready to betray it, and that hence the anti-imperialist struggle can be successful only if led by the proletariat, *is therefore a mistaken one.* The events of the post-war years show that in the new conditions—the presence of the world socialist system, a powerful anti-imperialist front and a general weakening of the imperialist position—the national bourgeoisie is able and willing to head the national liberation struggle and to fight for *political* independence.

This does not mean that the dual nature of the colonial bourgeoisie has disappeared and that its political vacillations have ceased. As a rule the bourgeoisie refuses to agree to radical land reforms even in the interests of the anti-imperialist struggle. These reforms have not as yet been carried out in any of the large colonial countries which have won political independence under the leadership of the bourgeoisie.[1] To an even less degree is the bourgeoisie willing to hand state power over to the proletariat voluntarily and to repudiate the system of private property.

"But as the contradictions between the working people and the propertied classes grow and the class struggle inside the country becomes more acute," the C.P.S.U. Programme says, "the national bourgeoisie shows an increasing inclination to compromise with imperialism and domestic reaction."

But in spite of this, the newly free countries play a progressive role in international politics even under bourgeois rule, and together with the socialist countries form the anti-imperialist front.

Too little time has passed since the liberation of the colonies to be able to draw any conclusions about the role played by the bourgeoisie in the countries proceeding along the capitalist road of development or are still hesitant as to what road to choose.

---

[1] Even in the U.A.R., where feudal relations were vigorously abolished, citizens were allowed to own 200 (since reduced to 100) feddans of land, which in conditions of irrigation farming is a large enough area for the establishment of large-scale capitalist farms.

Besides, the role and the importance of the bourgeoisie in the newly free countries differs according to the level of capitalist development achieved by the country before liberation. In India, for example, which even before the liberation had some large enterprises like the Tata and Birla works, closely resembling those of the monopoly type, the bourgeoisie played a different role than in countries like Ghana or Mali where there was no national bourgeoisie, or where it existed only in the incubation stage. Of great importance also are the specific features connected with the historical development of the peoples and their social and cultural level before and during their enslavement by the imperialists. In a number of newly free African countries inter-tribal warfare is still in progress. India and Pakistan were divided according to religious principles, but the Bengalis in India and in Pakistan are a single nation and their economic interests demand that they be united. In India, Indonesia, the U.A.R., the Yemen and other countries the fight of the feudal reactionaries against progressive forces has assumed a religious form.

Under these circumstances it is as yet too early to deduce a general formula which could be applied to all countries which have thrown off the imperialist yoke. We are only able to establish one principle which is typical of the development of all newly free countries having reached a comparatively high economic level. Namely, after reaching the objective which temporarily united *all classes* and layers of society (except the big landowners and the comprador bourgeoisie)—the liberation from the imperialist yoke—the unity of the people begins to disintegrate. A new attack by the imperialists may re-establish this unity, *but on the whole, class interests once again come to the fore and push aside national interests, with a resultant intensification in the class struggle.*

This can be seen clearly by the example of India. For more than 30 years the Programme of the Congress Party contained a clause on the development of Indian society "along socialist lines" after liberation. But, up to now, Nehru's Government has not only failed to develop socialism but has done everything possible to advance the state capitalist sector of the economy. The policy of neutrality and of friendly relations with the Soviet Union (which undoubtedly falls in with the interests of the Indian peoples) meets increasing resistance on the part of the bourgeoisie and all reactionary forces in the country. The big bourgeoisie is working hand in glove with the imperialist states in trying to change India's domestic and foreign policy.

This shows that the class struggle tends to become more acute. In moments of national danger, the classes in the newly free countries may consolidate their ranks to face the imperialist threat. But *the struggle over which road of development to take—the socialist or the capitalist—becomes decisive in the life of the newly free countries.* This struggle is often interlinked with the foreign political orientation of these countries on the capitalist or socialist world.

THE PROBLEM
OF THE PROLETARIAT'S RELATIVE
IMPOVERISHMENT

Theoretically, the problem of the proletariat's relative impoverishment poses no difficulties. By relative impoverishment Karl Marx meant a decrease of the working-class share in the country's gross national income. *In most cases this happens under capitalism* even when real wages grow. Marx wrote: "Relative wages can fall although real wages rise simultaneously with nominal wages, with the money value of labour. . . ."[1]

Proceeding from Marx's theoretical assumption that labour power, like all other commodities, is sold at value, it becomes obvious that a growth in labour productivity, i.e., a decrease in labour time per consumer goods unit, *decreases the share of the national income going to the working class* and increases the part being appropriated by the ruling bourgeoisie.

While this is unquestionable in theory, in practice it is very difficult to give figures corroborating this premise.

Marx's analysis presupposes a stable currency based on gold and free competition. Under such conditions the decrease in the value of consumer goods (their quality being unaffected) would be attended by a consistent drop in their prices and in a corresponding decrease in the cost of labour; in other words the share of the working class in the national income would diminish whether there is any absolute impoverishment or not.

However, during the 20th century the prices of consumer

---

[1] Marx and Engels, *Selected Works*, Vol. I, Moscow, 1962, p. 97.

goods instead of dropping have steadily risen. This can be seen by the example of the U.S.A.

Consumer Price Indexes[1]

(1947-49=100)

1913	1930	1933	1940	1950	1960	1962
42	71	55	60	103	126	128

In spite of their inaccuracy, these figures show that with the exception of the drop caused by the 1929-33 economic crisis, prices have grown steadily (among other reasons, as a result of the devaluation of the dollar in 1933) and continue to do so to this day. In other countries, where inflation and devaluation assumed a larger scale than in the U.S.A., there was an even greater rise in prices.

At first glance this seems to contradict the general theory of price formation, but a closer look explains that this is due to the following reasons:

a) the inflation and devaluation of currencies, which are the main cause of price increases during the general crisis of capitalism;

b) the monopolies fix the prices of commodities above their values, or to be more exact, above their prices of production, the buyers of consumer goods are made to pay part of this increase[2];

c) indirect taxes, duties, etc., which are also paid by the buyer;

d) other methods used by the monopoly capitalist state to raise prices—sometimes directly (the low price established for agricultural goods in all advanced capitalist countries is an example of direct methods); sometimes indirectly, by levying special taxes, imposing duties, restricting or prohibiting imports, granting subventions to encourage exports, etc.

---

[1] *Historical Statistics of the United States,* 2nd Edition, Washington, 1960, pp. 125-26; *Statistical Abstract of the United States,* 1961, p. 334; for 1962: *Federal Reserve Bulletin,* May 1963, p. 698 (recalculated by the author on the basis 1947-49 = 100).

[2] The other part is a deduction from the profits of non-monopoly enterprises (see below).

Obviously, a rapid rise in consumer goods prices must be paralleled by an increase in workers' wages.

We must therefore look for some other statistical method of assessing relative impoverishment. The best method is to trace the distribution of the national income among the classes. In dealing with such relative quantities price changes can be ignored.

But this, too, is easier said than done. Bourgeois statistical data on the national income is extremely unreliable, especially so since the bourgeoisie is interested in falsifying data to make it appear as if the share of the working class in the national income is increasing.

We must therefore make considerable amendments to the income distribution figures before they can serve any useful purpose. This means that we must deduct from the incomes of office and factory workers taxes and payments to the social security fund; set apart the income of the upper echelon of "employees", who in reality are capitalists (directors of enterprises, etc.); deduct the expenditure workers are forced to make not for themselves but on behalf of their capitalist bosses—fares to their place of work, which are very high in the U.S.A. and additional wear of clothes and footwear where workers are not provided with protective garments by their employers. On the other hand, we must add their benefits from social security funds, if these are not included in the sum total.

If we look carefully at the items in national income statistics other than wages, we shall discover considerable duplication. For instance, the income of professional people —lawyers, private physicians, artists, actors, writers, etc. —are derivative incomes, being paid predominantly out of the income of the bourgeoisie and partly out of that of the workers.

This illustrates that computations are unavoidably very approximate, and that we must not be surprised that there are considerable discrepancies between various estimates. The following three series, computed by different persons and institutions, show how great these discrepancies sometimes are. (See table on p. 105.)

A. Katz gives details on the corrections made by him in official American statistics. We shall not discuss them here: in most cases they are justifiable. His figures prove that

Share of Factory and Office Workers in the U.S. National Income
(percentages)

	1889	1900	1919	1920	1929	1939	1956	1960
I. Kuzminov[1]	70	. . .	61	. . .	47	45	40	. . .
A. Katz[2] . .	—	—	—	—	46.8	46.5	45.7	46.2
Official statistics	. . .	48.6	. . .	51.5	53.5	57.6	62.6	63.3

the share of factory and office workers in the national income is not growing and that the claim made by official U.S. statistics to the contrary is pure propaganda. Yet the author's calculations also fail to show a decrease in the workers' share.

To show the decrease of the factory and office workers' share in the national income, the author takes account of the growth in the number of wage workers and calculates the workers' share on that basis. This calculation gives the following result:

Share of the Proletarian and Proletarianising Population in the National Income Between 1900 and 1956
(percentages)

1900	1910	1920	1929	1940	1948	1953	1956
59.7	54.3	55.0	53.5	48.8	45.1	46.2	45.7

---

[1] See I. I. Kuzminov, *Obnishchaniye trudyashchikhsya pri kapitalizme* (Impoverishment of Working People Under Capitalism), Russ. ed., 1960, p. 19. The author does not disclose his sources and does not explain his method of computation. He says that this is a ratio of profit and wages in "industry", but does not mention whether it applies to industry as a whole or only to the manufacturing branches; as regards profits, he does not specify whether these are before-tax or after-tax. His figures cannot be checked and the reader is forced to take him at his word.

[2] See A. I. Katz, *Polozheniye proletariata SShA pri imperializme* (Position of the U.S. Proletariat Under Imperialism), U.S.S.R. Academy of Sciences Publishing House, Russ. ed., 1962, pp. 92, 97.

An enumeration of the number of workers to prove their relative impoverishment is permissible as a method, but the result does not show the actual share of the working class (and employees) in the national income, but the probable changes in the share of the average wage in the national income.

The modification introduced by Katz *fails to demonstrate a considerable relative impoverishment of the working class in the post-war years*, and hence, the conclusions drawn from these figures are the same as those which disregard the modification.

In general Katz's calculations are so intricate that a layman would be unable to check them and would have to accept the author's conclusions on trust.

Let us, in passing, discuss the attitude we should adopt towards bourgeois statistics.

Many of our authors have completely forgotten Lenin's remark about the " 'irrefutability' of bourgeois statistics"— they declare all bourgeois statistics falsified. This is a gross exaggeration. Data are falsified in some fields, including statistics on the distribution of the national income and social wealth and on the cost of living index, which often decide wage increases and wage cuts when long-term collective agreements are entered into, etc. But in many other fields, the bourgeoisie is interested in accurate information, for instance, data on production, reserves, total new orders, unfulfilled orders, etc.

In our opinion the practice of calling all bourgeois statistics "falsified bourgeois statistics", "obviously falsified data", etc., should be discontinued. This is an insult to the reader's intelligence. The author should either refrain from quoting data he considers falsified, or show why, how and to what extent cited data have been doctored.

It is even more ridiculous when some authors, who have already declared that all bourgeois statistics are falsified, use these very figures for computations with an accuracy of up to one or even two decimals.

Admittedly, no statistics are completely reliable and cannot picture reality with photographic accuracy. All statistics distort reality, the extent of the distortion depending on the method used to collect data. In countries where all births and deaths must be registered, birth and mortality statistics are *almost* completely accurate. Harvest statistics based on appraisals made by people who are often quite incompetent are generally accurate to about ten per cent. Such inaccuracies do not contradict Lenin's remark on the "irrefutability" of bourgeois statistics, when we are out to prove the correctness of the economic laws of capitalist development formulated by Marx. In that respect statistical inaccuracies are unimportant.

In short, we should make use of bourgeois statistics, especially since they are the only statistics on the economy of capitalist countries available to us, as Lenin did[1]. We should adopt a concrete and critical approach and should not adapt them in order to try to prove what seems desirable, for Marxism has no need to resort to such methods to prove its correctness.

* * *

The simplest statistical method for proving the relative impoverishment of the proletariat is to calculate the growth in the rate of its exploitation. Basically the two processes are identical: the appropriation of the surplus value forms the basis for the distribution of the national income among the classes.

The official census of the U.S. manufacturing industry gives data on the total wages paid, i.e., on the variable capital (v); on all expenditure on raw material, fuel, etc., i.e., on the circulating part of the constant capital (c) and the sum of the newly created value $(v+m)$, which has enabled us to approximate the rate of surplus value for the period 1899 to 1931. In presenting these data to the reader we mentioned: "It should be noted that the rate of surplus value given here is lower than the actual, since the profit of trading capital, which is also being created by industry, is not included.

"We believe it necessary to emphasise that *the above calculation is no more than an attempt at a rough evalua-*

---

[1] Here is a concrete example of how statistics are "adapted". Trying to prove the rapid growth of reserves in the U.S.A., Katz (p. 48) takes 1933 as the base year—a time when after the four-year-long crisis of overproduction reserves were abnormally low. To make his conclusions scientifically fair he should have based them on the *average level* for the cycle.

tion of the rate of surplus value and that it is based on far from adequate data. This calculation is undeniably far from accurate, but it may be categorically stated that the actual rate of surplus value *has been understated*."[1]

Our calculations furnished the following figures for the rate of exploitation:

1899	1909	1919	1921	1925	1929	1931
128	130	122	106	128	158	147

In spite of their inaccuracy these figures show: a) the correctness of Marx's assumption (formulated after consultation with Engels) that the rate of exploitation in England in the 1860s was 100 per cent; b) that the rate of exploitation grows as capitalism develops. This is irrefutable proof of the proletariat's relative impoverishment; c) that the rate of exploitation drops in crisis years and rises in the boom years. This seeming contradiction is easily explained. When production falls sharply because of a crisis, the expenditure on labour power not directly participating in the creation of new values, i.e., on the hiring of office workers, engineers, repairmen, store managers, guards, etc., changes but little, whereas the mass of the newly created value shrinks considerably. The opposite happens when the business climate improves; the profits of capital and the rate of exploitation rise to a peak, which is in keeping with the true nature of capitalism.

For the post-war years we have data only on wages paid out and on the newly created values.[2] On their basis we can compute the rate of exploitation $\frac{m}{v}$:

1947	1950	1955	1958
187	187	183	192

[1] Y. Varga, *Mezhdu VI i VII kongressami Kominterna. Ekonomika i politika 1928-1934 gg* (Between the Sixth and Seventh Congresses of the Comintern. Economy and Politics Between 1928 and 1934), Russ. ed., Partizdat, 1935, p. 188.

[2] *Statistical Abstract of the United States*, 1961, p. 777.

These far from accurate data show that the degree of exploitation has increased substantially since the war, and that it is continuing to grow slowly but surely. In spite of the declarations of bourgeois spokesmen about the levelling of incomes in the highly developed countries, the relative impoverishment of the working class continues.

A number of Soviet economists (V. Motylev, M. Smit-Falkner, A. Katz) declare that our calculations minimise the rate of exploitation and have therefore introduced various correction factors (both justified and unjustified ones) to find higher rates. We shall not bore the reader with an analysis of their corrections—for to prove the growth in the relative impoverishment we do not need the absolute magnitude of the rate of exploitation but only its movement, i.e., its growth over a long period (even though this is irregular rather than smooth). It is from this vantage point that we compare Katz's data with our data.

Dynamics in the Rate of Exploitation in the U. S. Manufacturing Industry

	1919	1931	1958	Growth of exploitation between 1919 and 1958 (per cent)
Our approximation	122	147	192	58
Katz's calculations[1]:				
first calculation	130	142	209	53
second calculation . . .	242	311	369	51
third and final			(1957)	
calculation	253	344	397	57
			(1957)	

Katz's extremely complicated calculations show the same growth in the rate of exploitation (even a slightly smaller one) than do our approximations.

We could stop our discussion here, but the reader could well ask why the figure in Katz's second calculation is about 100 per cent higher than in the first. This is because he regarded not only the profits of trading capital

---

[1] A. I. Katz, *Polozheniye proletariata SShA pri imperializme*, pp. 62, 70, 77.

but also the wages of commercial workers as deductions from the wages of the workers in the manufacturing industry and added the resulting sum to the surplus value. This is entirely unjustified—they are not deductions from wages,[1] but a *payment made by the buyer out of his income for trade services rendered*.

To make this clear let us consider *pure* services. The American worker sends a telegram and pays for it. Is that a deduction from his wages? Is the sum of wages received by the employees of the "American Telegraph and Telephone Co." a deduction from the sum of wages drawn by the workers of the manufacturing industry, as the author would have us believe from the example of commercial workers? This is carrying things a bit too far. Paying for the dispatch of his telegram the worker spends part of his wages on services rendered.

The same holds good for trade. Trading establishments render important services to the buyer, indeed it would be difficult to imagine life in the United States without such services. Buyers are paying for these services in the form of mark-ups on prices. This is the source of the wages of commercial workers and to consider it a part of the surplus value is ridiculous. The attempt to use all sorts of complicated methods to show a higher rate of exploitation does not make for a better understanding of the proletariat's relative impoverishment.

---

[1] This assumption also contradicts one of the keystones of Marx's teaching, namely, that labour power, like every other commodity, is bought approximately at value.

THE PROBLEM
OF ABSOLUTE IMPOVERISHMENT

The problem of absolute impoverishment is much more complicated than that of relative impoverishment. All Marxists agree that under capitalism relative impoverishment is a constant phenomenon, but hold different views on the methods that should be used to prove it and also on the rate of impoverishment. In general, there is a wide divergence of views on the problem of absolute impoverishment.

The apologists of capitalism, Right-wing Social-Democrats and a few renegades like Browder declare that there is no absolute impoverishment. This is obviously wrong, for there have always been countries in the bourgeois world where an absolute impoverishment of the working people could be observed. First and foremost this applies to countries where the penetration of the capitalist mode of production destroyed or disturbed the old social system without superseding it.

A hundred years ago Marx wrote about Germany: "...We, like all the rest of Continental Western Europe, suffer not only from the development of capitalist production, but also from the incompleteness of that development. Alongside of modern evils, a whole series of inherited evils oppress us, arising from the passive survival of antiquated modes of production, with their inevitable train of social and political anachronisms. We suffer not only from the living, but from the dead. *Le mort saisit le vif*!"[1]

Sixty years ago Lenin developed this view by declaring

---

[1] Karl Marx, *Capital*, Vol. I, p. 9.

that "...'the border regions' of capitalism (i.e., those countries and those branches of the national economy in which capitalism is only just emerging and clashing with pre-capitalist conditions) the growth of poverty—not only 'social', but also the most horrible physical poverty, to the extent of starvation and death from starvation—assumes a mass scale."[1]

This is no less true today. Even so staunch a supporter of capitalism as Stevenson admits that the per capita national income of the peoples in the less developed countries is falling with every passing year, i.e., that absolute impoverishment *is* taking place.

The diary of a Negro woman from the slums of the rich Brazilian town of Sao Paulo[2] gives a horrifying picture of the life of the poor there. A mother of three (two of them white), she was abandoned by her husband and left destitute. She was unable to find a steady job. With the baby tied to her back, she spent every day rummaging through garbage cans in the part of town inhabited by the rich, collecting waste paper and other refuse which she later sold for a few pennies. She was never able to earn enough to feed her three children. Her entry on August 26, 1959, reads: "Nothing can be worse than hunger." In addition to hunger she had to suffer the constant drunkenness, swearing and fights which are an integral part of slum life.

The proletariat of West Germany, France and the other European capitalist countries which participated in the Second World War, also experienced absolute impoverishment, i.e., an absolute decrease in real wages during the war and during the post-war inflation.

But we are concerned not with the question of whether absolute impoverishment exists under capitalism or not, but whether in the developed capitalist countries this impoverishment is a *constant, irreversible process*, similar to that of relative impoverishment (as quite a few authors assert and "prove"), or whether it is *neither constant nor irreversible*.

The first point of view is the more strange in that it contradicts the views expressed in the old Party Pro-

---

[1] V. I. Lenin, *Collected Works*, Vol. 4, p. 234.
[2] Carolina Maria de Jesus, *Beyond All Pity*, London, 1962.

gramme, written by Lenin, and the new Programme of the C.P.S.U., which in the main repeats the views on this problem given in the old.

During the 1902 discussion of Plekhanov's draft for the Party Programme Lenin wrote: "I am not proposing to speak of the absolute growth of poverty and destitution. . ."[1] and again: " '*Growth* of poverty of every description'—this borrowing from my draft is not a very apt one. I did not speak about the *growth* of poverty. 'Of every description' includes *'absolute'* too."[2] The Programme of the C.P.S.U. says: "Crises and periods of industrial stagnation, in turn, are still more ruinous to small producers, increase the dependence of wage-labour on capital and lead more rapidly to a relative, and sometimes an absolute, deterioration of the condition of the working class."[3]

It will be seen that the Programme of the C.P.S.U., like Lenin before it, says that the workers' position worsens absolutely "at times" due to crises. "At times" means in the minority of cases but not constantly.

Yet I. Kuzminov declares: "Unfortunately there are theoreticians who remember Marx's tenet on the impoverishment of the working people only during crises and tend to forget about it during booms, thereby allowing the basic tenets of Marxism-Leninism to become dependent on the capitalist cycle and the vacillations of the capitalist market."[4]

Our dogmatists also ignore other warnings of the founders of Marxism against a dogmatic, mechanical reiteration of Marx's law on the polarisation of capitalist society and the growth of poverty as a result of the accumulation of capital. Marx himself spoke of the counter-tendency modifying this law: "Like all other laws it is modified in its working by many circumstances, the analysis of which does not concern us here."[5] As early as 1891, Engels pointed out the root factors modifying the operation of the law of the impoverishment of the proletariat. He criticised the

---

[1] V. I. Lenin, *Collected Works*, Vol. 6, p. 48.

[2] Ibid., p. 65.

[3] *The Road to Communism*, pp. 452-53.

[4] I. Kuzminov, *Obnishchaniye trudyashchikhsya pri kapitalizme,* p. 26.

[5] Karl Marx, *Capital*, Vol. I, p. 644.

item in the 1891 draft programme of the German Social-Democratic Party reading: "The numbers and the *want* of the proletarians grow ever more." Engels wrote in this connection: "In so absolute a form this is incorrect. The organisation of workers, their growing resistance will create a certain obstacle to the *growth of poverty*. But what definitely does grow is the *insecurity of their existence.*"[1] During the general crisis of capitalism this "obstacle" is even more effective than it was 70 years ago when the organisation of the workers was incomparably weaker than it is now.

Our dogmatists are ignoring this. Between 1947 and 1953 the leading workers of the Economics Institute of the U.S.S.R. Academy of Sciences (after its merger with the Institute for World Economy) officially adopted the view that the absolute impoverishment of the working class was *constant* throughout the capitalist world. Some even spoke of a continuous progressive impoverishment, i.e., of a progressive decrease in real wages. At that time I wrote that even a very small progressive decrease in real wages would in a comparatively short historical period reduce wages *to zero* (as can be seen from a very simple mathematical calculation[2]), but my objection went unnoticed.

As distinct from the dogmatists, Marx adopted a very flexible approach to the problem. He established in a most general form that real wages must be equal to the *value* of the labour power, including the expenditure on the education of new workers.

Did Marx declare that the real wages are a constant magnitude, that they always coincide with the value of labour power? He did not. Marx not only emphasised that the capitalists are constantly trying to depress the real wages below the level of the value of labour power, and often with marked success, but he even *allowed for the possibility of real wages rising* above that level. "But hand-in-hand with the increasing productivity of labour, goes, as we have seen, the cheapening of the labourer, therefore a

---

[1] Marx/Engels, *Werke*, Bd. 22, S. 231 (italics mine.—*Y. V.*).

[2] If we suppose that in the first year real wages drop by 0.5 per cent and it decreases progressively by 0.1 per cent a year, the real wages would in 28 years amount to *50 per cent* of their initial size.

higher rate of surplus-value, *even when the real wages are rising.*"[1]

Even though the size of the real wages is based on the value of the labour power, its actual size depends on the outcome of the class struggle between capital and labour. *The concrete size of the real wages differs from country to country* and in any given period depends on the course taken by the class struggle. Besides, the real wages of the working class change regularly during the cycle.

Some people, who consider themselves orthodox Marxists, still continue to maintain that absolute impoverishment is a constant process, and that even in highly developed capitalist countries, such as Britain and the U.S.A., real wages are lower today than they were 60 years ago.

In the above-mentioned book I. Kuzminov writes (p. 148) that "in Britain ... real wages ... are at present [1958.— *Y. V.*] below the 1938 level, and hence below the 1900-01 level". He claims that the same is also true of the U.S.A. He also declares (p. 154) that in 1920 the wage level was "below the 1899 level", that before the Second World War it had not "caught up with the 1899-1900 level" (p. 157), that in 1952 it was 85 per cent of the 1939 level (p. 158), that in 1956 "the growth in real wages ... had at best drawn the general wage level to that of pre-war 1939" (p. 160), while in 1958 wages were 5 per cent below the 1956 level, i.e., that the wages of American workers in 1958 were about five per cent below the 1939 level, which was already below the 1899-1900 level. According to I. Kuzminov the wages of American and British workers dropped steadily during the whole of the 20th century, i.e., there was an absolute impoverishment of the working class. In other words, the absolute impoverishment of the proletariat did not take place "at times", as a result of a crisis as formulated in the Programme of the C.P.S.U., but proceeded constantly over the century.

A. Katz, even though he does it more carefully, also considers that absolute impoverishment in the U.S.A. is essentially a constant process. He writes: "In observing the dynamics of real wages over a long historical period, it should

---

[1] Karl Marx, *Capital*, Vol. I, p. 604 (italics mine.—*Y. V.*).

be borne in mind that the *absolute worsening of the conditions* of the proletarian masses in so developed a country as the U.S.A. *does not always assume the pattern of rectilinear motion.*"[1] Translated into simple language this means that in the U.S.A. absolute impoverishment is a constant, though not a rectilinear process.

Is this statement correct? Considering the great diversity of forms taken by the development of capitalism in different countries and at different times, the laws of capitalism cannot always be expected to operate identically. The statement about the uninterrupted and identical impoverishment of the working class in all capitalist countries precludes a scientific study of this problem, which has so important a bearing on the class struggle of the proletariat.

Dogmatists may argue as follows: statistics demonstrate that the real wages of workers in the U.S.A. and Britain have fallen during the 20th century. We shall reply by saying that this problem cannot be solved by statistics alone.

What are statistical data based on? They are based on a comparison of monetary wages with changes in the cost of living. This method can be used for short periods (not exceeding ten years), but is useless for long periods, especially for one as long as the whole of the 20th century.

The present pattern of the worker's family consumption differs so much from the 1899 pattern that the two are incomparable. Technological progress has given birth to new requirements, and conversely, new requirements have motivated technological progress. At the beginning of the century American workers did not have to spend money on motor cars, radios, TVs, dry cleaning, etc. They prepared their food at home from fresh products. Today they are buying cans, ready-to-cook foods, etc. In view of these changes, how can the cost of living index or the consumer price index be used as a yardstick of real wages?[2]

---

[1] A. I. Katz, op. cit., p. 168 (italics mine.—*Y. V.*).

[2] Statistical bodies in bourgeois countries try to get over this difficulty by periodically "adapting" the cost of living index to the changes in the consumption pattern. But this involves further computations and often serves to depict the position of the workers in a better light than it really is.

The following shows how quickly the type of food consumed in the U.S.A. changes: in 1962, as compared with 1947-49, the average American ate 45 per cent more beef, 60 per cent more chicken, 70 per cent more margarine, 312 per cent more fresh frozen fruit, 362 per cent more fresh frozen vegetables, 10 per cent less potatoes, 15 per cent less flour, 30 per cent less butter, 30 per cent less fresh vegetables.[1]

In approaching any study of this involved problem we should always remember Lenin's words that "... in view of the extreme complexity of the phenomena of social life it is always possible to select any number of examples or separate data to prove any proposition...".[2]

Even today millions of proletarians in the U.S.A. and Britain live in slums and are undernourished. People unemployed for a long time still sink into extreme poverty.

Lord Orr, a major authority on this problem, wrote in 1943: "Nutritional anaemia affects nearly 50 per cent of the women of child-bearing age amongst the poorest-paid working class. Infant mortality rate, tuberculosis and some other pathological conditions, which are affected by diet, are much higher amongst ill-fed people. Children do not grow to their full stature. The average height of adults amongst the poor is about 4 inches less than amongst the adequately-fed well-to-do."[3]

All this is true. But it still does not mean that *the bulk* of the British or American workers, the working class as a whole, is worse off today than it was at the end of the 19th century. A substantial change in the pattern of consumption, labour intensity and labour conditions, makes statistics useless.

The table on "Summary of Apparent Annual Real Wages" given by Katz[4] (travelling expenses and rents are excluded)

---

[1] *The Economist*, January 19, 1963. Based on *National Food Situation*, U.S. Department of Agriculture.

[2] V. I. Lenin, *Collected Works*, Vol. 22, p. 190.

[3] John Boyd Orr, *Food and the People*, London, 1943, p. 20. He points out that the much simpler and coarser foods the British workers (and peasants) ate 250 years ago contained more vitamins, iron and calcium than the modern town-dweller's far more exquisite diet. However, this is due not to a drop in real wages but to changed habits.

[4] A. I. Katz, op. cit., p. 230.

proves conclusively that such computations are useless.
Here is the table:

1884-1892 100	1950-196) 98.1
1893-1903 90	

Comparing the data for 1950-60 with that for 1884-92 we
find that real wages for 1950-60 *have dropped* by two per
cent; but if we compare them with 1893-1903, we find that
they *have grown* by eight per cent. What do such figures
prove?

Lenin rightly remarked that in dealing with such exceptionally complicated phenomena, the same phenomenon
can be interpreted in many different ways. Workers buy
cars because urban development has led to the emergence
of large cities. For this reason Katz excludes the money
American workers spend on the purchase of cars from their
"free" wages, i.e., from that part set aside for the satisfaction of strictly personal requirements.

Is he right in doing this? Partly yes, and partly no. Since
the car serves to convey the worker to his place of work,
the money spent on it decreases the part left to him for
the satisfaction of other requirements—lowers his real
wages. But he also uses his car for pleasure—drives in it
to the cinema, uses it for Sunday outings, takes it with him
on holiday, etc. Such expenditure should not be excluded
from his real wages.

Here is another example: the change in the consumption
of bread and potatoes. In poor countries a decrease in the
consumption of bread and potatoes may signify a worsening in the diet. In rich countries, on the other hand, it
indicates an improvement in the diet: the more meat,
vegetables, fruit people eat, the less bread they use.

Or take the decreased consumption of butter and the increased consumption of margarine. On the face of it, the
substitution in the average American's diet of margarine
for butter is a worsening of the diet. But American physicians (and life insurance companies which are interested
in having their clients pay their premiums for as long as
possible) have conducted a vigorous campaign against the
use of all animal fats. Can statistics tell us how great a
share in the decreased consumption of butter is due to the

fact that margarine is cheaper than butter, and how great a share is due to people following medical advice? Is it a worsening in the diet or an improvement?

In social life, tendencies are always fighting counter-tendencies. Let us look, for example, at working conditions. The capitalists assert that since workers have been freed of hard physical labour, working conditions are better today than they were before. This is untrue. The workers' muscles are probably taxed to a far less degree but the high tempo, monotony,[1] and constant concentration of attention needed for conveyor work strains their nerves. On the other hand factories are now better lit, better heated, the working day is shorter, and in a number of countries workers are receiving paid holidays. At first the capitalists fiercely resisted the demands of workers for better working conditions, now they have realised that a betterment of these conditions *may even be profitable for them,* for it raises labour productivity irrespective of their will. Thus we see that in this field, too, tendencies and counter-tendencies are in constant conflict. A truly scientific analysis requires that both be considered.

* * *

The worst fault of our dogmatists is that they *divorce economics from politics.*

We consider their view on the constant and inevitable absolute impoverishment of the working class not only wrong but even *politically harmful.* How can Communists mobilise the working class for the protection of their interests, for strikes, if they themselves state that a deterioration in their position is inevitable? Experience shows that political slogans are able to mobilise the large mass of non-Party workers only if they are linked with economic demands in which the workers themselves are vitally interested. What could a Communist striker answer if a strikebreaker asked him: "Why should I go on strike and refuse my wages today if you yourself say that our impoverishment is inevitable?"

In the above mentioned book I. Kuzminov writes: "We

---

[1] Experience shows that drivers tire much more on one-way highways without crossings than on ordinary highways.

must not forget that even the most successful struggle of the workers under capitalism cannot ... overcome the operation of the law of capitalist accumulation, which means that the working people's conditions will not improve but worsen."[1]

We Communists decisively refute the reformist assertion that the working class is able to change the capitalist system through economic and parliamentary struggle and that modern capitalism is no longer capitalism, but something in-between capitalism and socialism, as the proponents of capitalism, including the reformists, keep repeating. These are obvious lies. Under capitalism workers are as much slaves today as they were a hundred years ago. They can exist only by selling their labour power to the capitalists. But this does not mean that the conditions of their slavery are constantly worsening.

In analysing working-class conditions, the dogmatists completely ignore the intimate links that exist between economy and politics. They are forgetting Lenin's definition of politics as a concentrated expression of the economy. They ignore the new political conditions in the fight between labour and capital; ignore the fact that the very existence of the socialist world is forcing the capitalists and the statesmen of the capitalist countries to adapt their relations with the working class of their country to the conditions in which the struggle between the two world systems is now proceeding. Now as then, they are interested in exploiting the workers to the utmost and paying them the lowest possible wage. But, for *political* reasons, *the capitalist class as a whole* does not want *the class struggle in their country to become too intense* since this could lead to the workers embracing communism. A simultaneous fight against the socialist world and the working class in their country would endanger their rule. This is especially true of the highly developed capitalist countries such as Britain and the U.S.A. where the working class (factory and office workers) constitute the overriding majority of the population.[2] The presence of a powerful socialist world system

---

[1] I. Kuzminov, op. cit., p. 27.

[2] The history of German and Italian fascism is a warning to the bourgeoisie to avoid extremes as long as possible.

forces the U.S., British and other governments to concern themselves with the interests of their bourgeoisie as a whole. This forces them to intervene in the struggle between labour and capital and often even to take steps *against* separate capitalist enterprises which have aggravated the conflict with their workers to an extent greater than is permissible by the common interests of the capitalist class during the third stage of capitalism's general crisis.

The conditions under which the struggle between labour and capital proceeds are different from those of sixty years ago when the capitalist system still seemed invincible. The existence and strengthening of the world socialist system helps the working class in the capitalist, especially in the highly developed, countries in the struggle against the capitalists. Because of the struggle between the two systems, monopoly capital has to enter into compromises with the workers in order to prevent them from embarking on the road to revolution.

* * *

There is one more political question we should like to ask our dogmatists.

If the real wages of workers in the U.S.A. and Britain are lower than they were at the beginning of the century, if working conditions have worsened and are continuing to worsen, how can they explain the fact that neither in the U.S.A. nor in Britain have the Communist Parties yet been able to gain a hold on the minds of the masses; that in the U.S.A. there is not even a working-class reformist party and that millions of workers, in spite of great structural unemployment, vote for bourgeois parties; that in Britain where a reformist workers' party has been in existence since the beginning of the century, no less than six million factory and office workers in the 1959 elections voted for the Conservatives, who won the elections, even though more than 90 per cent of the gainfully employed population live on earned incomes?

Far be it from us to belittle the enormous influence exerted by bourgeois propaganda, the petty-bourgeois medium and the country's history on the political behaviour of the working class. But these ideological factors could hardly have such a telling influence if both the real wages and working conditions had deteriorated in comparison with the beginning of the century. After all, the economic position must exert a greater influence on the political behaviour of the working class than an ideology foreign to it.

How will our dogmatists answer this question?

* * *

Finally, by harping on the constant absolute impoverishment of the working class in the highly developed capitalist countries, these dogmatists are discrediting Soviet economic science abroad.

Many Marxist scholars in those countries have made a thorough study of the working class's position by combining statistical methods of research with on-the-spot observation. It is interesting to note that their computations contradict the views of our dogmatists.

The figures obtained by six British Marxist researchers in conjunction with workers of the editorial offices of the magazine *World Marxist Review*, provide the following data on the position of the British working class[1]:

Real Wages of Adult Male Workers in Industry

(1850=100)

1880	134	1930	212
1890	166	1938	222
1900	183	1960	335
1910	169		

These figures are greatly at odds with the picture painted by M. Smit-Falkner, I. Kuzminov et al.

The British workers pay for this increase in real wages. "This warrants the conclusion that much of the increase in real wages is due to more intensive work and longer hours."[2]

But in spite of all that, the authors of the survey say: *"The increase in the real earnings of the British working*

---

[1] *World Marxist Review* No. 8, Prague, 1963, p. 31.
[2] Ibid.

people in the post-war years can be rightfully regarded as a major success of the labour movement."[1]

In his report at the Moscow Meeting of Marxist Economists, A. Arzumanyan quoted the following figures:

Dynamics of Real Wages (weekly)[2]

(1938=100)

	U. S. A.	Britain	F. R. G.	France	Italy	Japan
1948 . .	89.4	101	91[3]	68	103	48.6
1958 . .	106.8	123	132	96	121	112.8
1960 . .	111.7	135	147	—	125	127.1

These figures are inaccurate and should not be compared with each other because of the different patterns of consumption in the various countries. However they do show that since the Second World War real wages have grown considerably in the highly developed capitalist countries, and there has definitely been no absolute impoverishment. True, labour intensity and the value of labour power have grown too. Also, a growth in real wages is *not* the same as a growth in the welfare of the workers; it is only *one* aspect of the workers' welfare, albeit an important one.[4]

Theoretically, there can be absolute impoverishment even when real wages are growing. This, Marx says, will happen when the labour intensity, i.e., the expenditure of muscular and nervous energy, etc., grows faster than real wages. But in modern times this does not happen in the developed capitalist countries.

---

[1] *World Marxist Review*, No. 8, Prague, 1963, p. 30.

[2] *Problems of Modern Capitalism and the Working Class*, Prague, 1963, p. 59.

[3] For the year 1950.

[4] A. A. Arzumanyan, a prominent Soviet economist, says (p. 60): "...The upper limit of the workers' living standard is determined by the value of labour power." This is neither very accurate nor quite understandable. According to Marx, wages (i.e., the payment for the value of the labour power) fluctuate around value—they can be higher or lower than their value, depending on the conditions on the labour market and the relation of forces in the class struggle, an important factor being the organisation and fighting efficiency of the working class.

* * *

After many years of resistance Kuzminov has finally changed his stand on this question. In October 1963 he wrote: "As for absolute impoverishment, neither Marx nor Lenin ever said this was an uninterrupted process. ... The living standard of the workers is subject to considerable fluctuation, it might rise or decline for more or less long periods."[1]

This is true. However it is strange that I. Kuzminov did not think it necessary to add a few critical words on his previous views.

---

[1] *International Affairs* No. 10, 1963, p. 53.

THE LABOUR ARISTOCRACY AFTER
THE SECOND WORLD WAR

The role of the labour aristocracy has been thoroughly studied by the founders of Marxism-Leninism. But the deep changes wrought by the development of capitalism, especially since the Second World War, have not failed to affect the labour aristocracy, its composition, and the sources of its privileges.

Under pre-monopoly capitalism only Britain had a labour aristocracy. The monopoly superprofits of British capitalists provided the funds ensuring its privileged position. Britain was then the workshop of the world and, in addition to ordinary profits derived from exploiting the working class within the country, British capitalists garnered huge superprofits from exploiting the enormous colonial empire. Engels said of Britain that "this most bourgeois of all nations is apparently aiming ultimately at the possession of a bourgeois aristocracy and a bourgeois proletariat *alongside* the bourgeoisie".[1]

"This aristocracy of labour," Lenin wrote, "which at that time earned tolerably good wages, boxed itself up in narrow, self-interested craft unions, and *isolated itself from the mass of the proletariat, while in politics it supported the liberal bourgeoisie*. And to this very day perhaps nowhere in the world are there so many liberals among the advanced workers as in Britain."[2] This and many other statements by

---

[1] Marx and Engels, *Selected Correspondence*, p. 110.
[2] V. I. Lenin, *Collected Works*, Vol. 19, p. 370 (italics mine.—*Y. V.*).

Lenin show that he regarded the labour aristocracy primarily *as a political factor.*

The feature typical of the labour aristocracy is its divorce from the mass of workers, its desertion of the working class and its siding with the bourgeoisie and the anti-revolutionary influence exerted by it on the mass of workers.

The principal reasons for its betrayal of the working class are the economic privileges enjoyed by the labour aristocracy.

A concrete historical analysis of this phenomenon shows that this problem is far more complicated than would seem at first sight.

It is not only colonial superprofits which are responsible for the comparatively good conditions of the labour aristocracy and for its defection to the side of the bourgeoisie. In economic respects the U.S.A. was for a long time a colonial country. But the American workers (except new immigrants) were economically in a better and more privileged position than their European counterparts. This was because there was practically no land rent in America, because large tracts of land were waiting to be cultivated, and anybody having worked a few years as a hired worker could become an independent farmer.

The labour aristocracy, formed of white workers in the colonies, stands on a different basis. The difference between their incomes and those of the native population (Rhodesia, South Africa, etc.) considerably exceeds that between the labour aristocracy and unskilled workers in metropolitan countries. Their function, too, is different. They have no ideological influence on native workers and are bribed by the white capitalists solely to make them allies in their oppression of non-white workers.

Often the bourgeoisie is supported not only by the labour aristocracy, but also by low-paid workers, the bulk of which has not yet been drawn into the trade union movement. These include farmhands, workers in villages employed by artisans, unskilled factory workers, especially women, etc. They are politically backward, irresponsible, badly organised and fall under the influence notably of religious parties. They also vote for these parties, in other words, for the bourgeoisie. Only a revolutionary crisis is able to stir them from the political lethargy into which they have fallen.

But it would be dogmatic and wrong to believe that the labour aristocracy always sides with the bourgeoisie. Historical events have demonstrated that it is not only economic conditions which determine the political behaviour of workers. Workers are able to suffer adverse conditions for a very long time, in fact they even get used to them. *Dissatisfaction is caused primarily by a worsening of conditions*, especially by a rapid worsening. The same also applies to the labour aristocracy. It holds the side of the bourgeoisie so long as its economic privileges are stable, *but, if its position sharply deteriorates, it may become an active participant in the revolutionary struggle*. This happened in Hungary in 1918-19 before the establishment of the dictatorship of the proletariat when a sharp inflation plunged down the living standard of the workers. Skilled workers who were receiving the highest rates reacted far more vehemently to the worsening of their position than did badly paid workers. They joined the Communist Party and often played a leading role in the fight to overthrow the bourgeoisie. Similar developments were observed in the workers' revolutionary movement in Germany.

Attempts to establish the numbers of the labour aristocracy are of a certain scientific interest,[1] but numbers do not decide the political influence of the labour aristocracy on the behaviour of the working class as a whole in a definite historical situation.

The reasons responsible for that influence changed during the course of capitalist development. In the 19th century, workers' skills played the decisive role. The labour aristocracy consisted exclusively of skilled workers, even though not all skilled workers were part of it. At that time the composition of the working class was comparatively simple.

---

[1] British scientists give the following figures for the composition of the British working class (per cent):

> Labour aristocracy (top level skilled workers)—about 15
> Skilled and semi-skilled workers—about 45-50
> Unskilled workers—about 35-40

The British Labour Movement. 1770-1920. A History by A. L. Morton and George Tate, London, 1956.

It consisted of two categories (excluding supervisors): skilled workers who had acquired their qualifications after three to five years of empirical study under artisans, and unskilled workers who worked under the skilled workers. The ideological influence of the labour aristocracy was based on their role in production—unskilled workers could not work without them; when skilled workers went on strike, unskilled workers could not work.

With the development of the machine industry and especially of conveyorised and automatic lines, the composition of the industrial working class changed substantially. The number of skilled workers became relatively small, that of "trained" workers rose steeply, and the term of training became much shorter. At the Ford Motor Works, for example, it took only one day to "train" a worker. This led to the emergence of a small layer of highly skilled workers who had acquired their skills not empirically but at special schools where they had been taught to adjust and repair automatic lines, appliances, etc. There is practically no difference between these workers, technicians and production engineers.

This change can be seen by the example of the U.S.A. and Britain.

The Gap Between Wage-Rates for Skilled and Unskilled Work in Britain[1]

(per cent)

Narrowing Differentials	1914	1960
Engineering (weekly rates)		
patternmakers'	184	133
fitters and turners'	170	119
Builders (hourly rates)		
bricklayers' . . . . : . .	150	114
Railways (weekly rates)		
engine drivers'	211	147

[1] *The Economist*, April 23, 1960, p. 363.

For the U.S.A. we have the following data:

**Average Weekly Earnings for Production Workers
in 25 Manufacturing Industries,
by Sex and Degree of Skill[1]**

(dollars)

	Unskilled, male	Skilled and semi-skilled, male	Percentage by which earnings of skilled workers exceed those of unskilled workers
1914 . .	10.7	15.0	42
1948 . .	50.0	63.5	27

It will be seen that in the U.S.A., too, wages tend to equalise even though this tendency operates exceedingly slowly.

The data given above shows that there is a tendency towards a levelling of the wages of skilled and unskilled workers. This shows that the position of the labour aristocracy (in the old sense of the word) is weakening for two reasons—the share of skilled workers is diminishing and the pay differential between them and unskilled labour is decreasing.

Yet in spite of this tendency there is still a great difference between some categories of American workers. According to official statistics,[2] in November 1962 industrial workers in the transport equipment branches were drawing the highest hourly rate—2.98 dollars; those in the garment industry, the lowest—1.67 dollars. Partly this is due to the fact that in the former branch only about 10 per cent of the workers are women, while in the latter they account for more than 80 per cent. Since the above figures give the average for the whole branch, and there are large differences within the branch itself, it follows that some workers in America earn twice as much as those in the low bracket. These figures show that even though wages tend to equalise, pay differences are still very high and a labour aristocracy continues to exist.

---

[1] *Historical Statistics of the United States*, 2nd Edition, p. 94. (More recent data is unavailable. Percentages computed by the author.)

[2] *Federal Reserve Bulletin*, December 1962, p. 1687.

In Britain women workers are still subjected to discrimination.

Weekly Wages in British Industry[1]
(shillings)

	October 1938	October 1948	1959
Men over 21	69	138	271
Women over 18	32.6	74.6	140

Now, as before the war, women are earning about half as much as men. Admittedly, they are generally less skilled, but even when they are doing the same work as men, they receive much less. In the U.S.A. this discrimination is less pronounced.

* * *

If we approach the problem of the labour aristocracy on a world scale we must consider most U.S. industrial workers (except Negroes, Mexicans, Puerto Ricans, etc.) as forming a labour aristocracy as compared with workers in other capitalist countries. This does not mean that there is no poverty among the U.S. working class. Even President Kennedy had to admit that more than 30 million Americans live in poverty. These are mainly Negroes, Mexican workers, new immigrants or homeless farm labourers who wander from place to place, the unemployed who have exhausted all legal sources of aid, etc. Nevertheless, the layer of the labour aristocracy is wider in the U.S.A. today than it was in Britain even during the period of its highest prosperity.

The average hourly wages of workers (men and women) in the manufacturing industry in 1961[2] amounted to:

---

[1] *United Kingdom Annual Absract of Statistics*, 1938-48, p. 116; 1961, p. 128.

[2] U. N. data. *Monthly Bulletin of Statistics*, January 1963, p. 116 (recalculated into dollars at the official rate of exchange.—*Y. V.*).

U. S. A.	West Germany	France	Italy	Britain (only men)	Britain (men and women)
2.32	0.72	0.45	0.40	0.95	0.80[1]

We are well aware that these figures distort facts in favour of the American workers. Computations according to the official rate of the dollar tend to lessen the purchasing power of West European currencies. Unemployment is much higher in the U.S.A. than in Western Europe. West European workers having children receive special benefits, are given aid in case of unemployment, disability due to illness, complete disability, etc., while in the U.S.A. only a minority enjoys such benefits. But even if we evaluate these additions at 50 per cent of their wages, the wages of West European workers are only a half or a third of those of their American counterparts. The difference in the hourly wage level in the American and West European manufacturing industries exceeds the difference in wages between the labour aristocracy and unskilled workers in Britain at any time in its history.

That the American industrial workers are the labour aristocracy of the capitalist world becomes even more obvious if we compare their wages with those of industrial workers in the less developed capitalist countries. U.S. workers earn as much in a week as workers in neighbouring Mexico earn in a month, and as much as African workers earn in two to three months.

* * *

Where does the big bourgeoisie of the highly developed countries get the money to bribe and maintain the labour aristocracy?

One often hears that the liberation of the colonies from the imperialist yoke has deprived, or at least considerably decreased, the bourgeoisie's possibilities of bribing a part of the workers.

In our opinion this is untrue. Only the former colonies and semi-colonies which liberated themselves under the leadership of the working class and the Communist Parties

---

[1] Our estimate.

(North Korea, North Vietnam, China and Cuba) and took the road of socialist development, have succeeded in freeing themselves from imperialist exploitation. In all other large Asian countries—India and Pakistan, the Middle East, the whole of Africa, Latin America (except Cuba), political sovereignty did not bring economic liberation from the domination of foreign capital. Britain's capital investments in India doubled after that country's liberation and profits grew correspondingly. The overt imperialist rule of old was replaced by neo-colonialism, mixed capitalist companies were set up, loans were granted by the World Bank, government "aid" was extended, etc. We are unable to give accurate data but there is no doubt that the *total capital investments* of imperialist countries in the less developed bourgeois countries and the *profits and superprofits* being pumped out of them are much higher now than they were before their liberation.

The profits the imperialists derive from trading with the developing countries have also grown considerably because the prices of goods being exported by them have risen steeply, while the prices of the developing countries' staple export commodities have dropped. In other words, the terms of trade[1] become worse for the former colonies.

Let us make an attempt to approximate the additional tribute exacted by the highly developed imperialist countries from the developing countries as a result of deteriorating terms of trade during the past decade.

Terms of Trade[2]

(1958=100)

	1950	1960	1962
Highly developed countries[3] . .	96	103	105
Less developed countries[4] . . .	108	99	95

[1] The "terms of trade" is the export price index divided by the import price index.

[2] *Monthly Bulletin of Statistics*, January 1963, p. XI.

[3] According to the U.N. classification these include the U.S.A., Canada, the West European countries, Japan, Australia, New Zealand and South Africa. This classification is not quite accurate for although Spain and Portugal are West European countries they cannot be considered highly developed.

[4] All other capitalist countries.

This shows that although during the past decade the terms of foreign trade have improved by seven per cent for the imperialist countries, they have worsened during the same period for the less developed countries by 14 per cent.

How much do the imperialist countries trading with the less developed countries gain from this disparity? In 1960 (the last year for which data are available) the highly developed countries sold the less developed countries commodities to the value of 21,200 million dollars.[1] Their profit, due to the worsening of the terms of trade for the less developed countries by 7 per cent, amounted to 1,400 million dollars. In 1960 the highly developed countries bought from the less developed countries commodities to the value of 19,800 million dollars. The losses incurred by the less developed countries due to the worsening of the terms of trade by 14 per cent (that is the buyers' profit) amounted to 2,800 million dollars. The total gain of the imperialists thus amounted to 4,200 million dollars in 1960 alone.

As we see, imperialist profits from capital investments in the less developed countries, in addition to the huge profits from their foreign trade with these countries, provide them with large sums of money with which to bribe the labour aristocracy.

But large as it is, this sum is not enough. This can be seen from the following comparison. Let us, for example, take the U.S.A., the richest capitalist country in the world, and Canada. In 1961 United States exports to the less developed countries amounted to 7,000 million dollars and its imports from them to 6,800 million dollars.[2] Even if we presume that their gain from the better terms of trade was equal to that computed above (and this is an exaggeration because the U.S.A. and Canada export a lot of foodstuffs to those countries), it would have amounted to 1,300 million dollars. Let us add to it the net profit on capital investments in the less developed countries, amounting to 2,300 million dollars.[3] To avoid any underestimation let us round the sum off to 4,000 million dollars.

[1] *Monthly Bulletin of Statistics*, August 1962, p. XVIII.
[2] Ibid., March 1963, p. XVI.
[3] *Statistical Abstract of the United States*, 1961, p. 865 (for 1960).

Undoubtedly, 4,000 millions dollars a year is a lot of money. Yet even so this sum is not large enough to transform the bulk of the American working class into a labour aristocracy. This can be seen from the following figures.

Assuming full employment, the total sum of wages and salaries paid by private business in the United States in 1951 comprised 142,000 million dollars.[1] The 4,000 million dollars of superprofits pumped out of the less developed countries amounted to only three per cent of that total.

In 1960 the average estimated income of a fully employed worker in the U.S. private sector amounted to 4,734 dollars.[2] These figures are a gross overestimation, for they include the income of highly paid employees and do not exclude losses due to unemployment, taxes and other payments. Yet it is obvious that even if the American (and Canadian) bourgeoisie had spent all the superprofits pumped out of the less developed countries on bribing its workers, this would have sufficed to transform only a small share of its 40 million strong army of workers and rank-and-file employees into a labour aristocracy.

The principal source of funds for bribing a considerable portion of the working class is the rapid growth in labour productivity which is not accompanied by a corresponding shortening of working time. This can be shown by the example of the growth of labour productivity in U.S. industry.

Output in Man-hours in the Manufacturing Industry as a Whole[3]

(1947-49=100)

1947	1950	1955	1960
97.6	109.5	125.6	135.7

---

[1] Statistical Abstract of the United States, 1961, p. 303 (for 1960).
[2] Ibid., p. 323.
[3] Ibid., p. 217, 1960—non-agricultural branches of production.

According to official statistics labour productivity has grown by almost 40 per cent since the Second World War.[1] At the same time the working week has decreased but very little, in any case, by less than 10 per cent.[2] The growth in the labour productivity has not been paralleled by a corresponding drop in prices; on the contrary, the "index of consumer goods prices" is now 25 per cent higher than it was in 1948 and continues to grow steadily.

All this means that American capital appropriates at present a far greater proportion of the surplus product (some 20 to 30 per cent more) than it did 15 years ago.

The rapid growth of labour productivity provides the bourgeoisie with vast reserves with which to bribe a considerable share of the working class.[3] On the other hand, it creates an ever increasing structural unemployment—the scourge of the working class.

The other advanced capitalist countries develop along similar lines.

Since the war labour productivity has grown considerably in all industrially developed countries, while the actual

---

[1] These figures are obviously inaccurate. They include office workers, artisans, etc. The labour productivity of industrial workers has undoubtedly grown to an even greater extent. On the other hand, the general effect of the growth in labour productivity is slightly less, since depreciation deductions have grown because of the introduction of more complicated and more expensive equipment.

[2] American statistics compute the duration of the working week not by the number of hours worked during the week by fully employed workers, but by the average number of hours worked per week by enterprises, i.e., the average working time (full, reduced or with the closure of enterprises taken into account) per worker. In crisis years the statistics therefore show a considerable decrease in working time.

[3] We have not been able to obtain concrete figures to show how much the American bourgeoisie gains from the growth in labour productivity. The following figures give a rough idea:

U. S. National Income Minus Incomes of Factory and Office Workers

(in thous. million dollars)

1947	1955	1961
70	107	126
	Or—corporate profits	
23.6	43.0	45.5

(*Survey of Current Business*, July 1962, pp. 6-7.)

working time has decreased little as compared with the pre-war working week of 48 hours.

In 1961 the number of hours actually worked per week was 45.3 in West Germany, 45.7 in France, 46.8 in Britain and 48.5 in Italy.[1]

Even though there were several hundred thousand unemployed in Britain during the week ending April 27, 1963, about 1.7 million British workers (or 28.6 per cent of the total) each worked an average of 8 hours overtime a week.[2]

* * *

The functions the labour aristocracy is expected to perform are to safeguard the capitalist system, and disseminate bourgeois ideology among the working class so as to keep it from taking the revolutionary road. In carrying out these functions, the labour aristocracy, whose importance in production and influence on other layers of workers has waned because of technological progress, is being increasingly assisted, and even superseded, by the *workers' bureaucracy*.

After the First World War Lenin wrote: "An entire social stratum, consisting of parliamentarians, journalists, labour officials, privileged office personnel, and certain strata of the proletariat, has sprung up and has become *amalgamated* with its own national bourgeoisie, which has proved fully capable of appreciating and 'adapting' it."[3]

Today the reformist workers' bureaucracy has become even more numerous and powerful. As distinct from the labour aristocracy, members of the bureaucracy tend to be clerical rather than production workers. The incomes of the lower bracket of the bureaucracy are no higher than those of the aristocracy of labour but they have the advantage of not having to fear unemployment, the ever-present scourge of the working class. The elite of the bureaucracy has an income which is as high as that of the bourgeoisie; its way of life is also that of the bourgeoisie. The leader of "Her Majesty's Opposition" receives a Minister's salary from the British bourgeois government. The

---

[1] *Monthly Bulletin of Statistics*, February 1963, p. 11.

[2] Data from the Ministry of Labour. *The Times*, June 8, 1963. During that same week 98,700 workers worked part time.

[3] V. I. Lenin, *Collected Works*, Vol. 21, p. 250.

incomes of the American trade union bosses are equal to those of millionaire rentiers, often reaching 100,000 dollars a year.[1]

The workers' bureaucracy has become very numerous. Its chief detachments are:

1. *The bureaucracy of the Social-Democratic parties*: members of parliament, the editorial staff, party functionaries and also those state, municipal and other officials who owe their jobs to party influence.

2. *The trade union bureaucracy*, which exerts a major influence on the workers. In co-operation with the bourgeois bureacracy in the factories, it often controls the fate of individual workers (within the framework of the collective wage contract): deciding upon who will lose his job first, who will be transferred to a better-paid job, what assistance will be given in the event of unemployment, etc. If a worker quarrels with somebody from the party bureaucracy or leaves the reformist party, he need not fear direct negative consequences, but if he quarrels with somebody from the trade union bureaucracy, this may be his undoing. A worker often cannot leave the trade union without losing his job. The trade union bureaucracy signs collective wage contracts with the bosses; the trade union members often do no more than endorse them by vote.[2]

3. *The co-operative bureaucracy*—also numerous—is closely linked with the reformist party bureaucracy but exerts a much smaller influence on the workers than the trade union bureaucracy.

It is difficult to establish how numerous the workers' bureaucracy really is. Although in the large countries it definitely reaches tens of thousands. But its importance and influence depends not only on its size, for in addition to the paid bureaucracy there are large numbers of "active" trade union members who strive for paid jobs in the trade

---

[1] In the middle of February 1963 the New Jersey Trade Union of Motor Transport Workers decided to raise the salary of A. Provencano, its leader, by 50,000 dollars a year. If he had received that increase his salary would have amounted to 113,000 dollars a year. He considered it expedient to refuse. (*The Times*, February 16, 1963; February 21, 1963.)

[2] In Britain shop-stewards sometimes oppose the influence wielded by the trade union bureaucracy.

union or party apparatus and therefore willingly fulfil all orders given by these bodies.

The principal function of the labour aristocracy and workers' bureaucracy is to disseminate bourgeois ideology and to struggle against Marxist or communist ideology within the working class. Their main ideological instruments are legal activity, the repudiation of all illegal activity, the embellishment of bourgeois democracy and parliamentarism, the teaching about the supra-class character of the democratic bourgeois state, chauvinism and religion, anti-Marxism and anti-communism.

Almost half a century ago Lenin wrote that: "*Opportunism and social-chauvinism have the same political content,* namely, class collaboration, repudiation of the dictatorship of the proletariat, repudiation of revolutionary action, unconditional acceptance of bourgeois legality, confidence in the bourgeoisie and lack of confidence in the proletariat. *Social-chauvinism is the direct continuation and consummation of British liberal-labour politics, of Millerandism and Bernsteinism.*

"The struggle between the two main trends in the labour movement—revolutionary socialism and opportunist socialism—fills the entire period from 1889 to 1914."[1]

Lenin does not mention the Church as one of the conductors of bourgeois ideology to the working class. This is explained by the fact that before the First World War religion was not used as widely in the class struggle as it is now. At that time there still existed liberal, anti-clerical tendencies in the bourgeoisie and the reformist labour movement. Since the First, and especially since the Second World War, religion and the Church have become one of the principal means of deceiving workers. Catholic parties were created or strengthened. In Britain a number of Labour Party leaders—Macdonald, Lansbury, Henderson— were devout churchmen. A multitude of religious sects in the U.S.A. are trying to obstruct the growth of class consciousness among workers.

When the people recovered from the shock of the Second World War, the influence of religion and the Church in

---

[1] V. I. Lenin, *Collected Works*, Vol. 22, p. 112.

politics waned. However, even today this influence is much stronger than it was before the First World War.

Trade union bureaucrats (at all levels) are of working-class origin; however, in the bureaucracy of the reformist parties, an increasing role is being played by bourgeois intellectuals. Attlee, Gaitskell, Wilson—all the past three leaders of the Labour Party are all of bourgeois origin; the same applies to Leon Blum, Guy Mollet, Ollenhauer, etc. This illustrates the close links between the reformist parties and the bourgeoisie.[1]

* * *

If we were asked in what measure the bourgeoisie, with the help of the labour aristocracy and the workers' bureaucracy, has succeeded in diverting the working class from the revolutionary path we should have to give the following reply: the bourgeoisie has, up to now, been successful in diverting the working class from the revolutionary path in the rich Anglo-Saxon and Scandinavian countries, but has not succeeded in doing so in other capitalist countries.

In the U.S.A., for instance, the working class does not even have a reformist mass party; tens of millions of factory and office workers vote for one of the two large bourgeois parties; the 40-year-old Communist Party has no mass influence, is persecuted and exists only semi-legally. The trade union leaders, serving the bourgeoisie, deceive the workers and propagate anti-Marxism and anti-communism. Identical conditions prevail in Canada.

Britain (as well as Australia and New Zealand) has a long-established working-class party which is, essentially, nothing more than a second bourgeois party.[2] The bourgeoisie is not afraid of periodically handing over to it the reins of government, knowing full well that this does not

---

[1] This does not mean that the leaders of the trade union bureaucracy are less obedient servants of the bourgeoisie. The British bourgeoisie still lauds Bevin as a great statesman. After Gaitskell's death the British bourgeoisie supported not Wilson's but Brown's candidature as leader of the Labour Party.

[2] Typical of the bourgeois spirit pervading this party is that Labour M.P. Jay recently suggested that the name of the Labour Party be changed because many voters considered it embarrassing to vote for a party so designated.

constitute a threat to the capitalist system. In Sweden the Social-Democratic Party has held office continuously for the past 25 years—either alone or in coalition with other bourgeois parties—and has ruled the country without detriment to Sweden's capitalist system. Communist Parties still do not constitute an important factor in the political life of those countries.

In these countries, the state Lenin described as the prerequisite for revolution, when the bourgeoisie is no longer able, and the proletariat no longer willing to live in the old way, has not as yet set in, despite mass unemployment in the U.S.A. and Britain.

True, in the U.S.A. there are long and stubborn mass strikes, which are often regarded as an expression of the revolutionary frame of mind of the American working class. But we believe that, in the present concrete historical conditions, this is a somewhat hasty conclusion.

During times of revolution, long mass strikes are a symptom and simultaneously a factor for the intensification of the revolutionary struggle, a sign that the workers refuse to live under existing conditions. Yet the mass strikes in the U.S.A. today only prove that the workers consider themselves strong enough to resist the worsening of their position due to the constant growth of consumer goods prices, and resort to strikes to improve their conditions within the capitalist framework.

The fact that these strikes are often headed by rabid anti-Communists, by champions of capitalism, is vivid proof that they are not a threat to the capitalist system in the U.S.A. The Kennedy administration has several times (for example during the iron and steel workers' strike or the dockers' strike) even found it expedient to intervene in the strike on behalf of the strikers to safeguard the interests of the big bourgeoisie as a whole. The American bourgeoisie is still able to rule by the old methods, and the bulk of American workers (and also British, Canadian, Australian and Swedish workers) still prefer to go on living as they do. *For the time being* the labour aristocracy and workers' bureaucracy in these countries are still managing to cope with the tasks entrusted them by the bourgeoisie.

But this does not apply to France and Italy, where the reformist workers' movement is much smaller than the communist movement, and where the Communist Parties exert a strong influence on the trade union movement. Even though the reformist and Catholic parties have succeeded in alienating a part of the workers and some trade unions, proletarian solidarity generally outweighs their ideological differences and in large strikes even the dissident trade unions co-operate with the communist trade unions. The mass strike of French miners in March 1963, which was supported by practically the whole of France's working class, had (irrespective of its outcome) quite a different political nature to the mass strikes in the U.S.A.

* * *

The above shows that in the richest capitalist countries the big bourgeoisie is *still* able to bribe wide layers of the labour aristocracy, and with their help and that of the reformist workers' bureaucracy, has so far succeeded in keeping most of the workers on its side. But this is a transient state of affairs. The development of the revolutionary workers' movement will obviously follow the pattern of the working-class movements in Italy, France, etc., which aim to destroy the influence of the bourgeoisie.

THE FLOW OF CAPITAL DURING THE LEVELLING OF THE RATE OF PROFIT. RATE OF PROFIT UNDER MONOPOLY CAPITALISM

Marx states that the constant flow of capital from branches yielding a lower than average rate of profit to branches with a higher rate of profit tends to equalise the rate of profit in the various branches of production.

He wrote that "... capital withdraws from a sphere with a low rate of profit and invades others, which yield a higher profit. Through this incessant outflow and influx, or, briefly, through its distribution among the various spheres, which depends on how the rate of profit falls here and rises there, it creates such a ratio of supply to demand that the average profit in the various spheres of production becomes the same...."[1]

Textbooks on political economy generally repeat this formula. Take the one edited by K. V. Ostrovityanov, for example, which says that "in pursuit of higher profits capital flows from branch to branch, and this results in the establishment of an average rate of profit..."[2].

In reality however, and especially in present-day conditions, the flow of capital from one branch to the other is a far more complicated problem than Marx's general formula seems to indicate. Developing this idea, Marx himself (as will be shown further in the essay) modified his general formula. By the flow of capital Marx understood changes in the distribution of the aggregate social capital in its func-

---

[1] Karl Marx, *Capital*, Vol. III, p. 195.
[2] *Politicheskaya ekonomiya* (Political Economy), Textbook, 4th Russ. ed., Gospolitizdat, 1962, p. 154.

tion of industrial productive capital. When an industrial capitalist sells his factory to another capitalist, he withdraws *his* capital from that branch. But this does not effect any changes in the distribution of the aggregate social capital and has no influence on the formation of the rate of profit, since this capital is replaced by an equally large capital belonging to *another* capitalist. This is also true of share transfers. Transactions in "paper duplicates of real capital" are also unimportant in this connection, for they too bring no real changes in the distribution of productive capital. Changes in the ratio between the sum total productive and sum total loan capital are also immaterial.

If an industry or an individual enterprise is using loan capital for which it has to pay out a certain part of profits in interest, it makes this payment *after* the average rate of profit has formed. Only changes in the distribution of productive capital between different industries affect the rate of profit.

Let us study the flow of capital in greater detail. The flow of capital from one branch to another was no problem under capitalism of the free competition era analysed by Marx. At that time there was no fundamental difference between this flow and the foundation of a new productive enterprise or the extension of an already existing one, i.e., the transformation of money capital into constant capital (both fixed and circulating) and variable capital, since the establishment of a new enterprise brought with it an expansion of production and an influx of capital to an already existing branch (the rare exception being when the production of an entirely new article was undertaken). The *outflow* of capital is a far more complicated matter. The outflow of circulating capital poses no problems—raw and auxiliary materials are processed, finished goods sold and the variable capital assumes a monetary form and can be invested in some other branch of production. But the outflow of fixed capital is a far more complicated matter—some buildings and power installations could be used in another branch, even though this would involve considerable additional outlay, but what of equipment? A sewing machine will do nothing but sew, a turning lathe is good only for turning, a ship can only carry loads over water. The outflow of capital *is therefore invariably linked with the loss of a part of it*.

Marx saw this clearly: "Yet with respect to each sphere of actual production—industry, agriculture, mining, etc.—the transfer of capital from one sphere to another offers considerable difficulties, particularly on account of the existing fixed capital."[1]

In Marx's time the share of fixed capital in the total capital of industrial enterprises was relatively small since technology was still on a comparatively low level; and the share of Department II in industry was much higher than that of Department I.

But even in Marx's time there were branches of economy from which an outflow of capital was practically impossible. The railways, for example, involved capital investments which in those days were considered huge. In the railways the share of fixed capital is very high in comparison with that of circulating capital invested in raw and other materials, and has a form that makes it useful only in railway transport—rails and sleepers, bridges, station buildings, engines and cars are useless in any other branch, except for the small amount that could be recouped as scrap. The same applies also to water transport.

In many cases the capitalist has only one way out—to export the equipment he no longer wants (engines, cars, ships) and to invest the resulting money in another branch. This will lead to an outflow of capital from that particular country, but nothing will have changed in the capitalist system as a whole—there will have been a geographical migration of capital but not a flow of capital from one branch of production to another.

It is not hard to see that nowadays the flow of capital is connected with far greater difficulties than it was in Marx's time. First, because technological progress has brought an enormous growth of the share of fixed capital in the aggregate capital, both in individual enterprises and on a world scale. Secondly, from the moment the enterprise is established, the fixed capital is adapted for production only in that particular industry. The buildings and plant of a modern chemical works can be used only in the chemical industry. An iron and steel works can produce only metal. The equipment of a modern motor works is adapted only for conveyor

---

[1] Karl Marx, *Capital*, Vol. III, Moscow, 1966, p. 208.

production, its automatic lines are no more than a heap of scrap if they cannot be used for the production of cars. This is true of most modern large enterprises. The flow of capital would entail enormous losses and become responsible for the bankruptcy of enterprises.

This naturally poses the following question: was Marx wrong when he said that the flow of capital tends to equalise the rate of profit?

No, he was not. Marx used his usual dialectical method of investigation—he first solved the problem in its most general form, and then worked it out in greater detail. He says that, "the general rate of profit is never anything more than a tendency, a movement to equalise specific rates of profit. The competition between capitalists—which is itself this movement toward equilibrium—consists here of their gradually withdrawing capital from spheres in which profit is for an appreciable length of time below average, and gradually investing capital into spheres in which profit is above average. Or it may also consist in *additional capital distributing itself gradually and in varying proportions among these spheres.*"[1]

The words given in italics show that the flow of capital tends to equalise the rate of profit. The outflow of capital is rare and is connected with huge losses. It would be more correct to say that the outflow of capital takes place when a business has incurred losses for a number of years and when the future, too, promises no profits.[2] The tendency towards the levelling of the rate of profit expresses itself in the gradual distribution of *newly invested capital* in different proportions among the various branches in conformity with the rate of profit they offer to the investor.

This applies in equal measure to pre-monopoly and monopoly capitalism. But, under capitalism of the free competition era, the influx of additional capital was unrestricted, while under monopoly capitalism this influx runs up against a number of *new* obstacles. The monopolies already existing in the given branch are able to expand their

---

[1] Karl Marx, *Capital*, Vol. III, p. 366 (italics mine.—*Y. V.*).

[2] After the Second World War many short-distance railway lines were closed down in Britain because they could not compete with road transport.

enterprises by investing additional capital if this expansion does not endanger monopoly prices, and raise the size of total profits. But the investment by *other firms* into branches controlled by one or several monopolies, united in cartels and trusts, runs up against strong opposition. The monopolies use various means to obstruct competitors, for new enterprises could endanger monopoly prices. The means they use for that purpose are known to the reader both from Lenin's works on imperialism and from everyday life. We shall therefore only touch upon the question in passing.

The primary obstacle to creating new enterprises in monopoly-controlled branches is the vast amount of capital needed to build a modern enterprise. It is very difficult to raise so large a sum without turning for help to the big banks. In view of the close links existing between these banks and the monopolies, the ruling finance oligarchy is generally apt to refuse this help. New enterprises can be set up in the monopoly-ruled branches (apart from enterprises belonging to these monopolies) only as a result of an invasion of the new monopolies into a branch controlled by the old, i.e., as a result of a war between them.

The investment of new capital is also obstructed by the fact that the existing monopolies control the raw material sources and monopolise production by a ramified system of patents. All this we know from Lenin's works.

A new factor is state intervention, which is a characteristic of state-monopoly capitalism. In most highly developed capitalist countries the state has the right to intervene in some form or other when large enterprises are set up, and it uses this right in the interests of monopolies.[1]

The above shows that while the influx of capital into monopoly-dominated branches is so difficult that it is practically impossible for outsiders to penetrate into them, the monopolies, on the other hand, can easily invest new capital in non-monopolised branches, driving weaker competitors

---

[1] Owing to the enmity of the masses against the monopolies, which jack up prices, the state from time to time proclaims (with a lot of horn-blowing) "strict measures and laws" against monopolies. This happened in the U.S.A. But the American monopolies suffer from these laws as little as the West German monopolies do from the "decartelisation" proclaimed by the Western occupation powers.

out of business by conducting a "price war", i.e., by first undercutting their competitors and then, having ruined them, establishing high monopoly prices and drawing high monopoly profits.[1]

The above poses the question: *to what extent does the tendency towards the levelling of the rate of profit promote the formation of a single rate of profit under present-day state-monopoly capitalism?*

This question will be answered further in the essay.

* * *

The tendency of the rate of profit to fall operates independently of the tendency for the formation of an average rate of profit as a result of the flow of capital.

From a purely theoretical point of view the existence of this tendency cannot be denied. Undoubtedly, the decrease in the share of variable capital in comparison with fixed capital must evolve a tendency for the rate of profit to decline. But unfortunately we have no figures to substantiate this theoretical premise. Bourgeois statistics do not give reliable data about the aggregate social capital functioning in the various spheres of production, nor about the total surplus value (profit) being appropriated. The income tax returns being published are deliberately minimised. This is done by exaggerating depreciation and by other methods of creating "hidden" reserves.

---

[1] A comparatively recent phenomenon in the activities of the monopolies is diversification. This means that the monopolies use newly accumulated capital to take over enterprises for the further processing of their output, or to ensure them with raw materials; for the production of packing materials; for the direct sale of goods to retailers, bypassing intermediate links, or set up their own retail networks, etc., in an attempt to expand the market for their main products and to achieve a better rate of equipment utilisation.

The diversification enables the monopolies to distribute capital among different branches of production and decrease the losses connected with the closure of some of their enterprises. But it does not eliminate the losses a given monopoly sustains when it transfers its fixed capital from one branch to another.

Alongside this diversification we observe the opposite tendency—American motor monopolies buy parts from other enterprises (often financially dependent on them) and themselves merely assemble the parts produced by hundreds of suppliers.

The decline in the rate of profit cannot be calculated directly.[1]

The decline in the rate of profit is also restrained because an increasing number of capitalists refuse to invest money in production (direct profits), but prefer to net a lower but more certain profit by investing money into bonds, privileged shares with a fixed dividend, etc. This means that a part of the aggregate profit assumes the form of interest. That part of the functioning industrial capital yields a rate of profit below average, while the other part yields a rate above average. This shows that the rate of profit would be lower if there were no loan capital and the total profit were distributed evenly over the aggregate capital.

This was noted by Marx, who wrote that "in stock companies the function is divorced from capital ownership. . . . Since profit here [in large stock companies.—*Y.V.*] assumes the pure form of interest, undertakings of this sort are still possible if they yield bare interest, and this is one of the causes stemming the fall of the general rate of profit, since such undertakings, in which the ratio of constant capital to the variable is so enormous, do not necessarily enter into the equalisation of the general rate of profit."[2]

Under monopoly capitalism the distribution of profits is greatly modified, and, as is shown below, the problem of the average rate of profit becomes even more complicated.

* * *

The above difficulties obstructing the outflow of capital and the influx into monopoly-dominated branches poses the

---

[1] Before the First World War we had already made attempts to show the decline in the rate of profit by indirect methods. We proceeded from the fact that capitalists have a choice of investing money into industry and netting a direct profit, or into gilt-edged securities, such as British Consolidated Annuities or French Rents, which pay a fixed interest. If the rate of profit were to decline steadily over a long period, there would be a corresponding increase in the quotations for government bonds. Since this did not happen we can presume that before the First World War the rate of profit did not decline. We avoid using the word "proves", for our reasoning does not take into account the influence exerted by many other factors. This indirect method cannot be used for the period following the Second World War because of the numerous and repeated inflations and currency stabilisations.

[2] Karl Marx, *Capital*, Vol. III, p. 437.

following question—to what extent does the tendency towards the levelling of the rate of profit operate under modern monopoly capitalism?

Before replying to that question, let us make the following two qualifications:

1. The rate of profit made by the monopolies is higher than the average rate of profit for non-monopoly enterprises. Indeed there would be no sense in establishing monopolies if they did not ensure a higher rate of profit.

2. Monopoly capitalism, as was repeatedly underlined by Lenin, does not remove anarchy of production and competition and does not result in the formation of an all-embracing monopoly, as believed by Hilferding. This means that *there is no constant and clearly defined limit between monopoly and non-monopoly enterprises.* Cartels and trusts form and disintegrate. A monopoly controlling a branch can lose its monopoly hold because of the penetration into that branch of an outsider. Technical innovations sometimes undermine the monopoly positions of enterprises. The economic sections of leading capitalist newspapers report such things every day. *The distinction between monopolies and non-monopolies, and hence between the monopoly and average rate of profit is unstable and cannot be clearly defined.*

Yet there are exceptions to this rule. In every highly developed capitalist country there is a group of giant enterprises which have an enormous fixed capital and huge internal reserves. Here are a few figures about some of the largest monopolies. In 1963 the profits of General Motors amounted to 1,592 million dollars.[1] This is equal to almost half of Austria's national income. Or to take another example, in 1964 the American Telegraph and Telephone Company intends to spend 3,250 million dollars on modernising its enterprises.[2] Such giants do not fear economic crises, nor do they fear competitors. Their monopoly profit cannot be halted by crises of overproduction or political upheavals within the capitalist framework, nor by wars and inflation. Technical innovations are also unable to undermine their position, for they control all scientific research

---

[1] *The Times*, January 28, 1964.
[2] Ibid., February 12, 1964.

and inventions in their fields of activity and protect themselves by an all-embracing system of patents. Other companies belonging to the group of giants are the Standard Oil Co., Du Pont's General Motors Corporation, United States Steel Corporation, etc., in the U.S.A.; Shell, Unilevers, Imperial Chemical Industries, etc., in Britain; the I. G. Farbenindustrie and Krupp in West Germany. During the crippling 1929-33 crisis a number of German Grossbanken, and some financial speculators like Samuel Insull in the U.S.A. and Ivar Kreuger in Sweden went bankrupt, but even that crisis was unable to undermine the position of the giant industrial monopolies. As regards political upheavals within the framework of the capitalist system, there has been no fundamental change in Krupp's position under Wilhelm I, Wilhelm II, the Weimar period, Hitler's regime, or Adenauer and Erhard.

It is impossible to establish statistically the share of monopolies in the economy or to compute the size of monopoly profits. The following data on the U.S.A. gives a very approximate picture[1]:

Thous. million dollars, pre-tax

	Profits of non-corporations	Corporation profits
1929	8.6	9.6
1939	7.5	6.4
1949	22.2	26.4
1959	34.8	47.0
1960	36.0	45.0

Since we are interested only in comparing the profits of non-corporations with corporations (joint-stock companies) we can ignore the devaluation of the dollar.

These figures (excluding those for 1939[2]) tell the following story.

---

[1] *United States. Economic Report of the President*, 1961, p. 138.

[2] In the 1930s the profits of the owners of non-corporations—farmers, artisans, merchants, lawyers, doctors, etc.—dropped less sharply than did those of joint-stock companies, many of which lost their monopoly positions during the crisis and depression.

1. The profits of joint-stock companies grew quicker than those of individually-owned enterprises. This was due partly to the constant transformation of individually owned enterprises into joint-stock companies.

2. The distribution of profits changes slowly: even in 1960 four-ninths of all profits were made by non-corporations and five-ninths by joint-stock companies. It can be assumed with a high degree of certainty that the actual profits of the joint-stock companies were higher, since they have more opportunities than individual enterprises for creating hidden profit reserves and for evading taxation.

With an even higher degree of probability we may assume *that all monopoly profits are a part of the profits of joint-stock companies*. True, there are also monopoly non-corporations like the Ford Motor Company (before its transformation into a joint-stock company) and Krupp in West Germany. But these are extremely rare exceptions and we need not consider them.

Of course, not all joint-stock companies are monopolies, in fact, quite a few are not. We do not know how the aggregate profit of joint-stock companies is divided between monopoly and non-monopoly enterprises. There are no statistics (and cannot be) to show us this division, for the line between monopolies and non-monopolies is unstable and constantly changing.[1]

In any case the above material shows that the share of joint-stock companies of the non-monopoly type accounts for about 35 per cent (this, we emphasise, is an approxima-

---

[1] If we assume that in the U.S.A. all joint-stock companies with a capital of 50 million dollars and up are monopolies, which is probably close to the truth, we can give the following data for 1959 (in thousand million dollars):

> Profits of all joint-stock companies 38
> including those of joint-stock companies with a
> capital of $50 million and up 24

(Statistical Abstract of the United States, 1961, pp. 487-88).

The substantial discrepancy between the figure for U.S. corporation profits for 1959—$47,000 million (according to the Report of the President) and $38,000 million (according to the *Statistical Abstract*) is explained by the fact that the latter source gives "taxable incomes". This by the way shows that one-fifth of corporation capital is officially exempted from taxes. In reality the share of the non-taxable profits is even higher.

tion) of the total corporation profits. Such is the structure of the monopoly profits in countries where the specific weight of the monopolies is very high. The figures for 1959 given below afford an idea of U.S. corporation profits[1]:

	'000 million dollars
Total corporation profits	47.0
Profits of 500 largest corporations	12.0
Profits of 100 largest corporations	8.2

This shows that the 500 largest companies are collecting a quarter of the profits of all joint-stock companies, and the 100 largest—one-sixth.

The annual survey published by *Fortune* magazine gives a somewhat more concrete picture of the distribution of profits in U.S. industry. It says that 57 per cent of the annual sales of industrial output falls to the 500 largest companies. They collect about 72 per cent of industry's total profits.[2] This means that the largest enterprises sell their goods at a higher profit than small firms. But this does not mean that their profit reduced to actually invested capital, i.e., their rate of profit, was higher in the same proportion. This would happen only if the invested capital per dollar of sales was equal for all enterprises. However we can assume with certainty that the organic composition of capital is above average in giant enterprises and that the ratio between their total capital (fixed plus circulating) and the sales volume is also higher. The difference in the rate of profit is therefore as great as the difference in profits compared with the sum of sales.

In 1960 the net worth of the capital of the 500 largest companies was $115,000 million, their net profits amounted to $11,600 million, i.e., they made an average profit of 10 per cent, which is undoubtedly above the average netted by non-monopoly enterprises.

At the same time it would be entirely wrong to regard these ten per cent as the average monopoly profit. We have shown above that between monopolies there is not any, or hardly any, migration of capital. Hence there is also no

---

[1] *Statistical Abstract of the United States*, 1961, p. 482.
[2] *Fortune*, July 1961, p. 167.

tendency towards the formation of an average monopoly profit.[1]

This can also be seen from data published by *Fortune* magazine. The highest profit on invested capital—43.4 per cent—was made by a comparatively small firm which accounted for only $1/_{481}$ of the total sales. Some giant corporations made a profit of less than ten per cent, 24 firms out of 500 showed losses, including Lockheed, the huge aircraft producer, which was no less than $43,000,000 in the red.

We should like to point out that the "net worth" of capital (essentially the subscribed share capital) given in the quoted statistical data by no means coincides with the capital actually invested. If a company shows too high a profit in comparison with its share capital it has to pay very high dividends. This is not profitable when wages are negotiated and tax returns are submitted. For this reason the size of the share capital is being artificially boosted without new capital investments. This is done by transforming old shares into new ones, of double or even quadruple the nominal value, or by issuing no par value shares. This makes the rate of profit and dividends appear lower, while the sum of distributed dividends remains the same or even increases. Identical profits on the subscribed share capital may therefore yield different rates of profit when reduced to the actually invested capital.

A study of the whole financial history of individual giant corporations from the moment of their foundation (take the Alcoa, for example) will show that the capital actually invested is comparatively small, and that the dividends on this capital are fantastically high. Capital, as has been shown by Marx, consists wholly of accumulated surplus value.

* * *

The profits made by the monopolies consist theoretically of two components: the average profit on the capital and the monopoly superprofit exceeding that average. We do not

---

[1] These figures indicate also the monstrous exploitation of workers. The total profit of the 500 largest corporations amounting to $11,600 million was produced by 9,178,511 factory and office workers. Hence every worker gave a profit of $1,250. As will be shown further in the essay, part of the profits, consists of appropriations of surplus value created in non-monopoly enterprises. The above figure for the labour force includes millions of employees who do not create surplus value.

and cannot know the concrete magnitude of these parts, since we are dealing with a tendency that is constantly changing under the influence of many economic factors.

We may now ask the question: what is the economic essence, the economic source of monopoly superprofits?

The usual explanation is that the monopolies are establishing high prices for their commodities and are making superprofits at the consumers' expense by jacking up prices. This is true only if we confine ourselves to studying competition. But this statement contradicts one of the fundamental tenets of Marxist economic theory, according to which under capitalism the total sum of values must be equal to the total sum of prices (provided, of course, that money is stable).

The assertion one often hears about monopoly profits being based on the purchase of labour power at a price lower than that paid by non-monopoly enterprises is also theoretically unfounded. This would mean that monopoly capital *always* pays for labour power less than its value. This statement contradicts the basic tenets of Marx's law of labour value, according to which all commodities, including labour power, are sold at value, even though prices constantly fluctuate around the value.

Under capitalism there is a tendency for wages to dip below the value of labour power. Marx wrote that "in the chapters on the production of surplus-value it was constantly presupposed that wages are at least equal to the value of labour-power. Forcible reduction of wages below this value plays, however, in practice too important a part for us not to pause upon it for a moment. It, in fact, transforms, within certain limits, the labourer's necessary consumption-fund into a fund for the accumulation of capital."[1]

This tendency, which was strongly pronounced in Marx's time, is still operating today in the developing countries. But in the highly developed countries it is opposed by a number of counter-tendencies, such as the power of the trade unions, the bourgeoisie's fear of the working class at a time of conflict between the two systems, the activities of the Communist Parties, etc.

The assertion that monopoly capital buys labour power more cheaply than non-monopoly capital is not borne out in practice. This can be seen from the following:

[1] Karl Marx, *Capital*, Vol. I, p. 599.

1. In all highly developed capitalist countries workers in small enterprises are constantly striving to obtain jobs in large enterprises.

2. The wages of workers in highly monopolised branches are higher than those of workers in the non-monopolised branches. Below are some figures pertaining to the U.S.A.

Official Average Weekly Wages[1]
(1960, in dollars)

Highly monopolised branches	Non-monopolised or relatively non-monopolised branches
Motor industry 115	Clothes industry 48-69
Iron and steel 116	Tobacco industry 53-80
Inorganic chemistry . . . 115	Carpentry output 66-81

The difference is to a great extent due to the larger share of women working in branches of the second group, even though the wages of men, too, are lower in them.

A similar survey by the British Ministry of Labour shows the difference in the earnings of workers in Britain's metal-working industry, depending on the size of the enterprise (figures include overtime and other additions, and do not exclude taxes and various payments—this, however, does not affect the ratio).

Workers' Remuneration in Big and Small Firms[2]
(average weekly earning, in shillings)

Size of firm according to number of employees	Workers on time rate			Workers on piece rate		
	Trained	Semi-trained	Unskilled	Trained	Semi-trained	Unskilled
25-99	313.9	264.3	242.2	328.3	295.8	253.2
100-499	335.7	279.4	243.0	340.3	301.0	262.8
500 and up	383.3	339.0	264.8	374.0	341.0	269.1
Average for all enterprises	354.3	316.6	253.8	362.2	331.5	265.9

---

[1] *Statistical Abstract of the United States*, 1961, pp. 220-22.

[2] *The Economist*, June 1, 1963, p. 922.

It should be emphasised that the *nominal* weekly wage of fully employed workers does not correspond to the sum the workers are actually receiving: high taxes and social security payments, chronic unemployment, etc., lower wages substantially. But this does not influence the difference in the workers' weekly wages. The intensity of labour is higher in heavy industry than in light industry, although in light industry, too, steps are taken to speed up production, and the lower piece rates raise the tempo and create what is aptly described as the "sweating system". Yet, in spite of all that, it is very difficult to believe that the American monopolies, paying often twice as much as non-monopolised enterprises, are buying labour power below its value.

In spite of higher wages, the rate of exploitation may be higher in monopoly than in non-monopoly branches, if the difference in the level of labour productivity and labour intensity in monopoly enterprises is higher than the difference in the remuneration of labour.

In view of the enormous economic and political might of modern monopoly capitalism, it is easy to draw the conclusion that the largest monopoly companies are able to force workers to agree to any terms they may choose to provide. In reality this is not so, as proved by the periodic and often prolonged strikes for wage rises in the highly developed monopoly capitalist countries. In analysing the relation of forces between the monopolies and the trade unions we should bear in mind that:

1. The larger an enterprise the higher is the organic composition of its capital; the smaller the share of expenditure on wages in the total production outlays, the larger the losses it incurs from stoppages resulting from wage conflicts. As technology and especially automation develop, the more important this rule becomes.

2. Intensive and long struggles for wage increases have also a political significance, for they worsen the relations between the bourgeoisie and the proletariat, and intensify the class struggle. In the cold war era this is entirely undesirable for the big bourgeoisie. The common interests of the capitalist class clash with the interests of the individual monopolies trying to dictate employment conditions to their workers. The explanation of monopoly profits by an increased exploitation of workers in monopoly-owned enter-

prises should not be regarded as a general law although in some cases this may be true, particularly for monopolies in economically underdeveloped countries where extremely low wages are paid to native workers.

A Marxist analysis of the essence of monopoly superprofits requires the application of methods which are no less consistent than those Marx applied in his analysis of profit. While such an analysis remains abstract, we can presume the existence of a pure capitalist society consisting only of capitalists and workers, and all capitalist countries can be considered as a single market, i.e., we can ignore foreign trade. All profit in such a society—both average and monopoly superprofits—is but another form of surplus value. There is no other source of profit except surplus value. The size of the surplus value determines the size of the aggregate profit—the latter cannot exceed the former.

This theoretical assumption leads to the conclusion that *in a pure capitalist society monopoly superprofits can evolve only as a result of an irregular distribution of the aggregate surplus value or aggregate profit, i.e., a distribution according to which profit does not correspond to the amount of capital invested.* There can be no other source of monopoly superprofits. Since monopolies make a profit above the average rate, non-monopoly enterprises are making profits which are lower than they should receive in proportion to their capital.

The redistribution of the aggregate profit in favour of the monopolies is effected through the mechanism of prices: monopolies are able to sell their goods at prices which are higher than the price of production, while non-monopoly enterprises are forced to sell theirs at a price below the price of production. But the sum total of prices is equal to the sum total of values, just like the sum total of surplus value is of necessity equal to the sum total of profits.[1]

In passing to a concrete analysis we must bear in mind that modern capitalist society incorporates not only capital-

---

[1] From time to time some monopolies (and monopoly capital as a whole) enrich themselves by a further centralisation of capital: they swallow up enterprises in financial difficulties through mergers, etc. But this occasional *appropriation of capital* is not a component part of *regular* monopoly superprofits.

ists and workers but also millions of small independent commodity producers—poor and medium farmers and artisans. They, too, have a part to play in the formation of monopoly profits. The relation of prices established by the monopolies—high monopoly prices on commodities bought from monopolies and low prices on commodities sold to them—forces small commodity producers to hand over part of their profits to the monopolies.

A more detailed analysis should also take into account the geographical location of capitalism. *Monopoly capital is almost completely concentrated in Western Europe, North America and Japan.* In other capitalist countries monopolies in the embryonic stage are found on rare occasions among the local bourgeoisie, like the Tata concern in India. The Latin American, African, and Asian capitalist countries are essentially economically less developed and their economy is based on millions of small independent owners: farmers and artisans. This division into monopoly capitalist and less developed countries is simultaneously a division into industrial and agricultural countries. About 90 per cent of the capitalist world's industrial output is to this day concentrated in Western Europe, North America and Japan. The tribute exacted by the monopolies from small commodity producers through unequivalent exchange flows *first and foremost* from the less developed countries to monopoly capitalist countries. The political liberation of the colonies has as yet wrought no changes in this respect. The fact that this tribute is being exacted can be clearly seen from the increasing difference between prices for raw materials and foodstuffs on the one hand, and industrial goods on the other.[1] The unequivalent exchange is a means by which rich

---

[1] In 1960 the price index was:

(1953=100)

	Export	Import
Highly developed capitalist countries	100	96
Less developed capitalist countries	94	99

During the seven-year period from 1953 to 1960, the terms of exchange have worsened for the less developed countries by nine per cent. (*Monthly Bulletin of Statistics*, April 1961, pp. VIII-IX.)

capitalist countries can constantly plunder poor countries, and is a constant source of monopoly superprofits, even though a certain share is appropriated also by the non-monopoly enterprises in the industrial countries.

The following facts demonstrate that this part of the monopoly profits is received mainly from the less developed countries.

1. In the economy of the monopoly capitalist countries the share of independent small commodity producers is negligible as compared with that of large-scale industry. In Britain, factory and office workers comprise 95 per cent of the gainfully employed population, in the other advanced capitalist countries—about 80 per cent. The aggregate income of independent small commodity producers accounts for only a very small part of the aggregate national income. For that reason only a very small portion of the monopoly superprofits can be formed at the expense of local small-scale commodity producers.

2. The perpetuation of the capitalist system and prevention of the spread of anti-capitalist propaganda are among the most important functions of the governments of the monopoly capitalist countries. They therefore go out of their way to keep independent small commodity producers (especially the peasants, who are the most numerous among that section) on their side. The monopoly capitalist countries—the U.S.A., Britain, France, West Germany—have therefore evolved a whole system of laws and measures to maintain prices on farm products at a reasonable level. Their import is restricted and special institutions have been founded to give credit to farmers, etc. In the U.S.A. farmers are at present receiving about $6,000 million a year in subsidies to support prices and limit production.[1] The lion's share is collected by capitalist farmers, but a certain share goes to the small commodity producers and staves off their final ruin.

But nobody protects the small commodity producers in the less developed countries against international monopoly capital. Yet, no matter how destructive the actions of monopoly capital in the economically less developed countries,

---

[1] See the essay "The Problem of Agrarian Crises".

the tribute it collects there forms only a small share of the total monopoly superprofits.

The monopoly capitalist countries charge high monopoly prices for the industrial goods they export to the less developed countries, and pay low monopoly prices for the raw materials and foodstuffs they import from those countries. Let us assume that the superprofits being derived by them through trade amount to 10 per cent of the foreign trade turnover, which is probably a somewhat exaggerated figure (Lenin evaluated the whole profit from foreign trade under imperialism at 10 per cent).

In 1959 the export of raw materials, fuel and foodstuffs from the economically less developed capitalist countries totalled $22,000 million, the import of industrial goods— $16,600 million.[1]

At the same time the less developed countries imported foodstuffs, raw materials and fuel to the value of $9,000 million and exported finished goods to the value of $3,000 million.

It follows that the net export of raw materials, fuel and foodstuffs from the less developed countries amounted to $13,000 million and the net import of industrial finished goods—$13,600 million, the total turnover amounting to $27,000 million[2].

Trade with the socialist countries accounts for part of that figure, and trade with those capitalist countries which cannot be considered highly developed also constitutes a small part. About $25,000 million of the total falls to the share of the monopoly capitalist countries, which at a rate of 10 per cent will amount to $2,500 million worth of superprofits. A certain part of that sum went to non-monopoly enterprises in those countries. It follows that the additional profit from foreign trade with the less developed countries constitutes an important part of monopoly superprofits but not a decisive one.

The fourth source of monopoly profits being reaped by monopolies owning enterprises in the less developed countries is the purchase of labour power at a price below value

---

[1] *Monthly Bulletin of Statistics*, March 1961, pp. XVI-XVII.

[2] The figures are rounded off, since they are not very accurate anyway: when ships change their destination en route this does not affect export statistics, etc.

and the more intense exploitation of labour there. (The wages of whites in Rhodesia, Katanga, etc., are much higher than those of native workers.) This does not contradict our former assertion that the purchase of labour power below value *cannot be* the source of monopoly superprofits. Our statement referred to the capitalist labour market in general where labour power is bought at value. This, naturally, is no more than a tendency, as are all the laws af capitalism. The price of labour power fluctuates around its value. It can therefore also be slightly above or below value, depending on the prevailing historical conditions and especially on the influence of the reproduction cycle. But in the final analysis the price of labour power is regulated by value. In this particular case we speak about the purchase of labour power not on the *labour market of the advanced capitalist countries*, but in countries in which the agrarian over-population creates an enormous surplus for the supply of labour power, and where, until very recently, there were no trade unions to help the workers fight the capitalists who squeezed the price of labour power to a level below value.

* * *

Let us now summarise the conclusions we have drawn from our analysis:

1. Under monopoly capitalism as under non-monopoly capitalism, the rates of profit in different branches tend to equalise and form an average profit. But the monopolies are also making additional profits which do not tend to equalise, and hence there is no such thing as an average rate of monopoly profit. This is inherent in the very nature of monopoly itself. At the same time, as far as non-monopoly enterprises are concerned, there has been no change in the tendency towards the establishment of an average rate of profit, proportionate to the size of capital. Marx mentioned that even if for some reason or other capital in some sphere stopped participating in the levelling process (he mentioned the railways as an example), this would not affect the general tendency. In such a case the average rate would establish itself for that part of the aggregate social capital participating in the levelling process.

The profits of the monopolies not only fail to participate

in the levelling of the general rate of profit but the monopolies even appropriate part of the profits of non-monopoly enterprises.

2. It is difficult to draw a line between the monopoly and average rates of profit, for enterprises which today are making monopoly superprofits may tomorrow lose their monopoly position and will then have to be content with the average rate of profit.

3. In spite of the differences between the monopoly and average rates of profit, their movement in the industrial cycle is identical: they drop during the crisis phase, but rise during the recovery and boom phases. Changes in the size of monopoly profits cannot be established because the monopolies accumulate large overt and covert reserves while conditions are favourable and use them in times of crises to pay out the usual dividends.

4. Monopoly superprofits are derived from three sources:

a) the main source is the distribution of aggregate surplus value out of proportion with the amount of capital invested in each separate enterprise (proportional distribution was typical of non-monopoly capitalism), and the redistribution of profits in favour of the monopolies and to the detriment of non-monopoly capitalist enterprises;

b) the appropriation of part of the value being produced by independent small commodity producers of the non-capitalist type in the country and outside of it;

c) the purchase of labour power in the less developed countries by the almost exclusively foreign monopolies operating there at a price below its value.

Naturally, we are unable to calculate the exact share of each source—we estimate very roughly that the first source accounts for 80 per cent, and the other two for 20 per cent of the monopoly superprofits.

* * *

In our analysis we have intentionally avoided Stalin's definition of maximum profit. Stalin's assertion that "it is not the average profit but the maximum profit, that modern monopoly capitalism needs for more or less extended reproduction" is entirely unfounded. Even the term "maximum profit" which Stalin substitutes for Lenin's term "monopoly superprofit" (a subject we have treated elsewhere[1]) is ambiguous and inaccurate.

The *striving* for maximum profits is not distinctive of *modern* capital, in fact, does not apply to capitalism alone. Phoenician merchants who traded along the shores of the Mediterranean, Roman usurers, Hansa merchants, Catholic Princes of the Church who in the Middle Ages engaged in usury, all strove as much for maximum profits as the monopoly bourgeoisie today. The fact that capital even in its pre-monopoly stage was ready to commit any crime for the sake of maximum profits was mentioned by Marx in his *Capital*.

The term "maximum profit" becomes even less understandable if we presume that it refers to monopoly capital as a whole, an assumption which most likely coincides with Stalin's point of view. He describes the "securing of the maximum profit" as the basic economic law of modern capitalism. In a mathematical sense the term "maximum profit" was intended to express that monopoly capital appropriates all the surplus value being created in capitalist society. This is sheer nonsense. Even in the U.S.A., the most highly developed capitalist country, millions of farmers, merchants, factory owners, entrepreneurs and joint-stock companies of the non-monopoly type are receiving approximately half the profits being appropriated by capital as a whole. This corresponds exactly with Lenin's well-known thesis (set forth by him during his controversy with Kievsky) that there is not, and cannot be, any "pure imperialism", i.e., a capitalism in which there are only monopolies. This does not in any way belittle the decisive role of the monopoly bourgeoisie, of the finance oligarchy, in the economy and politics of the developed capitalist countries. The absolutely meaningless term "maximum profit" renders Stalin's "basic law" useless (even if we leave aside the methodological and philosophical aspects of the problem which we have dealt with elsewhere). Stalin's "basic economic law" is an efficacious political indictment of monopoly capitalism but not a result of a Marxist analysis.

---

[1] See Y. Varga, *Osnovniye voprosy ekonomiki i politiki imperializma* (Basic Problems of the Economy and Politics of Imperialism), 2nd Russ. ed., Gospolitizdat, 1957, p. 23.

THE CAPACITY
OF THE CAPITALIST MARKET

In his *Economic Problems of Socialism in the U.S.S.R.* Stalin makes short work not only of Lenin's thesis that in spite of the decay of capitalism under imperialism "on the whole capitalism is growing far more rapidly than before", but even of his own (Stalin's) thesis on the stability of markets in the period of the general crisis of capitalism. "In view of the new conditions," Stalin wrote, "to which the Second World War has given rise, both these theses must be regarded as having lost their validity."

Among these new conditions he noted the geographic shrinking of the capitalist market as a result of the emergence and consolidation of the world socialist market and the fact that world resources have become less available to the principal capitalist countries (the U.S.A., Britain, France). This gave rise to the conclusion that "production growth in these countries will rest on a narrower basis, for the volume of output will decrease."

Stalin's statement is far from clear. In a single sentence we have both the *growth* and the *reduction* of production.

Stalin's unfounded assertion about the narrowing of the capitalist market over the years to come is to this day still echoed by some Soviet economists.

A comparison of capitalist development in the post-war years with that of the pre-war years proves conclusively that Lenin was right and Stalin was wrong.

In spite of the substantial geographic shrinking of the sphere controlled by capitalism, capitalist productive forces and capitalist production have, in the post-war years, grown at a quicker pace than before, while the capitalist market, far from narrowing, has expanded. This is true of capitalism as a whole and particularly of the U.S.A., Britain and France, i.e., the three countries mentioned by Stalin.

Before examining concrete figures we shall define the terms we are using to avoid ambiguity.

By *market* we understand the aggregate of all the intertwining sales and purchase transactions as a result of which commodities are channelled from the producer to the final consumer.

By *capitalist market* we understand those sales and purchase transactions which serve the capitalist production process directly (purchases of elements of the fixed capital), or sales of commodities produced in the process of capitalist production. A special position is held by the sale and exploitation of labour power, on which the whole capitalist system is based.

The *capacity of the capitalist market is smaller than that of the market as a whole*. In the highly developed capitalist countries this difference is small, though even there a certain share of the output of peasants, fishermen and artisans is sold directly to the consumer on local non-capitalist markets. In the less developed capitalist countries the capacity of the capitalist market is much smaller than that of the market as a whole, since the share of the non-capitalist trade turnover there is very high.

In his *The Development of Capitalism in Russia* Lenin pointed out that the capitalist market grows historically by drawing non-capitalist commodity producers into the capitalist trade turnover. This applies first and foremost to peasants who were formerly engaged in subsistence farming or sold their produce on local (non-capitalist) markets. In countries like Britain and the U.S.A. this "depeasantising" process has practically culminated, in other bourgeois countries it is still proceeding.

The best yardstick for the capacity of the capitalist market is the *volume of capitalist output*. True, part of the capitalist output may not find a buyer; in fact, this is what always happens during crises of overproduction, but if we consider a long enough period, embracing several trade cycles, the capacity of the capitalist market is determined primarily by the volume of output.

Under capitalism there is a peculiar dialectical interrelation between the volume of output and the market capacity. The growth in output is limited by the capacity of the market, i.e., by consumer goods sales. These in turn are depressed by the "proletarianisation" of the masses, their low effective demand resulting from the contradiction between the social character of production and the private capitalist appropriation of the fruits of labour. Conversely, the growth in the output of producer goods—the building of new factories, power stations, etc., and other expansion of fixed capital—entails a temporary increase in the variable capital, which results in a growth of the population's purchasing power and an expansion of the capitalist market's capacity. This expansion of the latter resulting from an expansion of fixed capital is temporary and leads eventually to a crisis of overproduction. It is not constant, as Tugan-Baranovsky erroneously asserted.

Let us now look at figures which demonstrate beyond a shadow of doubt that the thesis on the narrowing of the capitalist market since the Second World War is wrong.

Industrial Output of the Capitalist World[1]

(*1958 = 100*)

1950	1955	1961
70	95	122

Though not very accurate, these figures are convincing proof that since the Second World War there has been no narrowing of the capitalist market but a very considerable expansion. All commodities produced during that time have, in one way or another, been realised. (Changes in that part of the output which is being used by the producers themselves or sold by them on local non-capitalist markets are unimportant. In any case that part is smaller now than it was before the Second World War.) There are now larger commodity stocks than there were

---

[1] *Monthly Bulletin of Statistics*, June 1963, p. VIII.

before the war and part of the commodities is sold to consumers on credit. But considering that the industrial output of the capitalist world has increased by more than 50 per cent, this too can be discounted. Although the growth of agricultural output was smaller than that of industrial output, it was nonetheless considerable.

It is therefore apparent that the volume of output and the capacity of the capitalist market far from diminishing since the war, as predicted by Stalin, have grown substantially.

In spite of the breaking away from capitalism of a number of countries embracing over 700 million people, the foreign trade of the capitalist world has also grown. (The foreign trade of the socialist countries with the capitalist countries accounts for an insignificant share of their total foreign trade.)

External Trade of the Capitalist Countries[1]

(thousand million dollars)

	1948	1960	1961
Exports			
in current prices	53.6	112.7	117.7
in 1959 prices	51.8	111.5	116.7

From the table we see that exports have more than doubled not only in current prices but even in 1959 prices.

Stalin's prediction that the industrial output of the U.S.A., Britain and France will decrease has also not been corroborated by facts. The volume of output of all three countries has increased substantially since the war. In these three countries industrial output decides the general output volume, while it is common knowledge that since the war agricultural output has grown appreciably in the U.S.A. and, in particular, in France.[2] For this reason we shall give figures only for the dynamics of industrial output.

---

[1] *Statistical Yearbook of the United Nations*, 1962, p. 466.
[2] See the essay "The Problem of Agrarian Crises".

	1938	1948	1955	1960	1962[2]
U.S.A.	34	75	106	119	127
Britain	76	84	111	126	127
France	72	77	117	161	170

It should be noted that these data are inaccurate and tend to exaggerate the actual growth. Every time the methods for computing indices are changed, the results exceed those obtained before. The inclusion in U.S. indices of the rapidly growing servicing sphere has a particularly distorting effect. However, lack of space prevents us from making a concrete analysis of these distortions here. The growth in output in the U.S.A., Britain and France has been so large that with or without these exaggerations, it is clear that facts have not borne out Stalin's prediction.

Let us return to the problem of the capitalist market's capacity. Up to now volume of production was our main criterion for determining the capacity of that market. This is a correct approach since if there are to be sales, commodities must first be produced. But if we define the market capacity as the aggregate of sales and purchases, its capacity may differ from country to country, depending on structural features of their economies.

Let us take a simple example. Iron and steel works buy a worth of coal, b worth of ore and sell steel to engineering enterprises which in turn sell machinery to the final consumer.

The chain of purchases and sales will then be expressed by the following formula:

$$a + b + (a + b + x) + (a + b + x) + y = 3a + 3b + 2x + y$$

where x—the increase in value (or price) of coal and ore transformed into steel;

---

[1] *Statistical Yearbook of the United Nations,* 1961, p. 72 et passim.

[2] *Monthly Bulletin of Statistics,* July 1963, p. 18 et passim (recalculated by the author for 1953=100).

y—the increase in the value (or price) of steel processed into machinery.

The prices of coal and ore will pass into the price of steel, and together with the price of steel will once again be included in the price of the machinery.

Let us assume that instead of a number of independent enterprises engaged in the mining of coal, ore, the smelting of steel and the production of machinery, we have a complex (or vertical trust) which has its own ore and coal mines and its own iron and steel and engineering works. It sells only the machinery—the final product. Instead of two or three sales and purchase transactions there will be only one, which we can express as

$$a + b + x + y.$$

Thus, even though the volume of production remains unchanged, the market capacity will be lower in a country where vertical trusts are widespread.

Let us therefore ask ourselves if it is correct to define the market as the aggregate of *all* sales and purchase transactions. We think that certain qualifications should be introduced. In the capitalist world huge sums are spent on the sale and purchase of things having no genuine value—securities (fictitious capital), land, building sites in towns, patents, etc. It often happens that for speculative reasons the same commodities are sold over and over again. These transactions are purely fictitious—the seller has no commodities for sale and the buyer does not even intend to acquire them. Such transactions are essentially only a speculation on future prices.

To give an idea of the magnitude these fictitious sales and purchase transactions assume, let us point out that in 1959, for example, total sales on U.S. stock exchanges alone amounted to 54,000 million dollars.[1]

Banks also sell their clients securities directly, bypassing the exchange. Also in 1959, the total farm produce sold in the U.S.A. amounted to approximately half the above—30,600 million dollars.[2] The aggregate sales of the 500

---

[1] *Statistical Abstract of the United States*, 1961, p. 460.
[2] Ibid., p. 622.

largest industrial enterprises for that year amounted to 197,000 million dollars.[1]

If we include speculative sales and business transactions on the commodity exchanges, sales of land and real estate, etc., we shall obtain a sum of at least 100,000 million dollars a year.

Furthermore, the bulk of commodities is sold several times while en route from producer to consumer.

Sales in the U.S.A. in 1961[2]

(in '000 million dollars, average monthly)

Manufacturing	Wholesale trade	Retail trade
30.7	12.6	18.2

We think that the above proves that the capacity of the capitalist market should not be defined as the simple sum of all sales and purchases. This would give us a market capacity exceeding the sum total of prices of all produced commodities by 100-200 per cent, and would make it hard to understand why capitalists find it difficult to sell their commodities.

We think that it would be far more accurate to evaluate the capacity of the capitalist market as *the sum of initial sales of commodities and services,* i.e., the sales of farmers, industrialists, artisans, the expenditure of freightage and construction. Such data are available for a number of countries.[3]

The connection between the volume of output and the capacity of the market is thus a dialectical one—the growth of output does to some extent expand the capacity of the market, and the limited capacity of the market sets certain limits on the growth of output.

* * *

[1] Statistical Abstract of the United States, 1961, p. 482.

[2] *Survey of Current Business*, September 1962, p. S-4.

[3] See the essay "Theoretical Problems of the Common Market Economy" for data on West Germany.

The limit of the market capacity is a concrete figure that can be computed for each country, provided adequate statistical data are available.

The narrowness of the markets can be defined as the ratio between available productive capacities and possible goods purchases. Both members of this ratio are able to develop in opposite directions. An absolute growth of market capacity can go hand in hand with a relative shrinking of the market in comparison with the growth of productive capacities, i.e., it may become more difficult to sell goods in spite of increased market capacity.

In fact, this has become the dominating trend under capitalism. In pursuit of profits the capitalists steadily expand production capacities and thereby succeed in temporarily expanding the market. But under capitalism this expansion does not and cannot correspond to the growth of productive capacities.

In pursuit of profits capitalists expand the productive apparatus and, under pressure of competition, strive to lower the cost of commodities. Monopoly domination does not alter this. There are many methods for cutting costs— better utilisation of raw materials and fuel, the replacement of expensive raw materials by less expensive ones, and, in particular, the lowering of labour costs through direct wage cuts, through the introduction of "rational production methods", by increasing labour intensity, automating production, etc. In the final analysis *all* methods used to lower costs *decrease* the amount of labour time embodied in the commodity and thereby lower the factory and office workers' share in the national income. This naturally leads to crises of overproduction.

In an attempt to contradict historical fact some capitalist economists contend that the periodic crises of overproducion do not spring from the nature of the capitalist system, that there should be no crises at all, since production, they say, creates incomes both for capitalists and workers, the sum total of which is equal to the newly created value. This no one can deny. But they seem to forget, or maybe are loath to admit, that it is very relevant to capitalist reproduction who receives the income—the factory and office workers or the capitalists. The former spend their income immediately or soon after they receive

171

it on consumer goods. The capitalists, on the other hand, even though they live in luxury, plough back a large share of their income into new capital investments, that is, to expand and modernise the productive apparatus. Competition forces them to do this.

In the U.S.A. in 1961, which was no boom year, since industrial output rose by only one point above the preceding year (which is within the limits of statistical inaccuracy), capitalists spent 69,000 million dollars[1] of their profits on gross private domestic investments, including 25,500 million on new means of production (producers' durable equipment, as they are called in the United States). Similar conditions prevailed in other developed capitalist countries.

This means that productive capacities grow constantly, whereas the share of the national income going to the factory and office workers falls just as steadily. But since workers are the principal buyers of consumer goods, and since the sale of these goods decides the ultimate realisation of means of production, and hence the capacity of the capitalist market, crises and a dip in the production growth rate are an inevitable result.

Having analysed the results of the 1929-33 crisis we wrote in 1934: "The depression will not necessarily be followed by a recovery. In some countries it will progress irregularly and at certain periods be attended by a sharp deterioration in market conditions. . . . It would be a gross error to identify the depression resulting from the general crisis of capitalism and the end of stabilisation with a 'normal depression'."[2]

The course of the 1929-38 cycle has endorsed this prediction. But the Second World War (and later the Korean War) with the ensuing enormous destruction and the great excess of consumption over production, wrought deep changes in the post-war reproduction cycle.[3]

The long-term tendency of capitalism towards a

---

[1] *Survey of Current Business*, National Income Number, July 1962, p. 6.

[2] Y. Varga, *Noviye yavleniya v mirovom ekonomicheskom krizise* (New Developments in the World Economic Crisis), Russ. ed., 1934, pp. 113-14.

[3] See the essay "Changes in the Reproduction Cycle Following the Second World War".

decline in the growth of production is now clearly manifested in the rich capitalist countries whose territories were not invaded during the war.

Indices of Industrial Output

(1958=100)

	U.S.A.	Canada	Britain
1956	107	100	99
1959	113	108	105
1960	116	108	112
1961	117	112	114
1962	126	121	115

The growth of production in those countries was approximately two per cent a year. Since the yearly population growth in those countries was approximately one and a half per cent, there was practically no growth in per capita output at all.

In West Germany the end of the *Wirtschaftswunder* is also attended by a slow-down in production growth. It should also be remembered that even this modest growth of production is a result of the arms race.

As a result of this development a large share of fixed capital in the highly developed capitalist countries lies idle. In the U.S.A., Canada, and Britain at the beginning of the sixties, 20 to 30 per cent of all available capacities were idle (300 shifts a year being considered full employment).

Chronic mass unemployment is another concomitant of this development. It is particularly apparent in the U.S.A. and in Canada, even though a large share of the workers there is incorporated in the Army, Navy and Air Force. In Western Europe huge war losses, the drop in the birth rate during the war, the temporary expansion of the market, arising out of the need to create reserves, the building of new structures to replace demolished ones, the replacement of worn fixed capital, etc., have arrested this basic tendency of capitalism during the era of its general crisis.

Eighteen years ago I wrote: "The horrible fact is that during the past twenty-five years the world wars were the

173

only time when all those looking for jobs were able to find them. Only when millions of people were killing each other, and other millions were manufacturing death-dealing weapons was capitalist society able to provide full employment."[1]

Since then the general crisis of capitalism has deepened. The contradiction between the social character of production and private capitalist appropriation of the fruits of labour is aggravating. This contradiction makes itself felt in the further shrinking of the market, i.e., the relative insufficiency of its capacity, the growing underemployment of productive capacities, chronic mass unemployment and the general instability of capitalism.

In the past the expansion of the world capitalist market resulting from the development of capitalist relations in the less advanced countries has had a restraining influence on the tendency of production growth rates to fall. Such an expansion of the market can now be observed in Asia, Africa and Latin America. However the significance of this tendency is diminishing due to the growth of the number of countries which have freed themselves from imperialist rule and embarked upon the socialist road of development.

Neither Kennedy's "plans", nor the occasional upswing of production in some countries, nor the Common Market and West European integration will be able to check this slow-down in production growth.

* * *

Let us sum up: Stalin was wrong when he predicted a shrinking of the capitalist market. There is no such shrinking now, nor will there be any in future, except, of course, during crisis periods.

Stalin confused two concepts—the absolute capacity of the capitalist market and its relative narrowness. The market is becoming relatively narrower, i.e., the purchasing power lags behind growing productive capacity even though in absolute terms there is an expansion of the market.

---

[1] Y. Varga, *Izmeneniya v ekonomike kapitalizma v itoge vtoroi mirovoi voiny* (Changes in Capitalist Economy Brought by the Second World War), Russ. ed., Gospolitizdat, 1946, p. 319.

PROBLEMS OF PRICE FORMATION, INFLATION AND GOLD

We presume that the reader is familiar with Marx's theory of value and price formation. However, in our opinion it is often oversimplified and expounded dogmatically, in a way that does not throw enough light on the evolution price formation has undergone since the days when Marx formulated his initial theory. For this reason we think it necessary to give a short description of that evolution.

MAIN STAGES IN THE FORMATION OF PRICES

1. *Price corresponds to value,* i.e., to the labour time embodied in a commodity unit and expressed in terms of money, this being the measure of gold embodying the same amount of labour time.

Qualifications.

a) The labour time referred to above must be the socially necessary labour time, which in turn means that the labour power expended on the production of commodities must be of average skill, and the equipment used must correspond to the level achieved at the given stage of technical development. If the quality of equipment used is below the average social level, the price of the commodity will be below its individual value, and vice versa, if the equipment's quality is above the average, the commodity will temporarily be sold at a price exceeding its individual value.

b) The production of different commodities must tend to correspond to the effective social demand for these commodities. If the output of a definite commodity does not fill the effective demand, its price will temporarily rise above its value; if more than needed is produced, the price will sink below value.

c) *The money unit must be stable in relation to gold*. The sum of prices will, in that case, equal the aggregate value of all marketed commodities.

2. *Under capitalism commodities are not sold at value: prices become prices of production*. Because of competition, goods produced by capital whose organic composition is below the average social level are sold at prices below their individual value, while goods produced by capital whose organic composition is above the average social level are sold at prices above their individual value. This tends to ensure an average rate of profit for every enterprise.

But the sum total of prices is always equal to the sum total of values.

Industrial capitalists are selling their commodities to trading capitalists at a discount (i.e., *below* the price of production), enabling trading capital to make the average rate of profit. Without it there could be no capitalist trade. The sum of prices (which is equal to the total value of the commodities) therefore refers to the sum total of sales to consumers.

3. *Influence of the trade cycle*. During the crisis phase commodities are sold below the price of production; during booms—above that price.

Hence, *the sum of prices does not equal the sum of values every year, but only if taken on an average for the cycle*.

4. *Concrete market prices* (apart from the influence exerted by the cycle) also deviate from the prices of production due to the influence of many transient factors: the supply and demand situation at any given moment, the political situation, bad harvests, etc.

All the above refers to capitalism of the *free* competition era.

5. *Influence exerted on price formation by monopolies*. The monopolies are selling their commodities at prices which are above the price of production. This is the main source of their superprofits. From an abstract theoretical point of view this would mean that non-monopoly enterprises have to sell their commodities at prices below the price of production, for only in that case would the sum

of the prices equal the sum realised if all commodities were sold at their price of production. But in reality this is not so. Things have changed since the era of free competition gave way to that of monopoly capitalism. Non-monopoly enterprises buying commodities for productive purposes (raw materials, semi-manufactures, machines, devices, plant, services) from the monopolies at prices above production prices are generally unable to sell their output at current production prices as was the case under capitalism of the free competition era, for if they did, they would incur heavy losses and go bankrupt. They sell their commodities above the price of production and force the consumer to pay for the excess they have paid the monopolies. Whether they are able to shift the whole excess or only part of it to the consumer, and whether they are able to make the former average rate of profit[1] or not, depends on concrete market conditions. Every time commodities are resold, retailers and consumers have to pay a considerable share of the amount exacted by the monopolies over and above the price of production.

Thus, the sum of prices actually becomes higher than the sum of the prices of production and the sum of values even if the medium of exchange is a gold currency.

6. The influence *inflation* has on the formation of prices is, in many ways, similar to that exerted by the monopolies. During a heavy inflation, prices in terms of the nominal money unit may become hundreds of times higher than they would be if the money corresponded to its official gold content. Prices in terms of money are out of all proportion to the amount of gold the money officially represents.

7. *The influence exerted on price formation by taxes.* Taxes tend to boost prices because the capitalists try to shift the burden of their income tax onto the consumer. Whether they succeed in doing so or not depends on the market for the individual commodities. But there is one tax that is *automatically* shifted to the buyer—the turnover tax on *all* commodities. (When only *some* commodities are taxed, the consumer can buy commodities on which the tax is not levied.) All other conditions being equal, the sum of

---

[1] See the essay "The Flow of Capital During the Levelling of the Rate of Profit. Rate of Profit Under Monopoly Capitalism".

prices plus the sum of the turnover tax will be higher than the sum of production prices plus the increase in prices due to the machinations of the monopolies.

8. *The influence of speculation.* At times we observe a temporary speculative rise or fall in the prices of some commodities.

In the period of the general crisis of capitalism with its almost permanent inflation, concrete market prices deviate from values.

The following should be stressed in this connection. No matter how much the formation of prices is distorted by the above factors, *value*, i.e., the socially necessary labour time embodied in the commodity unit *remains the principal regulator of price relations.* No matter how much the general price level deviates from value, the commodity unit whose value is ten times higher than that of another commodity will always be sold at an approximately ten times the price of the latter, no matter how great the distortions in price formation. Marx's theory of labour value stating that the amount of socially necessary labour time embodied in a commodity unit serves as the basis for price formation, is correct and continues to apply.

Before the general crisis of capitalism, the stability of currencies, the identical purchasing power of banknotes and gold coins of the same denomination were the rule; inflation—the exception. But during the general crisis of capitalism, and especially since the Second World War, stable currencies are the exception and currency "chaos", inflation, devaluation, successful or relatively successful attempts to stabilise the currency have become the rule.

The depth of the third stage of the general crisis of capitalism can be seen from the fact that some 19 years after the end of the Second World War most capitalist countries, including the U.S.A., the richest of them all, are unable to stabilise their currencies and are constantly struggling against inflation.

Without a hard currency there can be no normal reproduction of social capital.

Thus the indices of wholesale prices indicate the depth of inflation.

	Neutral countries			Vanquished countries		
	Sweden	Switzerland	Spain	West Germany	Japan[2]	Italy
1938 . .	38	47	16	46	—	2
1948 . .	106	102	57	103	36	104
	(1952)			(1952)		
1960 . .	111	101	152	107	101	99
1962 . .	116	104	164	110	100	102

	Victor countries		Less developed countries		
	U.S.A.	Britain[3]	Brazil	Argentina	Egypt
1938 . .	46	53	13	25	29
1948 . .	96	102	53	66	93
		(1952)			
1960 . .	109	113	399	150	118
1962 . .	109	117	. . .	224	121

These figures are not very accurate because varying methods have been used for their computation in different countries. Frequent devaluations also distort the picture. Nevertheless the following deductions can be made:

a) prices soared in all countries either during the war or immediately after;

b) the price level rose between 1938 and 1949 by an average 100 to 300 per cent. In Italy prices increased 52 times;

c) since 1948 the movement of prices was even more irregular than before. In a number of countries prices stabilised or advanced slowly, but in Japan and Spain they rose another 100 to 200 per cent;

---

[1] *Statistical Yearbook of the United Nations*, 1958, p. 408 et passim; 1961, p. 474 et passim. *Monthly Bulletin of Statistics*, June 1963, p. 118 et passim (recalculated by the author to 1953=100).

[2] No earlier data available.

[3] Finished goods.

d) in a number of developing countries, the inflationary growth of prices continues to the present day, in spite of the dip in the price of raw materials on the world market.

The rise in prices is not the result of a change in the value of goods. This can be proved in two ways:

1. Let us assume that the value of commodities, i.e., the labour time embodied in them, has grown between 1938 and 1962 by 100 per cent and more and that prices have therefore shot up. But quite the opposite is the case: owing to the rapid development of technology, labour productivity has grown substantially during that period. At present a commodity unit embodies less labour time than it did in 1938, and prices should therefore be lower, not higher.

2. Theoretically the growth of prices could be the result of a sharp decline in the value of gold. But this too is impossible. There has been no technical revolution in gold mining, and the labour time embodied in gold has certainly not decreased several-fold.

The index of consumer goods prices and the cost of living index computed by the National City Bank[1] show that between 1950 and 1960 prices rose in all capitalist countries and that this resulted in a steady decline of the purchasing power of the currencies of 43 capitalist countries.

Annual Devaluation of Currencies *(per cent)*

(between 1950 and 1960)

Below 1 — 4 countries (Philippines, Ceylon, Portugal, Guatemala)

From 1 to 2 — 3 countries (Switzerland, Belgium, Ecuador)

From 2 to 3 — 10 countries (among them — U.S.A., West Germany, Italy, India)

From 3 to 4 — 6 countries (among them — Britain, Japan)

From 4 to 5 — 5 countries (among them — Sweden, Norway)

From 5 to 6 — 5 countries (among them — France)

From 6 to 10 — 6 countries (all developing)

From 10 to 38 — 8 countries (all developing, except Israel)

The irregularity is very pronounced; in all highly developed countries price increases fluctuated between two and

---

[1] *National City Bank Monthly Letter*, May 1961, p. 59.

five per cent. The devaluation of money continued at approximately the same rate between 1961 and 1963.

None of the above factors can explain these price increases. If their increase was due to a rise in the value of commodities or to a drop in the value of gold, the increase would have been approximately equal in all capitalist countries. But the actual increases differ from country to country, ranging from double to 100-fold.

The price increases have an obviously inflationary character, i.e., market prices have lost all connection with value, with the prices expressed in the gold content of the currency units (the nominal, but not the actual).

During the war and the post-war chaos this would not have been surprising. For many years the effective demand for all sorts of goods outweighed their supply, and therefore one of the basic conditions for the sale of commodities according to value was absent: namely, the dynamic equilibrium between supply and demand. Hence, the growth of the money supply in circulation was a consequence and not a cause of price increases.

The problem of inflation has a very important bearing on the living conditions of factory and office workers in the capitalist countries. The constant growth of prices—inflationary and otherwise—has become a decisive factor in the deterioration of the workers' living conditions in many countries. When, as a result of the class struggle, the workers succeed in obtaining a wage increase to compensate for the price advance, inflation reduces this success to naught.

Bourgeois economists explain the constant growth of prices by an "excessive" growth of wages. They are constantly harping on the "wage-price" spiral. Inflation makes the struggle of the working class for better working conditions more difficult and creates the impression that the workers are constantly on the offensive, whereas in reality they are only defending themselves from the damage wrought by inflation. The lie that the workers' unjustified demands raise the cost of living and thereby bring about inflation is used by the bourgeoisie to deceive the petty bourgeois in town and country and to bias them against the workers.

This vitally important problem of inflation has, during the past fifteen years, been studied only superficially in the

Soviet Union, and new developments in this field have not been thoroughly taken into account.

It is difficult to study inflation because we are never able to observe the movement of commodity values directly, i.e., the socially necessary labour time embodied in the commodity unit, expressed as a definite weight of gold. What we are able to observe is not the value of commodities and not their price of production but only concrete market prices,[1] which deviate from the price of production because of competition and market conditions.

From the multitude of causes responsible for the growth of prices, we shall first single out those which are not of an inflationary nature, for this will show that inflation is the decisive factor in the present high price level.

In spite of what bourgeois economists say, not every price increase is inflationary.

The prices of practically all commodities rise when the trade cycle enters an upward phase and, in particular, during booms. But this is not an inflationary growth, for it can be observed even when a genuine gold currency is in circulation and when the central banks are still willing to exchange their banknotes for gold or when gold coins are in circulation together with banknotes and their purchasing power is equal to the latter. The price advance at a definite phase of the cycle is neither caused by changes in the money being exchanged for commodities nor is it a permanent excess of prices over value.[2]

Price increases of short duration due, for instance, to

---

[1] Often *not* even *actual* market prices, but official prices (depending on numerous factors, the *actual* prices at which commodities are sold can be higher or lower than official prices).

[2] The value of commodities is probably higher in the prosperity phase than in other phases, because many of the workers being drawn into production are new workers or workers who have lost some of their skill during their enforced idleness. For this reason the socially necessary labour time embodied in a commodity unit and deciding its value, is higher during the prosperity phase (all other conditions being equal) than it is during the crisis and depression phase, when huge labour reserves enable capitalist enterprises to employ only the most skilled and experienced workers. This cannot be proved statistically, because technical progress also decreases the socially necessary labour time contained in a commodity unit, especially during booms when new factories (built in the revival phase) are being put into operation.

a bad harvest must also not be regarded as inflationary. These increases are due to a temporary increase in the amount of social labour per unit of agricultural produce. Increases in the prices of some commodities due to stock exchange speculations are also not of an inflationary nature. Only a more or less permanent increase in the prices of commodities above their values in gold can be considered inflationary.

As has been pointed out above, under monopoly capitalism those superprofits which make for an enduring rise of prices above value are also not of a truly inflationary nature. Every intermediate purchaser pays a part of the excess charged by the monopolies, the final consumer paying the part not covered by the preceding buyers.

But let us turn to historical facts. Even at the beginning of the 20th century, before the First World War, when all currencies were based on gold, there was a universal price advance. What caused it? It would be ridiculous to presume that the value of all commodities grew or, in other words, that twenty years before the outbreak of the First World War there was a steep rise in the amount of socially necessary labour per commodity unit. Technological progress lowers the value of commodities.

We might assume that the value of gold decreased and that this was the reason for the rise in prices. But there was no major technical advance in gold mining at that time. Besides the value of gold tends to grow as it becomes increasingly necessary to extract it from deeper and less rich deposits.

In analysing the reasons responsible for the high prices prevailing over half a century ago, we came to the conclusion that the principal cause for this price advance lay in the high prices charged by monopolies for the commodities they produced.

The reason why monopoly prices cause a general price advance can be explained by the following. The monopolies are especially powerful in heavy industry—the oil, iron and steel, chemical and engineering industries, i.e., in those branches whose output is included in the cost of articles produced by nearly all other branches of economy—agriculture, the manufacturing industry, transport and the building industry. It is therefore easy to see that if the non-monopoly enterprises which buy part of the means of production (raw materials and instruments of production) at monopoly prices above the price of production or value, were to sell their commodities at a price below or equal to the price of production or value, and the sum of prices remained equal to the sum of values (as it should be theoretically), this would lead to mass bankruptcy of the non-monopoly enterprises. However, this did not happen in practice.

The accumulation and centralisation of capital under capitalism is attended by a steady concentration of production. The largest monopolies account for an ever increasing share of the output. But at the same time there is no decrease in the number of enterprises.

If the huge sum comprising the monopoly superprofits were a deduction from the average profit of the non-monopoly enterprises they would have gone bankrupt long ago.

Annual Average Number of Firms in the U.S.A.[1]
(thousands)

	Operating	New businesses	Discontinued businesses
1929	3,029	275 (1940)	318 (1940)
1957	4,471[2]	405	341

Naturally, the bulk of small enterprises somehow manages to make ends meet, even though they are handing over part of their profits to the monopolies. But in the main they are shifting the increase in the price levied by the monopolies onto the shoulders of their buyers.

Agriculture is the only branch in the highly developed capitalist countries in which there is a decrease in the absolute number of enterprises. This is due to the mass ruination of the peasants (see the essay "The Problem of Agrarian Crises"). Farmers and peasants are punished by the monopolies in two ways: by having to buy means of production and partly articles of consumption at high mo-

---

[1] *Historical Statistics of the United States*, 2nd Edition, pp. 570-71.
[2] 4067 of them hire labour.

nopoly prices, and by having to sell their commodities at low monopoly prices. The mass ruin of the peasants is also a result of the agrarian crisis, and in the less developed countries—of unequivalent exchange.

Under imperialism the sale of the key types of means of production at high monopoly prices leads to a general price advance, even without inflation. Enterprises using these means of production are compelled to raise the prices of their output above value in order not to incur losses. If market conditions are unfavourable, they go bankrupt and the supply of the commodities manufactured by them decreases. Sooner or later the demand for these commodities catches up with and outstrips their supply, and then prices are raised to a level which enables producers still functioning at that time to make the usual minimum profit. Thus they are able to make the consumer pay for at least a part of the excess they have to pay for the raw materials and instruments of production they buy from the monopolies.

The extra charges for monopoly-produced commodities boost the prices of consumer articles and, in the final analysis, of all commodities, thereby lowering the real wages of factory and office workers. They demand higher wages and succeed in getting them through strikes. But, all other conditions being equal, wage increases bring about a certain growth in the cost of some commodities produced in the affected enterprises, which in turn leads to a further price advance.

Non-monopoly enterprises generally do not succeed in making their buyers pay the full amount of the monopoly surcharge. For that reason the profit they net is below the average rate, i.e., the rate they would obtain if there were no monopolies. This explains our statement that monopoly superprofits are partly created at the expense of the profits of non-monopoly producers.

In this way high monopoly prices gradually cause a general price advance. In practice the mechanism is far more complicated than has been described above. The struggle between monopolies often takes the form of drastic price cuts. The price formation in individual countries is also influenced by government policy—by customs tariffs, export and import restrictions, indirect taxes, etc., etc.

The effect the monopolies exert on the formation of prices warrants a special study. Studies are made difficult because during the period of the general crisis of capitalism this influence and the effects of inflation on prices are interlinked, and it is almost impossible to separate one from the other. But we are certain that any deep and detailed analysis will corroborate our view on the mechanism by which the monopolies bring about a general increase in the retail prices of all commodities.

Finally, in *some countries* the general price advance may be due to a *prolonged* passive balance of payments. Many consider such price advances an inflation. We have no wish to quibble, but this type of price advance should be distinguished from the price advance at present operating in all capitalist countries, including those having active balances of payments. Besides, under capitalism the rise in import prices, the expansion of the exports and the imports of capital have a spontaneous positive effect on the balance of payments and tend to restore the former price level. Modern universal inflation does not have this tendency.

* * *

Let us now take a closer look at inflation and its effect on price formation. Marxist writings continuously reiterate Marx's proposition that inflation is a congestion of the conduits of circulation with paper money. It is generally said that an inflationary rise in prices is due to the fact that to cover the budget deficit, the government issues more banknotes than the total amount of gold coins needed to ensure the commodity turnover at existing prices and the obtaining rate of money circulation.

In studying modern inflation we cannot confine ourselves to Marx's proposition, for much has changed in the field of money circulation since then. In Marx's day there were four fundamentally different types of money in circulation:

a) *Gold coins*—money which has a value of its own and is able to fulfil *all* the functions of money. There could not be a surplus of gold coins causing inflation.[1]

---

[1] This does not mean that a surplus of gold can *never* become responsible for a violent rise in prices. Twice in the history of capital-

b) *Silver coins.* In Marx's time a system of a bimetallism prevailed in a number of West European countries and in the U.S.A., i.e., silver and gold were the principal currency and silver coins served as money units on a par with gold coins. This resulted in great complications, for silver dropped below the value officially fixed for it in relation to gold. For this reason silver coins ceased to be a sound money and lost their standing as universal money.

c) *Banknotes,* which had no value of their own, were issued by emission banks (at that time most countries had several emission banks) on the basis of commercial credit. They were a phase of the as yet uncompleted circulation process. Goods rarely pass directly from the producer to the consumer without an interim distribution phase—they pass through the "sphere of circulation"—in other words through warehouses, factories for further processing and wholesale or retail traders. Until goods reach the final consumer, banks grant commercial credit secured by bills of exchange. These bills were discounted by emission banks which issued banknotes on their basis.

These genuine banknotes, "credit money", could not become surplus in circulation since they returned automatically to the emission bank. When a commodity reached its final consumer, it was sold for cash which passed from the retailer to the wholesaler, then to the manufacturer, and finally to the bank in redemption of the commercial bill of exchange, whence it was returned to the emission bank issuing banknotes.[1]

d) *Paper money* in the narrow sense of the word, i.e., banknotes issued by the state to cover budget deficits. As distinct from banknotes issued by emission banks these cannot leave the sphere of circulation but can be withdrawn

---

ism—in the 16th century following the discovery of America, and in the middle of the 19th century, following the discovery of the rich American and Australian goldfields—there was a price revolution: a large mass of low-value gold was thrown into circulation, and since commodity production did not expand correspondingly, prices rose sharply.

[1] The above shows that the stability of genuine banknotes *does not* depend on the size of the gold backing. The currencies of some countries, that of the Austro-Hungarian monarchy, for example, were stable even though they had no gold backing.

from circulation by the state as taxes (exceeding government spending), or through state loans.

Under certain conditions the emission of paper money may cause inflation, under other conditions no inflation will follow. When commodity production and the volume of trade turnover grow, while the sum of gold coins and banknotes in circulation does not, and if the supply of money units becomes insufficient at an unchanged rate of their turnover, the issuing of paper money by the state does not necessarily cause an inflation. But if the government prints and circulates more paper money than the sum of gold or banknotes needed in circulation, this inevitably results in inflation.[1]

Under these conditions Marx's definition that inflation is a congestion of the circulation conduits with paper money was perfectly adequate. But capitalist circulation today differs in many respects from the days when Marx developed his money theory in *A Critique of Political Economy*.

What has changed?

a) *Gold is no longer in circulation*. It is concentrated in the funds of the central emission banks and is used only as universal money to settle balance of payment deficits. Gold coins sometimes circulate in countries where inflation progresses at so rapid a rate that people refuse to sell their goods for paper money. They are also hoarded, especially in the less developed countries.

b) *Silver is no longer money*. Silver coins are used only as small change.[2]

c) *Paper money* in the narrow sense of the word, i.e., treasury notes (or banknotes issued by the state) has formally disappeared from circulation.

d) Under modern capitalism *banknotes* have become the main form of money in circulation. Their economic nature

---

[1] It follows that the so-called "quantitative theory" of money declaring that prices always change (in an inverse relation) with changes in the supply of money in circulation is wrong: an increase in the circulation of gold coins or genuine (full-value) banknotes does not result in a price increase.

[2] In North-East Africa, especially in Ethiopia, silver coins (the Maria Theresa Thaler) still serve as money. But this exception does not contradict the rule.

has changed substantially. Now it is difficult to tell wheth-er banknotes are genuine credit money, issued to cover credit operations, or not. A very large proportion of bank-notes, probably the bulk of the money now in circulation in the capitalist world, was issued directly on the basis of the enormous credits granted by central emission banks (mostly state banks) to various governments, primarily for the purpose of covering budget deficits.

Credits Granted by the Central Banks to Governments[1]

('000 million currency units)

U.S.A. (dollars)		West Germany (marks)	
1954	28.6	1954	4.3
1962	35.8	1962	5.9
Britain (pounds sterling)		Sweden (kronor)	
1954	2.1	1954	3.0
1962	2.7	1962	4.6
France (francs)			
1954	9.9		
1962	10.6		

Quite obviously, banknotes issued for the government are not genuine banknotes but paper money, bearing only an external resemblance to banknotes.

This change in the economic nature of banknotes was brought about mainly by the Second World War. In 1929 credits granted by banks to the U.S. Government accounted for only 10 per cent of private credits, in Sweden and Germany they were practically nil, and only in Britain did they equal private credits.

Indirectly, a portion of the credits granted by banks to private persons is state credit. Private firms obtain credit on government stock (military and other loans). In the U.S.A. banks are obliged by law to grant credit on U.S. military loans.

e) In Britain and the British dominions, and especially in the U.S.A., *an ever increasing role is being played by per-sonal cheques*, which are paid or compensated through the drawer's bank deposit. In circulation, cheques substitute

---

[1] *International Financial Statistics*, April 1963, pp. 112, 116, 230, 256, 260.

largely for banknotes. In Britain and the U.S.A. they are used for large payments and are widely accepted even in shops. Indicative of the great role played in modern circulation by deposits and cheques drawn on them, is the fact that in bourgeois statistics deposits are called "deposit money"[1] and are placed on a par with banknotes.

Thus Marx's definition of inflation is correct even today inasmuch as state budget deficits still remain the decisive reason for inflation.

But as "paper money", i.e., treasury notes, are no longer issued, and only banknotes are in circulation, part of which according to their economic essence is paper money, Marx's tenet that inflation is a congestion of the conduits of circulation with paper money needs additional explanation. The role of paper money has now been taken over by banknotes (which have lost their former economic content), bank deposits, short-term state loans, etc.

Our economists often interpret Marx's tenet to mean that the congestion of the channels of circulation with paper money is the *cause* of inflation. In our opinion this is wrong. The causes of inflation are economic and not technical.

Marx did not go into this question. He did not say whether the state resorts to the issue of paper money to cover budget deficits because it is unwilling or unable to take other measures. The reason for it is not hard to see. In Marx's time the problem of inflation was an important part of the money *theory*. But as we have already pointed out, inflation was rare in practice. At that time it could be observed only in a few countries, and its effects were neither deep nor enduring.

But, during the general crisis of capitalism, and particularly since the Second World War, *inflation* has spread to all capitalist countries and *has become an acute economic and political problem*. It is of *particular importance to the working class* since it affects both its living conditions and the success of its struggle against the capitalists. It is, therefore, necessary to reveal the economic and political

---

[1] An example are official U.N. data. They show that in most capitalist countries the sum of deposit monies comprises about half the sum of the banknotes in circulation, in the U.S.A.—the two are almost equal.

conditions responsible for universal inflation, to find out *why* all bourgeois governments (using loans from the central emission banks as a cover) had to put large sums of surplus money into circulation.

A distinction should be drawn between inflation as a process, expressed in the rise of prices, and an inflated price level, persisting even after a stabilisation of money has been achieved. The stabilisation of money in present-day conditions does not mean a return to the price level prevailing prior to the beginning of the inflation process, does not mean a restoration of the pre-inflation purchasing power of money. The gap between prices expressed in monetary units, which formally represent the former amount of gold, and the value of commodities remains even after the money has been stabilised. The economy adjusts itself to these new price levels, and only a deep economic crisis of overproduction can narrow the gap created by the inflationary process.

* * *

We are using U.S. data to illustrate these conditions because in most other capitalist countries there has been a devaluation of money after the Second World War, i.e., an official reduction in the weight of gold represented by the money unit circulating in the country. In France, for example, the dollar rate has changed repeatedly since the war.

These data prove that a simple repetition of Marx's definition of inflation does not explain the course taken by inflation in the U.S.A. either during or since the Second World War. (See table on p. 192.)

Between 1937 and 1945 the total money (banknotes) in circulation increased by 300 per cent, deposits by 200 per cent, while the state budget deficit amounted to the enormous sum of 200,000 million dollars. However, the official index of wholesale prices grew by only 20 per cent. But the index does not reflect the real state of affairs, for it fails to take account of military deliveries and black market sales. The correct price index was probably not 62 but ranged between 80 and 100.

The opposite applied between 1945 and 1950. The total money in circulation decreased by 1,000 million dollars,

Data on Post-War Inflation in the U.S.A.[1]

('000 million dollars at the end of the year)

	1937	1945	1950	1955	1961
Currency in circulation	6	26	25	28	30
Deposits in commercial banks . .	24	76	92	109	119
State budget deficit, summed up for a period between years . .		200	17	11	10
Gold stock	13	20	23	22	17
Index of industrial production (1953 = 100)	46	80	84	106	120
Wholesale price index (1953=100)	51	62	94	101	108[2]

total deposits grew by only 20 per cent and the official wholesale price index by 50 per cent.

Between 1950 and 1961 the movement of all these factors became more normal. Money circulation grew by about 16 per cent. This could not have an inflationary effect since the decisive factor in U.S. economy—industrial output—grew by more than 75 per cent during that period. The commodity turnover grew in approximately the same proportion, and hence, assuming that the rate remained stable, the need for money increased. Yet, the price index grew by about 15 per cent.

For the whole period between 1937 and 1961 the state budget deficit amounted to about 238,000 million dollars, while the sum of banknotes in circulation grew by only 24,000 million dollars or 10 per cent. Obviously, only a very small part of the budget deficit could be covered by the increased issue of banknotes, and therefore it could not have been responsible for the inflation, especially since

---

[1] *Historical Statistics of the United States*, 2nd Edition, pp. 647, 649, 711. *Statistical Yearbook of the United Nations*, 1956, pp. 452, 484, 490; 1961, p. 72. *Monthly Bulletin of Statistics*, May 1962, p. 126; June 1963, pp. 22, 128.

[2] Recalculated by the author from base year 1958=100 to base year 1953=100. All figures in the table are rounded off to thousand millions.

the substantial growth in commodity circulation would have made it necessary to increase the supply of banknotes in circulation even if there had been no price advance.

We think that the following are the main factors responsible for the above:

1. *Price limits enforced by the government.* This is an entirely new factor, which did not exist under the pre-monopoly capitalism studied by Marx, with its mechanism of free price formation through competition on the market, based on the price of production.

State price regulations kept *official* prices much lower than they would have been if they had corresponded to a greater increase of banknotes in circulation. When state regulation of prices was abolished in 1946, prices soared to a level roughly corresponding to the real state of affairs.

In Britain, where price regulation was not abandoned immediately after the war and where the black market played a far less important role than in the U.S.A., the price advance proceeded more regularly:

Official Wholesale Price Index in Britain[1]
(1953=100)

1937	1945	1948	1950	1955	1961[2]
33	52	67	80	104	105

The devaluation of the pound sterling by 30 per cent in 1949 had very little effect on price formation.

2. *The money turnover rate decreased during the war.* Large sums of cash were in the hands of black market speculators. Black market transactions (at prices higher than the official ones) were made in cash so as to leave no records.[3] U.S. armed forces, stationed far from the U.S.A.,

---

[1] *Statistical Yearbook*, 1956, p. 460; *Monthly Bulletin of Statistics*, June 1963, p. 118 et passim.

[2] Recalculated by the author from base year 1958=100 to base year 1953=100.

[3] During the war the supply of money in circulation grew rapidly, especially of banknotes of a high denomination.

had large cash sums at their disposal. Thus a part of the banknotes was deposited abroad, where devaluation set in earlier and more violently than in the U.S.A.

In this manner conduits of circulation were filled with paper money even though it differed from that used in Marx's time.

* * *

The real reason for universal inflation both during and after the Second World War stems from the *deep changes in the economy* of the participant capitalist countries as a result of the war. War expenses eat up as much as half the national product—arms and other war materials are destroyed in battle and thus become a deduction from the national income and wealth, also the real national wealth and national incomes of the warring countries, especially of those devastated by the war, decrease while the nominal national income and national wealth, expressed in money terms, grow because the government pays for all military deliveries at a much higher price than the price of production. This *contradictory movement of the real and nominal* national wealth and national income is the real economic reason for war-time inflation, while the blocking of the channels of circulation with paper money is the consequence.

Present-day methods of financing wars, and peace-time military expenditure make it possible to cover the enormous state budget deficit without a large issue of additional paper money. At present it is not a direct issue of additional paper money that corresponds to the inflated post-war sum of prices but the increase in deposits, used in the wholesale commodity circulation turnover instead of paper money, and the issue of war loans and other substitutes for paper money.

All these problems require further study. One thing is clear, however, that the genuine reason for inflation is not the filling up of the conduits of circulation with paper money but a discrepancy between the real and nominal national income during the Second World War and after it.

* * *

Inflation brings great changes in the distribution of the national income between the different classes and layers of capitalist society. It brings sufferings to the worker, whose real wages rapidly fall because money devaluates quicker than wages rise and it brings even more suffering to salaried workers, officials and pensioners, whose wages are fixed for a long time ahead. Rentiers also suffer losses. Huge losses are incurred by creditors because the purchasing power of the money they receive in settlement of debts is much lower than the purchasing power of the money they originally lent. Inflation also affects artisans and petty traders, who by force of habit continue to sell their commodities at the purchase price plus the usual mark-up. Their books show a profit, but the money realised for their commodities enables them to buy less goods than they sold.

Inflation is profitable for the ruling class—the industrial bourgeoisie—which buys labour power below its value, and purchases raw materials from "independent" producers below the price of production, settles its debts in devaluated money and receives ever greater credits from the banks (in the final analysis these come from the central emission bank). The industrial capitalists buy material values on credit and settle their debts with devaluated money. Land-owners, kulaks and house-owners also gain from inflation, for it automatically pays off mortgages. Large-scale specu-lators—bankers, who engage in currency and commodity speculation—also benefit.

Seeing that the ruling classes profit from inflation, our economists often contend that such a state of affairs is always profitable for the bourgeoisie. However, they are wrong.

Inflation is only profitable to the bourgeoisie at a certain stage in its development. But every inflation produces a progressive and accelerating devaluation of money. At a certain stage of development the disturbance to capitalist reproduction caused by the inflation assumes so large a scale that it becomes unprofitable even for the bourgeoisie.

"Excessive", "uncontrollable inflations" tend to disturb the commodity turnover since nobody wishes to sell com-modities knowing that their prices will rise on the next day. The links between town and country are disrupted when peasants find that they are unable to buy the commodities they want in town, they quickly stop supplying towns with food, refuse to sell their products for rapidly depreciating money and are interested only in barter—a shirt for meat. The labour discipline in factories suffers too, since the workers lose interest in wages which are paid in rapidly depreciating money. Many workers even stop working because they have to leave town in search of food. Factory owners are forced to supply their workers with basic food-stuffs or to pay them partly in kind, in the output of the factory, which the workers can then use for barter with the peasants. Paper money thus loses its value and its place is taken partly by some stable foreign currency, gold coins or even gold bars. All capitalists are forced to take up currency speculation to counter the devaluation of money, etc.

At a certain point every inflation becomes unprofitable and harmful not only to the working people but, with the possible exception of a handful of professional speculators, also to the ruling classes. The bourgeoisie therefore finds it necessary to put an end to the inflation and stabilise the currency.

We can draw on many historical facts to prove that this is so. There have been over a hundred major inflations in various capitalist countries since capitalism emerged. They all ended in stabilisation. This stabilisation was effected by the ruling bourgeoisie in its own interests. The fact that in a number of countries the bourgeoisie was unable to stabilise the currency for as long as 15 to 18 years shows that capitalism has weakened in the present stage of its general crisis. A number of highly developed countries are now deliberately carrying through a slow, regulated inflation according to John Maynard Keynes's recommendations.

In the second half of 1963, France and Italy were compelled to take strong measures to stop the rapid price advance, including the establishment of price limits for many commodities in France. This had to be done in spite of the fact that there were huge gold reserves in the central banks of both countries and that these reserves were growing. To maintain its remaining gold reserves, the United States was compelled to ask the West European central banks not to demand gold in exchange for their dollar deposits in the U.S.A. and had to cut down on its foreign spending, even though this harmed its role as the leading imperialist power.

Inflation generally ends with a stabilisation of money, even if a temporary one, but its consequences do not disappear without trace. The purchasing power of the money unit becomes smaller than it was before the inflation, even if the official gold backing remains unchanged, i.e., stabilisation is effected without devaluation. After a protracted inflation, the capitalist economy adjusts itself to the new, higher price level. The formation of monopoly prices, cyclical changes and price fluctuations on the market proceed at the new and higher level. The distribution of the national income, which changed greatly during the inflation is gradually restored and approaches the pre-inflationary pattern. Capitalist reproduction continues to function "normally" but at a new price level.

We said above that the price advance since the Second World War was not of a purely inflationary nature, since a part of it can be accounted for by monopoly price boosting. This can be seen from the following: if the price advance were purely inflationary, it would have applied in a more or less even measure to all commodities. Only changes in the value of commodities could have accounted for such differences.

A more or less proportionate increase in the price of all commodities would have indicated changes in the value of the commodities. But actually the prices of monopoly-produced commodities rose much higher than those of non-monopoly producers. This can be seen from the price movement in the U.S.A., where the nominal gold content of the dollar has remained unchanged.

Price per Ton[1]
(dollars)

	1939 (January)	1961 (December)
1. Monopoly produced commodities Steel ingots	34	80

---

[1] *Morgan Guaranty Trust Survey*, January 1962, pp. 10-11.

	1939 (January)	1961 (December)
Pig iron	20.5	66
Petrol (Oklahoma)	1	3
2. Non-monopoly produced commodities		
Steel scrap	15.5	36
Pigs (Chicago) per hundredweight	7.35	16.35
Heavy skins (cents per pound) . . .	11.5	14.5

The commodities in the first group increased by an average of 200 per cent, those in the second—by about 100 per cent.

A similar trend can be observed in industry.

Index Numbers of Wholesale Prices[1]

(1957-59=100)

	1953	1962 (June)
1. Highly monopolised commodities		
Fuel	95.9	99.6
Metals	83.6	100
Machinery	82.2	102.2
2. Non-monopolised or less monopolised commodities		
Farm products	105.9	95.3
Textiles	102.8	100.8
Miscellaneous	105.4	105.4

True, these figures are far from accurate, but the tendency is clearly visible. Changes in the value of the commodities cannot account for a different growth in the price of commodities produced at monopoly and non-monopoly enterprises. And the fact that we observe such changes primarily in the first group of commodities, where technical progress advanced much quicker than in the second, shows

[1] *Federal Reserve Bulletin*, August 1962, p. 1052.

that our reasoning is correct. It also shows that non-monopoly enterprises were unable to make the consumers of their commodities pay the whole of the monopoly surcharge.

* * *

This poses a new question—how can we explain the fact that even now, when the currencies of most capitalist countries have been stabilised, a kilo of gold will buy far fewer commodities of the same quality than before the war?

At present we are unable to give an exhaustive answer to this question, even though it is of the greatest consequence to the Soviet Union, itself a large-scale producer of the gold that is often used as universal money for commodity purchases on the world market. It is most important from a theoretical standpoint.

We know that whenever and wherever there is a *regular* exchange of products, be it barter or a commodity turnover by means of any universal equivalent—cattle, iron, silver, gold—the products or commodities are exchanged (sold) according to their value, i.e., according to the socially necessary labour embodied in the commodity unit and the universal equivalent.

For what reason then does a kilo of gold fetch less than half the amount of commodities it did before the war?

Gold imported into the U.S.A. is exchanged (as in other highly developed countries) at the rate of 35 dollars an ounce. But 35 dollars will now buy only 50 per cent of what they did before the war. Theoretically we could assume that each commodity unit now contains twice as much labour time as it did before the war. But this is obviously wrong. Since 1938 the productivity of social labour has grown by at least 30 to 50 per cent. Hence, a commodity unit now contains less labour time.

We could also assume that the labour time embodied in a kilo of gold is now half of what it was before the war. But this, too, is out of the question—there has been no technical revolution in gold mining and a kilo of gold contains no less, or at least not much less, labour time than it did before the war.

What we do see is that gold being exchanged for commodities fetches less than its value and that this has made gold mining unprofitable, as can be seen from the drop in gold production in the capitalist countries as compared with the pre-war level, while the production of nearly all other commodities has grown substantially.

Volume Index Numbers in Capitalist World[1]

(1953=100)

	Primary commodities	Production in manufacturing
1938	77	50
1960	120	140

Industrial production has nearly trebled, the production of primary materials (agriculture, fishing, mining, etc.) has grown by 50 per cent. Gold is almost the only product whose output has not grown.

Gold Production in the Capitalist World[2]

(thousand kg)

1938	1941 (maximum)	1945 (minimum)	1960
993	1,108	654	1,044

Owing to the present low rate at which gold is being exchanged for commodities, enterprises mining it under adverse conditions are unable to make the average rate of profit.

How can we explain the strange fact that gold, which even today serves as universal money, i.e., the only universally accepted form of currency, is being exchanged below value?

This could be due to the following causes: during the

---

[1] *Statistical Yearbook of the United Nations*, 1961, p. 59.

[2] Ibid., 1957, p. 174; 1961, p. 153. The sudden drop during the war is probably due to labour shortage.

Second World War, and a few years after it, all capitalist countries had a passive trade balance and balance of payments with the U.S.A. This brought on the dollar deficit. The U.S.A. seized a considerable portion of the capitalist world's gold reserves. Other countries having a chronically passive balance of payments were unable to maintain their gold reserves.

Gold Reserves of the United States
(thousand million dollars at the end of the year)
(at 35 dollars an ounce)

1929	1938	1949 (maximum)	1955	1962
4.0	14.5	24.6	21.8	16.0

The U.S.A. accepted gold at an unchanged rate—at 35 dollars an ounce. This was profitable for U.S. business since owing to the inflationary devaluation of the dollar they were giving far fewer commodities per kilo of gold than they had before the war—less than they would have had to give if the exchange of commodities for gold proceeded at **value.**

This can be proved by two facts.

Until very recently an ounce of gold was sold on the black markets of New York, London, Paris, etc., not at 35, but at 40 to 45 dollars an ounce. In 1951 the Republic of South Africa, the world's principal gold producer, sold about 40 per cent of its output as industrial gold at a price higher than the 35 dollars an ounce being paid by the U.S.A. and all the banks of the capitalist world.[1] In the U.S.A., too, more than the official rate was paid for newly mined gold.

The gold producing countries, such as the Republic of South Africa and Australia, insistently demanded an increase in the "price" of gold, but the U.S.A. no less insistently refused to fall in with this demand.

---

[1] See Y. Varga, *Osnovniye voprosy ekonomiki i politiki imperializma posle vtoroi mirovoi voiny*, pp. 66-67.

All these issues are concealed in bourgeois economic writing. Instead of quoting commodities in gold, the universal measure of value, bourgeois papers quote the "price" of gold in different currencies. Instead of expressing the rate of currencies in gold, they are officially quoted in dollars and cents.

By selling gold, the central banks support the rates of their currencies not in relation to gold but in relation to the dollar. Everything seems to have turned upside down.

This is all the more strange since the U.S. dollar is not a gold currency. Dollar bills are not exchanged for gold, even though they formally have a 25 per cent gold backing. U.S. citizens (except jewellers) are not allowed to store gold, either at home or abroad. Gold is paid out only to foreign countries and central banks in payment of U.S. debts. The gold reserves of the United States are lower now than they were in 1939. In 1962 the per capita gold reserves of Switzerland or the Netherlands were higher than those of the U.S.A.

But in spite of the fact that officially the dollar is being equated to gold, the true rate gradually re-establishes itself. The bulk of newly mined gold is sold not to the central banks at the official rate of 35 dollars an ounce, but is bought by private persons, at a much higher rate and hoarded.

According to the report of the International Monetary Fund[1] for 1961 over 50 per cent of the gold mined in the capitalist countries between the beginning of 1950 and the end of 1961 has not been sold to the central banks at the official rate but been bought up by private persons for hoarding or for the production of jewellery. In 1960 private gold purchases accounted for 1,035 million dollars, while the increase in the gold reserves of the central banks, for only 340 million dollars. Even though the United States has concluded agreements with most West European central banks obliging them to grant the U.S.A. temporary credits to artificially maintain the dollar at its official rate, these banks too are trying to exchange dollars they accumulated during the dollar shortage.

The tendency to exchange the dollars in bank reserves

---

[1] *Neue Zürcher Zeitung*, October 21, 1962.

for gold has become universal and can be seen particulary in Switzerland, the Netherlands, Italy and West Germany.

Reserves of Emission Banks[1]
(million dollars at the end of the year)

		1951	1960	1962
Belgium	gold	635	1,170	1,365
	foreign currency	419	252	257
France	gold	597	1,641	2,587
	foreign currency	19	429	1,023
West Germany	gold	28	2,971	3,679
	foreign currency	427	3,766	2,768
Italy	gold	333	2,203	2,243
	foreign currency	441	876	1,198
Netherlands	gold	544 (1952)	1,451	1,581
	foreign currency	379	291	162
Switzerland	gold	1,451	2,185	2,667
	foreign currency	193	139	205
Britain[2]	gold	—	2,800	—
	foreign currency	—	431	—

The devaluation of currencies is another way of re-establishing a normal rate of exchange. According to the report of the International Monetary Fund, 23 countries have lowered the nominal gold content of their currencies during 1962 alone.

Since the artificially maintained official rate of exchange between the dollar and gold does not correspond to the law of value, it is to be expected that it will soon be changed and that the rate between them will be dictated directly by the law of value and not in the roundabout way it is now. *Sooner or later there will be a devaluation of the dollar—this is inevitable.* The abnormally high rate of the dollar could exist only so long as the U.S.A. was econom-

---

[1] *Statistical Yearbook of the United Nations*, 1961, p. 521 et passim; *Monthly Bulletin of Statistics*, June 1963, p. 171 et passim.
[2] Figures for other years are unavailable.

ically strong enough to force all other capitalist countries to accept the exaggerated rate.[1]

* * *

We should also like to touch upon another problem that has been given little attention in Marxist studies and calls for further research.

Gold is the universal equivalent and measure of the value of commodities. It is a better equivalent than all the other commodities which have, during the course of history, fulfilled this function. A small weight of gold contains a large amount of embodied labour time, it is easily divisible, of equal quality in all its parts, etc. Like all other commodities, the value of gold changes. Marx shows this in *A Contribution to the Critique of Political Economy*. The value of an ounce of gold differs in various gold mining enterprises as does the actual labour time embodied in extracting it. Furthermore, gold may be produced both from rich and from poor ore; may be produced by primitive manual techniques or with the most up-to-date machinery. Some gold mining enterprises are paying extremely high mine rents. The dividends paid by some South African enterprises have covered invested capital a hundred times over; many, on the other hand, have gone bankrupt or have stopped production.

The point is that in gold production expenditure depends almost exclusively on the mass of ore extracted and not on its gold content, which differs within wide limits. In 1962 the ore extracted at the South African Geduld mines contained 20 dwt of gold per ton of ore, while that extracted in the Breakpan mines contained 2.17 dwt or slightly more than one-tenth of the gold content of the former.[2]

What economic mechanism transforms gold, which is mined in different places and under different conditions and

---

[1] The following shows how distorted the present situation really is. Gold coins, even those being minted now and therefore no rarity, stand considerably above mint par because it is convenient to hoard them. The Swiss gold coin (minted in 1925) for 100 francs is quoted at 957 per cent above mint par; the British sovereign at 20 per cent, the American ten-dollar coin at 30 per cent, the 1915 Austrian gold coins at 7 per cent above mint par. (*Neue Zürcher Zeitung*, October 26, 1962.)

[2] *Neue Zürcher Zeitung*, October 27, 1962.

initially differs in value, into a world currency or universal money with a unified value per kilogram? In other words, which of the different values at which gold is actually produced, determines the value of the end product? Or, to put it in other words—what determines the presence and scale of the differential mine rent in the gold-mining industry?

This problem cannot be solved by drawing a parallel with other commodities whose price includes differential rent (metals or wheat, for example). The price of the mass of these commodities still necessary to satisfy effective social demand is determined by the value of "marginal" units, produced under the worst possible conditions, i.e., in conditions in which the highest labour time is contained per commodity unit. For the sake of simplicity we shall disregard absolute rent.

But as far as gold as a world currency is concerned, the problem of the amount needed to satisfy social demand does not exist. In this sense gold has no marginal value determining the value (price) of the total output—all mined gold is needed. There are not and cannot be difficulties over its realisation since gold, as the universal equivalent, is exchangeable for all other commodities.

The problem is simple enough for each individual gold-mining enterprise. If the production of a kilo of gold costs more than the gold itself the enterprise runs at a loss and must be closed. If expenditure is lower than the cost of production and the invested capital yields the average rate of profit, the enterprise is viable. If, for example, only half a kilo of gold has to be spent to produce a further kilo, mine rent is formed. This rent is expressed in terms of gold, and naturally also in the currency of the relevant country.

The problem is to establish what individual value becomes the *universal* gold value and by what economic mechanism this transformation is effected. The problem is complicated by the following. Only very little of the gold mined is used as industrial gold. The bulk of the annual yield becomes world currency. The known gold reserves of the capitalist world (excluding the gold hoarded by private persons) amounted, at the end of 1960, to 40.5 thousand million dollars. This is about 50 times the annual yield and about 100 times the amount of gold being added annually to the gold reserves. This shows that the currency funds contain gold mined a hundred, and even more years ago. There can be no doubt that the value of gold mined 100 years ago by predominantly primitive methods was much higher than that of the gold being mined today.

This gives rise to the following question: does the value of the gold being mined today determine the value of all the gold stored in the currency funds? Or is there some sort of historically established average value for all the gold in stock, which is exerting an influence on the value of the gold being mined today?

We are merely raising this question without being able to give a satisfactory answer. So complicated a question needs detailed study by Marxist financists.

CHANGES IN THE REPRODUCTION
CYCLE FOLLOWING
THE SECOND WORLD WAR

In investigating this problem Marxist economic science has to answer the following questions:

1. Why does the reproduction cycle of the 20 years following the end of the Second World War differ substantially from that of the inter-war period? Is this difference due only to the far-reaching changes in capitalism during and after the Second World War or are other reasons responsible for it?

2. Why are there such striking differences in the development of that cycle, on the one hand in the U.S.A., Canada and to a certain extent in Britain, where slight improvements rapidly alternated with shallow crises, and in the continental European countries (France, West Germany, Italy), on the other, where no crises of overproduction (the drop of industrial output below the level for the preceding year) have as yet set in?

Admittedly, never in the history of capitalism have cycles fully complied with Marx's scheme. The laws of the reproduction cycle, like all laws, are no more than scientific abstractions, and are determined by the different tendencies and counter-tendencies at work in capitalist economy. But the history of capitalism has never before known so great and enduring a divergence between the two main parts of the capitalist world—North America and continental Europe.

3. Finally the most important question—will capitalist reproduction, so long as capitalism continues to exist,

follow the pattern of development of the U.S.A. or of the West European capitalist countries?

*　*　*

Let us remind the reader that during the inter-war period the production cycle was running relatively normally. There were three world crises of overproduction: 1920-21, 1929-33 and 1937-38. Of them the 1920-21 crisis was not long-lived and not deep; the 1929-33 crisis the longest and most prostrating in the history of capitalism, and the 1937-38 crisis of average intensity.

Below are the indices of world industrial output during that period.

General Index of the Capitalist World's Industrial Output[1]

(1929=100)

1913	68.2	1933	71.9
1920	66.9	1934	77.7
1929	100.0	1935	86.0
	(pre-crisis	1936	96.4
	peak)	1937	103.7
1932	63.8	1938	93.0
	(minimum)		

Though these data do not claim absolute accuracy, they are accurate enough to show the cyclic course of reproduction. If we had monthly figures, the amplitude of oscillation would be even greater. The figures show that between 1920 and 1938 production grew by about 50 per cent, or by an average of 3.5 per cent a year. But growth was confined to the period between 1920 and 1929. From 1929 to 1938 there was practically no growth; nor was there any real upswing after the 1929-33 crisis.[2] The 1937 peak exceeded the 1929 level by only 4 per cent.

The 20 years since the end of the Second World War differ considerably from the two decades following the end

---

[1] *Mirovoye khozyaistvo* (World Economy), Russ. ed., 1938-39, p. 362.
[2] The exception was Germany where war preparations altered the reproduction cycle.

of the First World War. World industrial output grew at a more rapid pace, the cyclical movement was expressed much less clearly and the oscillations were less pronounced.

Index of the Capitalist World's Industrial Production[1]

(1953=100)

1937	1938	1946	1947	1948	1950	1952	1955	1956	1957	1958	1959	1960	1961	1962[2]
56	51	61	68	73	84	93	112	117	121	118	130	139	144	153

During the post-war period industrial output more than doubled. The average yearly growth was 5.5 per cent, i.e., higher than during the inter-war period.

As mentioned above, production growth was not the result of industrial development in the less developed countries, but was due almost exclusively to an expansion of output in the highly developed capitalist countries.

The U.N. gives the following percentages for the shares of groups of countries in the world industrial output between 1953 and 1958[3]:

	U.S.A. and Canada	Western Europe	Japan	Enumerated countries in corpore	Rest of capitalist world
1953	55.0	32.6	2.1	89.7	10.3
1958	49.5	36.3	3.5	89.3	10.7

During the five years in which the imperialist countries were beating the drum about the development of productive forces in the less developed countries, the share of the

---

[1] U.N. data. *Statistical Yearbook of the United Nations*, 1955, p. 115; 1961, p. 60. *Monthly Bulletin of Statistics*, May 1962, p. VI; June 1963, p. VI.

[2] Recalculated by the author from 1958=100.

[3] *Statistical Yearbook of the United Nations*, 1961, p. 62 et passim; *Monthly Bulletin of Statistics*, February 1963, pp. XII-XIV.

latter in the capitalist world's industrial output increased by only 0.4 per cent—a figure well within the limits of statistical error. The highly developed countries continue to account for the bulk of the world's industrial output.

During that same period the cyclic movement of *world* capitalist production was expressed only feebly. In the crisis year of 1958 the industrial output of the capitalist world dropped by only 3 per cent below the 1957 level. There was no depression phase—indeed the 1959 output level was considerably above the preceding peak.[1]

And yet development remained *extremely uneven* in the highly developed capitalist countries. It depended on the degree to which their economies had been dislocated during the war and, in particular, on the state of their productive apparatus (fixed capital, raw materials, etc.). The countries which were not exhausted by the war and had not been devastated, began to increase their output as soon as they had overcome the difficulty of shifting from war to peace-time production; but the countries which had been devastated by war and whose productive apparatus had been seriously damaged, needed several years before they were able to expand their output.

Below we give figures on industrial output in the important capitalist countries, grouped according to the 1947 production level. (See table on p. 211.)

The table shows that:

a) the vanquished countries, whose post-war output was extremely low, managed to raise their output without an interim critical drop; the 1958 crisis affected their production growth rate only to a very slight degree;

b) in 1962 the industrial production level in these countries was about 200 per cent higher than it had been in 1937—i.e., they had developed quicker than the U.S.A. and Britain. The causes for this rapid development will be explained below;

c) as distinct from the vanquished countries, a number of comparatively slight crises hit the U.S.A. During the past eight years production has grown very slowly both in the U.S.A. and Britain.

---

[1] A consideration of monthly data would furnish a slightly greater difference.

Index Numbers of Industrial Production
(1953=100)

	Japan	West Germany	Italy	France	U.S.A.	Britain	Canada
1937[2]	80	78	63	78	46	76	43
1947	29	...	...	71	75	76	76
1948	38	40	62	81	78	83	79
1949	48	57	68	88	72	88	80
1950	55	72	79	88	84	94	85
1951	74	85	90	99	90	97	91
1952	82	92	91	103	93	94	94
1953	100	100	100	100	100	100	100
1954	108	112	109	109	93	107	98
1955	116	129	120	120	106	111	110
1956	144	139	128	133	109	112	120
1957	167	147	137	144	110	114	120
1958	168	151	142	150	102	112	120
1959	208	162	158	156	116	118	129
1960	261	180	180	174	119	126	130
1961	317	191	200	184	120	128	133
1962	345	200	206	196	122	129	141

Marxist economists are divided on the interpretation of these facts, some declaring that the cycle following the 1937-38 crisis continued right through the war and ended with the regular crisis of overproduction in 1946.

We disagree. The Second World War, like every other great war,[3] interrupted the normal course of the cycle and created an enormous demand for war materials and a corresponding reduction in civilian production, with the

---

[1] U. N. data. *Statistical Yearbook of the United Nations*, 1955, p. 117 et passim; 1961, p. 71 et passim. *Monthly Bulletin of Statistics*, May 1962, p. 16 et passim; June 1963, p. 16 et passim (1962 recalculated by the author from 1958=100).

[2] We are comparing with 1937 and not 1938 because the latter was a crisis year, and 1939 marked the outbreak of the war.

[3] Even the comparatively small war in Korea exerted a considerable influence on the post-war cycle—reserves of strategic raw materials were created, military spending increased steeply and prices soared.

result that, for a number of years, the effective demand outweighed supply. In conditions when nearly half the gross national product of a capitalist society goes to satisfy war needs, when enormous wealth is destroyed by the war, when the main problem of capitalist enterprises becomes not how to sell their goods, but where to get the necessary raw materials, machines and labour force to produce them, there can be no overproduction of commodities and no crises of overproduction, and hence no cyclic movement of reproduction. Thus world war interrupts the cyclic movement of reproduction; indeed cyclic reproduction and crises of overproduction are simply inconceivable.

The main function of the cycle, of both its course as a whole and its separate phases, is to create the conditions for a crisis of overproduction. During the war years no such conditions are created. For this reason periods of prolonged war must not be included in the cycle.

There are those who object to this argument. They say that the cyclical nature of reproduction stems from the operation of the general laws of capitalism and that capitalism remains capitalism even in times of war. For this reason, they say, the cyclic course of reproduction continues even during the world wars.

We consider this approach too dogmatic. It lacks what Lenin called "the living soul of Marxism"—a concrete analysis of a concrete situation. After all, Marx established the laws of the capitalist economy *in peace-time.* Even though there were wars in his time, they did not exert a great influence on the economy and "military economy" simply did not exist.

Some of our economists expressed the opinion that the war itself creates the conditions for a crisis of overproduction because of the excessive development of the war industry and its associated branches (ferrous and non-ferrous metallurgy, the metal-working, chemical and other industries) and the lagging behind of industries producing consumer goods, i.e., creates a major disproportion within the economy. This theory echoes the bourgeois and revisionist view that it is not capitalism itself that is responsible for the crises of overproduction, nor is it the contradiction between the social character of production and the private capitalist form of appropriation with the ensuing poverty and proletarianisation of the masses, but a disproportion between the various branches of production.[1]

This is incorrect. The fact that after a period of war the productive capacity of some industries is too high, and that of others too low, may cause a *partial* crisis in some war industries, but cannot bring about a general crisis of overproduction. In many important industries, especially those producing consumer goods, demand continued to exceed supply even after the war.[2]

The only fact which could be interpreted as an indication of overproduction during the war was the drop in the general index of industrial output in the U.S.A. in 1944 from a peak 244 (1935-39=100) in February to 230 in July[3]. However this drop was due primarily to an overestimation of the requirements for means of transport and heavy armaments; the drop in production therefore affected mainly engineering (including the production of tanks, guns, etc.) and transport machinery building.

The facts show that this drop in production was not of a cyclical nature: a) in 1946 there was still a general

---

[1] This theory is based on the tenet of English classical political economy stating that every commodity includes wages, profit and rent, i.e., that the production of a commodity in itself creates the purchasing power ensuring its sale, and that a general crisis of overproduction is therefore impossible.

This tenet is wrong—indeed it was refuted by Marx. Even so it continues to circulate to this day. In the mouthpiece of the Guaranty Trust, the largest American bank, we read that every bit of the cash value of any article produced or any service rendered represents somebody's income or purchasing power.... If goods are unsold this is not an indication of low purchasing power but of the fact that this power is not utilised to the full.

[2] Even in the U.S.A., where the organic composition of capital is much higher than in the other capitalist countries, the share of Department II is not smaller than that of Department I. During 1957 an equal amount of durables and non-durables was sold—about 170,000 million dollars worth of each (*Survey of Current Business*, February 1958, p. S-3). The durables included consumer goods such as cars, furniture, etc. On the other hand, American statistics include coal and petrol, which are used predominantly as means of production, in the non-durables group. But on the whole, the division of goods into durables and non-durables more or less corresponds to the division into Departments I and II.

[3] *Statistical Abstract of the United States*, 1944-45, p. 796.

shortage of peace-time goods in all capitalist countries; overproduction was observed only in war materials; b) there was a drop in production in the second half of 1945 and in 1946 not only in the capitalist countries, but also in the Soviet Union, in spite of Soviet economy's planned and crisis-free development.

There was little difference in the manner in which the transition from war to peace-time economy was made in the capitalist countries and in the Soviet Union: war production stopped; millions of people had to be moved over enormous distances (soldiers, the evacuated population, POWs); people who normally did not work in industry quitted their jobs; production had to be adjusted in all industries which had ceased operating during the war, etc. Thus, even though this adjustment proceeded according to plan, the level of Soviet industrial output (1913=100) dropped from 782 in 1945 to 652 in 1946 in spite of the *growth* of the production of consumer goods from 295 in 1945 to 335 in 1946.[1]

In all countries, the industrial output level was lower in the second half of 1945 and in 1946, and partly in 1947 than it had been during the war. This is not a cyclic phenomenon but the natural result of the switchover from war-time to peace-time economy. Part of the military plants was temporarily put out of use, part was re-equipped and transferred to the production of peace-time goods, while a part continued to produce weapons. Industry had to adjust itself to the production of a new range of goods. This transition took time and was attended by a drop in output. Thus, *1947 should be regarded as the beginning of a post-war cycle lasting from 10 to 11 years.*

In this respect the first cycle following the Second World War differed greatly from that following the First. Then the crisis set in 2 to 3 years after the end of the First World War. True, the 1920-21 crisis was not long-lived and not very deep. The difference is explained by the fact that the First World War was comparatively short, less war materials were needed, fewer countries were involved and the damage wrought to productive capacities was smaller,

---

[1] See *Narodnoye khozyaistvo SSSR v 1960 godu*, p. 219.

The changes world capitalist economy underwent as a result of the First World War were therefore much smaller than those wrought by the Second.

This poses a theoretical question: what determines the difference in the length of individual cycles?

The expansion and renewal of fixed capital is the material basis of the reproduction cycle. If we disregard extraordinary events—wars, crop failures, etc.—the length of the cycle depends on the size of the fixed capital being renewed or expanded and the use to which it is put. The larger the amount of new capital investments, the longer the upward phases of the cycle—revival, boom (and overstrain).

In studying the cycles we generally consider only the sum total of new capital investments and pay little attention to their nature. This is wrong: equal amounts of new capital investments can exert different influences on the cycle's duration depending on:

1. Whether capital investments are made predominantly into factories, etc., i.e., projects which immediately upon completion directly increase the supply of commodities on the market, or (as was the case in the middle of the 19th century) into projects which increase the supply of goods on the market only indirectly, such as railways, ports, vessels, highways, bank buildings, department stores, etc. In the former case the conditions for a crisis mature much quicker.

2. The ratio between the new capital investments and the value of commodities being put on the market after the new projects are commissioned. Thus, for example, the building of a hydropower station requires large capital investments, but it supplies only a comparatively small amount of new commodities and investments are recouped very slowly. At the same time factories with a lower organic composition of capital supply the market with more commodities (in relation to the amount of invested capital) and overproduction sets in much sooner.

3. The length of time during which projects are under construction. On the one hand, technical progress and the concentration of capital make for the building of large factories and groups of factories, the designing and building of which takes much longer than the small factories of a

century ago. On the other hand, the rate of construction is now much higher than ever before.

The factors which have caused this speeding up in the cycle are described below.

DISTINGUISHING FEATURES
OF THE FIRST POST-WAR CYCLE

Even though for the past hundred years trade cycles have assumed a definite regularity, and are all identical in their causes and nature, each has its own particular features, dependent on the concrete historical conditions in which it unfolds.

The principal features of the cycle following the Second World War were:

a) the existence of two world systems, the continuous influence on world economy exerted by the cold war;

b) the disintegration of the colonial system of imperialism;

c) the changes in the world capitalist economy wrought by the six-year long world war;

d) the different economic (and political) circumstances in which various capitalist countries—neutral countries, the U.S.A., the West European countries, the victorious countries and the vanquished countries—found themselves after the war and consequent difference in the length of the cycle in the various countries;

e) the general inflation and steady and rapid price advance in all but a few neutral countries resulting partly from an artificial boosting of prices by the monopolies, and partly from the usual increase accompanying such economic upswings;

f) the dollar deficit experienced by most capitalist countries;

g) the marked intensification in the agrarian crisis.

Let us try to analyse briefly the influence exerted on the cycle by concrete historical conditions.

The principal result of the cold war was that the capitalist countries, and notably the U.S.A., took up large-scale production of arms soon after the end of the war. This continued throughout the cycle at a steadily increasing rate.

According to our computations military spending as a percentage of the national income comprised[1]:

	1937-38	1948-49	1953-54
U.S.A.			
percentage of official national income	1.5	6.5	15.8
percentage of national income after exclusion of double entries	—	—	ab. 22
Britain			
percentage of official national income	4.1	7.7	9.5
percentage of national income after exclusion of double entries	—	—	ab. 12
France			
percentage of official national income	5.9	6.1	13.3
percentage of national income after exclusion of double entries	—	—	ab. 16

The share of war production in the national income continued to grow in later years.

The bulk of the military spending was channelled to the production of arms, which themselves were becoming steadily more intricate and expensive. Military technology developed so rapidly that weapons were often obsolete even before their serial production was taken up (this happened to the British atomic weapons Blue Streak and Skybolt). This means that even in peace-time the monopolies producing armaments are getting new and highly profitable orders. Continued international tension and the cold war policy thus become extremely profitable for the monopolies. The share of military deliveries is much higher in the aggregate industrial output than it is in the national income, and it is even higher in the sum total of profits.

The influence war production exerts on reproduction in peace-time depends on the concrete historical conditions. If, owing to a lack in effective demand, there are surplus productive capacities, raw materials and labour force in the country (during the general crisis of capitalism this is

---

[1] See Y. Varga, *Osnovniye voprosy ekonomiki i politiki imperializma posle vtoroi mirovoi voiny*, p. 42.

the normal state)[1], military orders promote production and economic growth, extend the market, lengthen the revival and boom (and overstraining) phases of the cycle, and hence the whole cycle. However, at the same time they produce or strengthen inflation. If, on the other hand, there are no idle production reserves, military production does not increase the aggregate industrial output but is effected at the expense of the output of the civilian branches and, finally, if the scale of war production is greater than that warranted by the country's economic resources, the result will be an overstrained and unbalanced economy similar to that in times of war.

The influence exerted by war orders on the cycle can be clearly seen from the example of the 1948-49 crisis in the U.S.A. (In this connection it is not particularly important whether it was an interim crisis or whether the war in Korea stopped it from developing into a real crisis of overproduction.) The war in Korea gave an impetus to production growth. The index of industrial output rose from its lowest point of 95 in July 1949 to an average 112 in 1950 (1947-49=100), i.e., by 18 per cent.[2] This shows that under certain conditions a steep increase in war orders can produce a revival and upswing in the economy.

However Britain's economy in the last three years of the post-war cycle indicates that not all war orders produce a general expansion in production and market capacity. Even though the volume of war production was considerable, the volume of aggregate production did not change throughout 1955, 1956 and 1957. Production capacities were used almost to the full and the high share of war production became responsible for an inflation and currency crisis. On the other hand, the comparatively low war expenditures

---

[1] Idle capacities in the U.S.A. (per cent):

1954	1955	1956	1957	1958
16	8	14	22	20

(Data from 12th *MacGrow Hill Survey*). In practice even more of the fixed capital stood idle, for the above figures are based on only 300 shifts a year.

[2] *Federal Reserve Bulletin*, various issues.

of West Germany and Japan greatly contributed to the rapid rehabilitation in these countries of destroyed productive capacities and to an expansion of the fixed capital, resulting in substantial production growth during the upward phase.

All these facts show that war production exerted a major influence on the course of the first post-war cycle. As regards the system of capitalist economy as a whole, we find that war production is able to lengthen the upward and overstrain phases, and hence the whole cycle, but cannot avert a crisis of overproduction, as has been conclusively proved by the 1957-58 crisis.

In their newspapers, the monopolies, which are thriving on war orders, propound the theory that such orders have a stabilising influence on the course of reproduction. This is pure fantasy. The feverish development of military equipment intensifies anarchy of production.

The data below show how quickly the expenditure on the main kinds of war materials changes in the U.S.A.[1]

Percentage Expenditure

Year	Vessels	Tanks, ammunition	Aircraft	Electronics	Missiles
1953	6.8	50.0	31.5	11.2	0.5
1961	7.8	12.4	28.2	18.0	33.6

Such leaps do not stabilise the economy but disorganise it and often bring mass unemployment to U.S. towns.

The disintegration of the colonial system also had a telling influence on the course of the cycle. The export of all capital to the former colonial and semi-colonial countries which embarked on the socialist road of development—China, North Vietnam and North Korea—ceased. Politics became all-important in deciding to which country capital should be exported. This meant that capital could be exported only to countries in which there was "law and order", in which there was no threat of nationalisation, i.e., in which there existed conditions favourable to a profitable

---

[1] *The Economist*, October 13, 1962, p. 144.

investment of new capital. The disintegration of the colonial system also changed the volume and geographic destination of the capital exports. During the post-war cycle the sum of private capital exported (especially if we consider the drop in the purchasing power of all currencies) was much smaller than it had been during the 1921-29 cycle. Geographically, too, there were changes: capital was exported primarily to countries which from a capitalist point of view were safest—to Canada, the Latin American countries, and, in some cases, Africa.

A recent development is the large-scale export of capital in the form of economic and military subsidies by various governments, especially the U.S.A. As regards the course of the cycle there is no difference between the export of private and state capital or subventions.[1] All it means is that commodities are exported from a country while no commodities are imported, as distinct from normal foreign trade. This brings a temporary expansion of the market and, all other conditions being equal, a lengthening of the trade cycle.

The loss of resources brought about by the formation of the world socialist system and the disintegration of the colonial system did not produce a shortage of raw materials in the capitalist world. During the post-war cycle a shortage in some raw materials and a steep increase in their price was observed only in 1950 when the United States was feverishly buying up various strategic raw materials to create military reserves. Modern technology helped the capitalists to open up many new deposits in Canada, South America, Central Africa and even in the imperialist countries themselves (oil in Texas, West Germany and France), which provided a new source of raw materials for those in short supply.

The false assertion that the capitalist world is short of raw materials can be seen from the fact that the over-production and a drop in prices of industrial raw materials began before the industrial crisis.

---

[1] The effects of capital export and subventions are identical only as regards the course of the cycle. Actually subventions, in spite of the contentions of some Soviet economists, are not an export of capital, since they do not possess what Marx described as the essence of capital—self-increasing value.

	1956 peak	1957 January	1958 January
Copper (cents per pound)	45.9	35.8	24.8
Steel scrap (dollar per ton)	67.0	63.0	33.0
Zinc (cents per pound)	13.5	13.5	10.0
Lead " " "	106.5	102.2	92.2
Rubber " " "	37.2	33.5	27.2
Hides " " "	13.5	10.0	9.2

This shows that the prices for some types of raw materials (copper, lead, rubber, hides) began to drop in 1957.

The Second World War in which all industrial countries in the world, except Sweden and Switzerland, participated, *exerted a decisive influence on the course of the first post-war cycle*.[2]

During the war the consumption level—military and civilian with due account being taken also of the devastation wrought by the war—was considerably higher than the production level. The volume of national wealth decreased.[3] Commodity stocks diminished. Fixed capital, excluding that in the military branches, wore out and became obsolete. Consumer demand, especially for durables (housing, furniture, cars, household appliances), was not satisfied for years, since the production of these articles had been prohibited in order to free the productive forces (workers, raw materials and machines) for war production. The food consumption of the urban population (excluding

---

[1] *The Morgan Guaranty Trust Survey*, January 1958, pp. 12-13; February 1958, pp. 12-13.

[2] Even the economy of the neutral European countries was upset by the war: the warring countries, and notably Germany, were buying from them all types of goods at high prices.

[3] According to American economists, even in the U.S.A., which suffered no devastation in the war and which participated in it for a far shorter time than the European countries, the national wealth (excluding that part which was government-owned) was no larger in 1945 than it had been in 1929 (in 1929 prices). (S. Kuznets and L. Goldsmith, *Income and Wealth of the United States*, Cambridge, 1952, pp. 327-28.)

the rich, who bought what they needed on the black market), was limited by the rationing system. By the end of the war there was a tremendous unsatisfied demand for means of production for the "peaceful" branches and for consumer goods.

This extraordinarily high demand was effective. The government paid the capitalists high prices for military supplies. Profits, accumulated depreciation funds and accumulations resulting from the decrease in stocks took the form of bank deposits, bonds (which could be readily converted into money) and cash. The well-to-do part of the population and even some categories of industrial workers could not spend the whole of their income because of the shortage of consumer goods and whether they liked it or not, were forced to save part of it.

The following U.S. data show clearly that owing to the consumer goods shortage during the war the population was unable to spend all of its income.

Personal Savings in the U.S.A.[1]

(thousand million dollars)

1939	1942	1943	1944	1945	1947
2.9	27.8	33	36.9	28.7	4.7

The picture is so clear that no further comment is needed. At the same time money circulation and deposits were growing, due partly to the war-time inflation.

Money in Circulation[2]

(thousand millions at the end of the year)

Year	U.S.A. dollars	Canada Can. dollars	Brazil cruzeiros	Britain pounds sterling	Sweden kronor	France francs	Italy lira	Japan yen
1938	5.8	0.24	3.6	0.46	1.04	112	19	2.9
1945	26.5	1.06	14.3	1.34	2.79	577	368	54.8

[1] *United States. Economic Report of the President*, 1961, p. 145.
[2] *Statistical Yearbook of the United Nations*, 1956, p. 484 et passim.

Both in industrial and less developed countries (Brazil), those which participated in the war or remained neutral, the supply of money in circulation grew by 200 to 400 per cent, in the vanquished countries (Italy and Japan) it grew nearly 20 times over.

Bank deposits should be added to the above.

Deposits[1]

(thousand millions at the end of the year)

Year	U.S.A.[2] dollars	Canada Can. dollars	Brazil cruzeiros	Britain pounds sterling	Sweden kronor	France francs	Italy lira	Japan yen
1938	26	0.9	8.5	1.2	1.9	80	21	4.7
1945	76	2.5	27	3.1	3.8	436	290	36

The deposit growth rate coincided roughly with the money circulation growth rate.[3] Taken together they show that, as a result of the war, the purchasing power of society increased enormously. To this we should also add the deposits in savings accounts and the war bonds held by private persons and companies. Naturally there could have been no growing effective demand if prices had risen in proportion to the supply of money in circulation, long- and short-term deposits in savings banks. However they did not.

Average Yearly General Wholesale Price Index

(1953=100)

Year	U.S.A.	Canada	Brazil	Britain	Sweden	France	Italy	Japan
1938	46	46	13	31	37	4	2	0.4
1945	62	60	40	52	65	14	39	1.0

---

[1] *Statistical Yearbook of the United Nations*, 1956, p. 484 et passim.

[2] *Federal Reserve Bulletin* gives even higher figures. The difference is probably due to the fact that the sum of deposits includes inter-bank and state deposits.

[3] In Italy and Japan there was a strong inflation at that time and the growth of deposits was therefore smaller than the growth in the supply of money in circulation.

In the countries which were of overriding importance to the industrial cycle (U.S.A., Britain, Canada) at that time, prices advanced during the war far less than the supply of money in circulation, long- and short-term deposits in savings banks. In other words, *by the end of the war the postponed demand in these countries was fully effective,* even though black market prices were higher than official ones. The situation differed in France and Italy, which had already been stricken by a deep inflation during the war.

Following the end of the war the capacity of the capitalist market was above "normal" both as regards the output of Department I and Department II, and this above all determined the course of the post-war cycle. The capitalists began to renew the worn fixed capital at an extremely rapid rate and also began to expand it: in the victor countries this took place immediately after the war, in the vanquished countries[1] a few years later. This was the main reason for the length of the revival and boom phases in the post-war cycle. This can be seen from the figures for the U.S.A., Britain and West Germany given below.

Expenditure on New Equipment in the U.S.A.[2]
(thousand million dollars, average per year)

1929-38	1945-49	1950-54	1955	1956	1957
3.5	14.4	25.5	28.7	35.1	37.0

The expansion of fixed capital continued steadily until the first half of 1957. Even taking into account the falling purchasing power of the dollar throughout the post-war cycle, the scale of the expansion was several times larger than it had been in the pre-war cycle.

The same state of affairs obtained in Britain and West Germany.

---

[1] The neutral countries and especially the less developed ones which did not participate in the war directly also experienced a shortage of fixed capital towards the end of the war. The reason was that the warring industrial countries were unable to supply them with means of production.

[2] *Statistical Abstract of the United States*, 1951, p. 444; 1956, p. 498; 1961, p. 492.

Gross Fixed Capital Formation in Britain[1]
(million pounds sterling)

	1938	1950	1955	1956
Current prices	656	1,702	2,855	3,139
1948 prices	1,559	1,641	2,124	2,234

In West Germany capital investments in means of production and construction comprised (thousand million marks)[2]:

1938	1950-55 average yearly	1955
7.1	27.8	39.8

Funds which had accumulated during the war were used to expand the fixed capital and to replenish commodity stocks, which by the end of the war had fallen to a very low level. In the U.S.A., for example, commodity stocks in industry, wholesale and retail trade had by the end of the war fallen to 25,000 million dollars; during the subsequent cycle they grew to 91,300 million dollars (August 1957). Similar conditions obtained in the other industrial countries. Production for the replenishment of stocks played a major role in lengthening the revival and boom phases of the post-war cycle. In the U.S.A. stocks began to decrease only in the fourth quarter of 1957. But the enormous growth in commodity stocks as compared with the sum of sales indicated even earlier that stocks were too high and that there was an overproduction of commodities.

The third factor which made for a lengthening of the upward phase had nothing to do with the war, but was due to an artificial expansion of the consumer goods market by

---

[1] *United Kingdom Annual Abstract of Statistics*, 1956, p. 249; 1957, p. 252.

[2] *Statistisches Jahrbuch für die Bundesrepublik Deutschland*, 1957, S. 561.

considerably extending consumer credits. This step was taken when the additional demand of the first post-war years was satisfied and the effective demand ceased to correspond with the volume of production. It was then that the future income, the future purchasing power of capitalist society, was used to save the present situation. This was practised particularly widely in the U.S.A., where consumer credit grew from $5,700 million at the end of 1945 to $45,300 million in November 1957. On a smaller scale, consumer credit also grew in Britain and other capitalist countries.

These three factors—the extraordinarily large volume of the renewal and expansion of fixed capital (in the war-devastated countries also the reconstruction of destroyed factories, houses, etc.), the creation of large commodity stocks in production and trade, and sales on account of future incomes—were responsible for the length of the post-war cycle.

In this connection we should also explain why the 1957-58 crisis of overproduction which completed the first post-war cycle did not spread to such highly developed countries as France, West Germany, Italy and Japan.

In the light of the present discussion it is interesting to look into the mechanism by which a crisis emerging in one or several countries spreads to other industrial countries.

Countries afflicted by a crisis attempt to ease their position at the expense of other countries by expanding exports[1] and restricting imports. The development of a crisis stops new capital investments.

The fall in share quotations caused by a crisis is registered on the stock exchanges of all capitalist countries.

In the event of a credit-monetary crisis the withdrawal of short-term loan capital from other countries may even cause a monetary-credit crisis there.[2]

Other factors can also lead indirectly to the same result.

---

[1] Indicative in this respect is the steep increase in the active side of the U.S. trade balance in 1957. It rose from 2,900 million dollars in 1955 to 4,700 million dollars in 1956 and to 6,500 million dollars in 1957 (excluding the export of arms). (*Statistical Abstract of the United States*, 1961, p. 865.)

[2] The crash of the German Grossbanken in 1931 following the withdrawal of American short-term loans serves as an example.

A crisis may become responsible for a sharp drop in raw material prices in some countries, and force countries with a mono-cultural economy to cut down on the import of manufactured goods.

Prevailing conditions in the various countries decide which of these factors becomes the most active. The influence exerted by foreign trade in bringing about a crisis is felt most strongly in countries having high export and import quotas, for example in Britain and Belgium. But, as a rule, *a crisis of overproduction spreads to new countries only if the conditions for a crisis have to a greater or larger extent already matured in their domestic economy.* This becomes clearer if we consider that, even with an export quota of about 25 per cent (as in the case of Britain), a 10 per cent drop in exports comprises only 2.5 per cent of total production. In most countries this percentage is smaller.

Even the sharp increase in industrial output between 1948 and 1958 to a level exceeding the pre-war by about 100 per cent did not fully abolish the economic consequences of the Second World War, nor did it create the conditions for a crisis of overproduction.

Thus, although by the end of the cycle the industrial output level of the capitalist world as a whole nearly doubled the 1937 level, there were considerable differences between individual countries as regards their level of production and the rate at which the production cycle developed. If the war in Korea had not given an impetus to U.S. industry (and that of a few other countries) the differences in the development of the cycle between the victorious and the vanquished countries would have been even greater.

An important feature of the first post-war cycle was the constant devaluation of the currencies of all capitalist countries as a result of inflation—a feature that was absent in all the 19th century cycles. This devaluation could be seen from the fact that in all countries, including the U.S.A., industrial gold was sold above its official dollar rate of 35 dollars an ounce. This in turn depreciated all other currencies and resulted in an increase in prices, which to some extent continued even after the crisis in the U.S.A. had set in. Owing to rapid technological progress the value of commodities, i.e., the labour time embodied in a commodity unit, decreased during the course of the cycle, and the price advance therefore indicated an inflationary break-away of commodity prices from true value.

A price advance stretching over many years lengthens the boom (and overstrain) phase and, with it, the whole cycle. Entrepreneurs, expecting a further growth in prices, increase their stocks and strive to invest their money-loan capital into material values. The consumer, expecting a further growth in prices, hurriedly lays in goods (often on credit) for the future. The boom phase extends. There can be no doubt that inflation was one of the factors responsible for the longer duration of the first post-war cycle.

Nearly all capitalist countries experienced a dollar deficit during the cycle.[1] This was the result of various governmental measures taken in the interests of the monopolies to restrict imports, state dumping of monopoly-produced goods on the world market, and the extremely favourable U.S. balance of payments resulting from it, and finally the steady increase in U.S. gold reserves at the expense of the other capitalist countries. The dollar shortage was an important contributory factor to the inflation in many capitalist countries, for example, Britain.

The cycle was attended almost throughout by a sharp agrarian crisis. This was characteristic not only of the present cycle but of all cycles in the era of the general crisis of capitalism (as we hope to prove in the next essay).

DISTINGUISHING FEATURES
OF THE SECOND POST-WAR CYCLE

Typical of the second post-war cycle is the continued struggle of the two systems; the completion, in the main, of the political liberation of the colonies, and a deepening of the agrarian crisis.

The most important features distinguishing the second post-war cycle from the first are the following:

a) the vanquished countries are no longer lagging behind in industrial output; all highly developed countries entered

---

[1] The exceptions were: 1) large gold producers; 2) large-scale exporters of strategic raw materials to the U.S.A., and 3) Switzerland, which became a haven for all capital of doubtful origin (nazis and speculators from all over the world deposit their money in Swiss banks, which take care not to divulge "bank secrets").

the new cycle at an approximately equal level, as compared with 1937;

b) the economic supremacy of the U.S.A. over all other capitalist countries has decreased considerably. Instead of the dollar deficit typical of the first cycle, the U.S.A. now has a considerable balance of payments deficit and a steady drain on its gold reserves. It has even been compelled to seek financial aid from the West European countries. The long-term settlements by France and West Germany of their state debts to the U.S.A.; the agreement obliging the West European banks to back the dollar; the sale of U.S. government bonds on the West European money market; the 500 million dollar loan given to the U.S.A. by the International Monetary Fund, etc., were some of the measures taken to stop this gold drain and to stabilise the dollar. The unusually high share of the U.S.A. in world industrial output, exports, and the volume of gold reserves, and also its political weight in world affairs proved to be only temporary conditions brought about by the Second World War. It turned out that in spite of the natural riches of the U.S.A. and high labour productivity based on up-to-date equipment, its economic might is insufficient to enable it permanently to play the role of the defender of capitalism on a world scale;

c) the inflation in the highly developed countries characteristic of the first post-war cycle has lifted; the currency rates expressed in dollars relative to gold have stabilised; but this stabilisation does not mean that prices have stopped advancing, especially the retail prices being paid by consumers.

Index of Consumer Prices[1]

(1958=100)

	France	West Germany	Italy	Britain	U.S.A.	Japan
End of 1961	114	105	104	105	103	110
End of 1962	119	109	109	110	105	118

The price increase was due to the activities of the monopolies and their state, which raises indirect taxes and

[1] *Monthly Bulletin of Statistics*, April 1963, p. 146 et passim.

duties and thus shifts an ever increasing share of the state expenditure on to the shoulders of factory and office workers;

d) there were great changes on the world market. During the first post-war cycle, and especially immediately after the war, American goods dominated the world market. The vanquished countries produced goods predominantly for home consumption, and exported very little. This is no longer true in the second post-war cycle. Sharp competition reigns on the world market, and the U.S.A. and the Common Market are introducing penalty duties. Japanese electronic products are infiltrating into the American market. Cotton cloth and other products of the less developed countries are in demand on the British market. Complaints about dumping are heard everywhere. All this shows that the world market is once again becoming too narrow for the steadily expanding productive capacities;

e) increasing structural unemployment is becoming the scourge of the working class, and a persistent worry to the big bourgeoisie in the U.S.A., Britain, etc. By resorting to stubborn class struggle, the working class is able to fight the high cost of living more or less effectively, but cannot combat the structural unemployment resulting from technological progress, and, in particular, automation. The only measure that could, albeit temporarily, solve this problem, would be to reduce the working time of the whole working class to about 30 hours a week. Naturally the capitalists are unwilling to agree to such a radical decrease in surplus value.

The statement made by William McChesney Martin, Chairman of the Board of Governors of the Federal Reserve System, to the Joint Economic Committee of the U.S. Congress, shows extent to which monopoly capital is concerned with the rapid and incessantly growing structural unemployment. "The number of people having jobs rose 1.2 million in 1962.... Yet the average rate of unemployment declined only to 5.6 per cent in 1962 from 6.7 per cent in 1961. Furthermore, despite an increase in industrial production to a level 8 per cent above the previous high in the first quarter of early 1960, the number of workers on the production lines of the nation's factories declined 500,000, or 4 per cent, in the same period."[1]

---

[1] *Federal Reserve Bulletin*, February 1963, p. 123.

The honourable banker is less worried about the fate of the millions of unemployed, than about the consequences mass unemployment would have for U.S. economy and the domestic market. He says: "We also face the inescapable challenge of a faster growing population of working age. Many more jobs will have to be found each year. About a million and a quarter persons are expected to be added to the labour force in each of the next 5 years compared with only about 800,000 in the past 5 years. By 1965, the burgeoning population of 18-24 years of age will account for more than half of the annual growth in the labour force. Unemployment rates are now very high among these young people, especially those with insufficient education. The long anticipated expansion in demand for homes, cars, and all sorts of goods and services will hardly materialise if we fail to find job opportunities for our growing population."[1]

This is one of the most important problems for the future course of reproduction in the U.S.A., Britain, and the other highly developed countries.

Even though the second post-war cycle develops in conditions differing considerably from those of the first, there still are distinctions between the way it unfolds in the victorious and in the vanquished countries. In the victorious countries (the U.S.A., Britain, Canada) the growth rates are slower and there have already been crises—in the U.S.A. in 1960-61, in Britain in 1962-63—but no upward phase worth mentioning.

Index of Industrial Production[2]

(1958=100)

Year	Japan	West Germany	France	Italy	U.S.A.	Britain
1959 . .	124	107	101	111	113	105
1960 . .	156	119	110	128	116	112
1961 . .	186	126	116	142	117	114
1962 . .	201	132	123	156	126	115

[1] Ibid., p. 128.
[2] U.N. data. *Monthly Bulletin of Statistics*, June 1963, p. 18 et passim.

The table shows that in the second post-war cycle, too, there are differences in the type of cyclical movement in the U.S.A. and Britain, on the one hand, and the large industrial capitalist countries of continental Europe, on the other.

* * *

How then will the reproduction cycle under capitalism develop in the future?

At present the cycles differ in the two decisive parts of the capitalist world. We think it illogical for this state of affairs to continue within the single framework of monopoly capitalism. Sooner or later a cycle of a single type[1] will be established throughout the capitalist world. In our opinion *this cycle will resemble the post-war development of the U.S.A.*

The tendency for the cycle to shorten is based on the general laws of capitalist reproduction. The contradiction between the social character of production and the private capitalist form of appropriation, which forms the basis of the cyclical movement, or to be more exact, the contradiction between the striving of the capitalists for an unlimited expansion of production and the limited consumption capacity of capitalist society becomes steadily deeper.[2] For this reason crises of overproduction will become more frequent.

A hundred years ago Marx discovered this tendency of the cycle to shorten. He wrote: "Up to now the cycle usually lasted ten to eleven years. But we have no reason to believe that this is a constant figure. On the contrary, the laws of capitalism we have described give us reason to believe that

---

[1] This should not be understood dogmatically; there are and will be deviations from this rule in individual countries.

[2] The social consumption capacity is the sum spent on consumer articles, i.e., $v+m-a$ (where a is accumulation). This is less than the social effective demand, which is $c+v+m$ (c in this case being the share of the worn-out fixed capital). But since all production in the final analysis serves to produce consumer articles, the social consumption capacity is the decisive factor in the contradiction between the striving of capital for a boundless expansion of production and the narrow limits of consumption.

Lenin proved that Tugan-Baranovsky's theory was wrong because it ignored the difference between consumption capacity and effective demand.

this is a changing figure and that it will gradually decrease."[1]

Right through the history of capitalism cycles tended to shorten. Between 1825 and 1857 when regular crises of overproduction could be observed only in Britain, then the most highly developed capitalist country, the cycle lasted 11 years. In the second half of the 19th century, when crises had already assumed a world-wide scale, the following sequence was observed—1857, 1866, 1873, 1882, 1890, 1900.

According to Marx's theory of crises and cycles, the crisis is the final (and initial) phase of the cycle.

Between 1857 and 1900 there were five cycles with an average duration of 8.5 years each.

In the early 20th century there were crises in 1907, 1914, 1920, 1929. This shows that over 29 years there were four cycles of an average length of 7 years each. It should also be remembered that in 1914 there was no noticeable crisis because of the outbreak of the First World War. Thus even though there actually were four crises during these 29 years, only three were noticeable.

We may well ask whether in future, too, the cycle will tend to shorten.

We think that this tendency will persist and that the cyclical movement in the whole capitalist world will acquire an ever closer resemblance to that of post-war U.S.A., i.e., there will be *shorter intervals between less serious crises, and real boom phases will be less pronounced.*

Some of our colleagues tried to bypass this question, styling all post-war crises in the U.S.A. and Britain (except the 1958 crisis) "interim", "partial", "preliminary" or "post-crisis". All these expressions have been used by Marx, especially in his letters. But in *Capital* Marx developed only the theory of genuine crises and cycles.

In our opinion there are no real grounds for regarding all post-war crises in the U.S.A. (except the 1958 crisis) as interim. Marx says that "false" crises occur within the

---

[1] *Le Capital* de Karl Marx, Paris, p. 288. These lines are an addition by Marx to the French translation of *Capital*. Engels (for reasons unknown to us) did not include them in the complete German edition; for this reason they do not appear in the second Russian edition of K. Marx's and F. Engels's *Works,* published by the Institute of Marxism-Leninism.

normal cycle, but are not part of it, for they may occur in one cycle, and fail to appear in another. However what we observe in the U.S.A. and Britain is a constant, regular and relatively rapid succession of minor crises. We therefore should not call them interim, although whatever we style them does not affect their nature.

We therefore maintain that the regular cycle for the capitalist system as a whole will come to resemble the post-war cycles in the U.S.A. and Great Britain, i.e., will be shorter than it was before the Second World War.

We think that in addition to a general aggravation of the contradictions of capitalism, *in the post-war period some new factors have tended to shorten the duration of the cycle.*

It is commonly known that the reproduction cycle is determined by the fixed capital, or to be more exact, every crisis is the starting point for a mass renewal and expansion of the fixed capital undertaken for the purpose of lowering production costs. This is because every capitalist thinks that the difficulty of selling his commodities is due to their high cost of production. Similarly, the laws of competition operating under monopoly capitalism force capitalists to renew and expand their fixed capital. This means that they buy equipment (machines, devices), commodities for the building of new factories, for the accumulation of new stocks of raw materials, etc., and this in itself effects an extension of the market.

But the position changes as the renewal and expansion of the fixed capital draws to a close. Capitalists stop buying the commodities and equipment they previously needed to build and equip new factories, just as the new capacities begin to supply the market with an additional mass of commodities.

During the post-war period the renewal and expansion of capital is characterised by the following important new factors:

1. Owing to speedy methods of construction, factories are built and put into operation much quicker than before the war.

2. Owing to rapid technological progress, equipment becomes obsolete sooner than it did before.

3. The rapid replacement of equipment and of the whole fixed capital is encouraged under state-monopoly capitalism. The governments of the highly developed capitalist countries allow the monopolies to deduct from profits depreciation sums which are often two to three times larger than the actual wear. In the U.S.A., for example, any equipment at enterprises, which are considered important from a defence point of view, is written off in five years and less. This provides capitalists with an ideal opportunity of renewing their fixed capital frequently at the expense of the taxpayer and tends to shorten the cycle.

4. Capital investments in the developed capitalist countries are used mainly for the modernisation of equipment in operating factories and not for the building of new factories. In the U.S.A. spending was distributed as follows (per cent)[1]:

	Expansion	Replacement and modernisation
1959	37	63
1960	35	65

The reason is that capacities are underemployed and result in the following: a) the same amount of new capital investments enables capacities to be enlarged to a far greater extent than if these funds were spent on the building of new factories[2]; b) the time between the investments into capacities and the time when the capacities start producing is reduced. Both these factors accelerate the maturing of the prerequisites for a crisis of overproduction and shorten the cycle.

Since these factors operate not only in the U.S.A. but in all highly developed capitalist countries, a further reduction in the length of the cycle can be expected throughout the capitalist world.

---

[1] *Business Week*, April 30, 1960, p. 28.

[2] A thorough study of German pre-war industry (made in connection with the reparation problem) showed that machines and equipment account for an average of 45 per cent of the total value of industrial enterprises.

It is also interesting to establish which of the cycle's phases is becoming shorter. If we look at post-war development in the U.S.A. it becomes obvious that, first and foremost, it is the depression phase. This is only logical. If capitalists are able to renew and expand their fixed capital out of their depreciation funds, the phase of depression, i.e., the period when production stagnates, must become less enduring.

But *the upward phase is also reduced and sometimes does not even set in at all.* Under conditions when a large portion of available equipment is constantly underemployed, even the introduction of small new capacities results in overproduction. For this reason the upward phase is shorter and the rise a very small one. The curve describing the cycle flattens out.

We may expect subsequent crises to deepen in comparison with the first post-war period—indeed the post-war crises in the U.S.A. exhibited a definite tendency to deepen. The economists of the American National City Bank determined the depth of the crises of overproduction in the U.S.A. according to monthly indices. The figures below clearly express this tendency of crises to deepen.[1]

Year	Depth of Crises (percentage drop of production)
1948-49	8
1953-54	10
1957-58	14
1960[2]	10

It is to be expected that in future the large monopolies will be even more determined to shift the burden of these crises onto the shoulders of small capitalists, farmers, the working class and especially the populations of the less developed countries, by capitalising on the further deterioration of the terms of trade between them and the highly developed countries—the drop in raw material prices and unchanged high prices on the commodities produced by the industrial monopolies.

---

[1] *First National City Bank Monthly Letter*, March 1960.
[2] Based on data from the *Federal Reserve Bulletin*.

A substantial growth in unemployment is also likely to ensue for two reasons: 1) the number of people coming of age and qualifying for work is increasing since the population movement of the war and early post-war years has stopped; 2) the rapid development of automation constantly decreases the number of people needed to produce the same amount of commodities. Especially important in this respect is the mechanisation of office work—copying machines, computers, accounting machines, etc., etc. All this means that unemployment is coming also to the "white-collar workers". This is very important from a political point of view since this layer of the proletariat, which has grown steeply during the past century and at present comprises 30 to 40 per cent of all employed, formerly considered itself nearer to the bourgeoisie than to the manual workers. We may therefore expect this huge army of office workers and civil servants to become far more revolutionary than it is at present. Such indications can already be observed in Britain and France.

A general intensification of the class struggle is to be expected, for the big bourgeoisie will attempt to counteract the drop in commodity sales by lowering production costs through wage cuts.

Nor should we forget the contradiction between the direct economic interests of the capitalists and their political interests. Their direct economic interests demand that they advance on the working class and cut down the wages and living standard of the workers. But because of the struggle between the two world systems, the bourgeoisie is unable to devote all its attention to direct economic interests alone. Struggling tooth and nail against the socialist world system, the bourgeoisie must take full account of the political consequences any offensive against the working class would have, especially in those countries where the proletariat comprises a large slice of the population, such as the U.S.A., Britain and West Germany.

Last but not least, researchers into this cycle should pay particular attention to the peculiar change in the crisis phase over recent years. Formerly the crisis generally took the form of an explosion—there was a sudden transition from the boom to the crisis phase. In America and Britain we now see that the outburst is delayed, that instead of an outburst there is often *a marking of time on the achieved high level of production,* which lasts for months, sometimes up to half a year, until a drop in production finally sets in.

The capitalists now have a far deeper knowledge of the overproduction following a boom and also of world market conditions than they had in Marx's time or even 30 years ago. At that time, much less relevant information was available and it was published only after great delay. Most important of all it was *retrospective* and recorded only past events.

Now we have efficient *projected* statistics.

In the highly developed industrial countries information on new orders, unfulfilled orders, contracts on new building work, proposed capital investments by joint-stock companies, questionnaires on projected car sales, records of commodity stocks at factories, in wholesale and retail trade, etc., are now being published regularly (and expeditiously). Many large enterprises and monopoly cartels have special organisations engaged in full-time market research for their commodities. This information enables capitalists to pre-gauge consumer demand and thus avoid an overproduction of commodities.

The monopoly capitalist state also takes steps to this end. It publishes forecasts on the national income, on total wages, on future state expenditure, etc., for several years in advance. These predictions, though inaccurate, afford a certain guidance to the capitalists.

Besides, when a recession is in the offing, the state can accelerate the placing of orders, increase their volume, lower taxes to increase effective social demand, etc. But it is easy to overestimate the importance of state "anti-crisis measures", for their potential value is extremely limited. Under capitalism there can be no state planning, no crisis-free capitalist reproduction. State measures are, however, able to slightly reinforce some of the factors which lower the intensity and duration of the upward phase and the depth and duration of crises in future cycles.

In any case, the long and powerful growth in output observed up to the present in the vanquished industrial countries is unlikely to continue in the future. This is recognised also by many bourgeois economists. Per Jacobs-

son, Director of the International Monetary Fund, address-
ing young economists in New York said:

". . .A new situation has arisen which shows certain simi-
larities with what happened in the early 1930s. . . . I do not
intend to convey the idea that we must repeat the sad
experiences of those years, but I do think we will have to
take definite measures to see that they are not repeated."[1]

The deepening of the general crisis of the capitalist system is expressed by the growth in the number of industries
which are in a state of perpetual crisis, such as the coal,
textile and ship-building industries, and those being gradually drawn into this state—the iron and steel and motor
industries.

---

[1] *The Times*, February 20, 1963, p. 10.

THE PROBLEM
OF AGRARIAN CRISES

More than half the population of the capitalist world is engaged in agriculture. The working peasantry is the proletariat's main ally in its struggle with capitalism. The problem of agrarian crises, essentially an economic problem, is therefore also of enormous political importance. The problem is gaining in significance as the marketability of the peasant economy grows, as the whole agriculture of the bourgeois world is being drawn into capitalist relations.

This important problem has been given insufficient study by Soviet economists.[1] In fact, there is not even enough material for such a study—no data has been collected on agricultural production, on prices and foreign trade in agricultural produce, on changes in ownership or on rents during the past 100 years and arranged systematically on the basis of Marxist-Leninist theory.

---

[1] L. I. Lyuboshits's book *Voprosy marksistsko-leninskoi teorii agrarnykh krizisov* (Problems of Marxist-Leninist Theory of Agrarian Crises) published by Gospolitizdat in 1949 is a serious Marxist attempt at analysing agrarian crises. But it is now obsolete, for it does not embrace the period since the Second World War, when the agrarian crisis of the 20th century assumed its final shape. Besides, in explaining agrarian crises, the author mistakenly draws a parallel between them and industrial crises. On page 35 he says: "Long agrarian crises, like industrial crises, are not only a sharp explosion of capitalist contradictions but also a means for their forceful levelling. It follows that ... they are neither permanent nor chronical and can therefore be overcome..." This statement is unsubstantiated by facts. To this day the agrarian crisis that followed the First World War has not been overcome (except during the period of the Second World War and the years immediately following it); at present, it embraces a greater number of agricultural branches than ever before.

The problem of agrarian crises is far more complicated than that of industrial crises of overproduction—primarily because agriculture itself is more complicated than industry, namely:

a) industry works only for the market; the proportion of total output consumed by the producers themselves is insignificant. Agriculture on the other hand produces only partly for the market. In the less developed countries (except on plantations) it is conducted mainly to satisfy the personal needs of the direct producers. Even in the highly developed countries there are millions of factory and office workers, artisans and small peasants who grow vegetables and fruit or keep pigs and fowl for their own needs. Besides, a large portion of farm produce (fodder) is used for on-farm production purposes. In industry these conditions prevail only in vertical trusts;

b) in industry social relations are more or less simple— the capitalists are faced by the hired workers. Of course there are also artisans, but in the developed capitalist countries they play only a minor role.

In agriculture, on the other hand, almost the same social relations that existed in the course of the whole of human history continue to prevail today. There are large capitalist enterprises in the capitalist countries and capitalist plantations in the less developed countries; there are independent peasant economies; feudal latifundias in Asian and Latin American countries, in Spain, Southern Italy, etc., preserving all the forms of money rent and rent in kind, and even labour rent; there is semi-slavery in South Africa, the Portuguese colonies, etc.;

c) in agriculture (and in mining) there is a special factor, missing in industry, namely absolute and differential rent, which, in lease agreements, is often fixed for many years (up to 10-12 years) in advance. This factor is reflected in the price of land, which depends not only on the size of the rent but also on the rate of interest yielded by loan capital;

d) in industry, production is usually continuous: new commodities reach the market every day (only construction, ship-building and the manufacture of large special-purpose machines and structures do not continue throughout the year).

Because of climatic conditions, agricultural production has a yearly cycle (half- or thrice-yearly in tropical countries). The major countries reap only one harvest a year. It is very difficult to change production during the agricultural year and, therefore, this is done only in the case of natural disaster;

e) climatic and weather conditions are of little importance to industrial production, to agriculture they are of overriding importance. Climatic conditions decide what crops are to be sown, and which are economically rational.[1] Unfavourable weather—dry winds, early or heavy frosts, etc.—may destroy most of the harvest and inflict considerable losses for the year in question.

All these factors make a study of the agrarian crisis extremely difficult. The multitude of often contradictory phenomena makes it difficult to divide the important from the unimportant, to determine the general trend of development.

Let us give a few examples.

A sharp drop in the price of agricultural products damages all enterprises producing them for the market. But it does not affect those who produce them for their own needs.

The drop in fodder prices leads to a systematic expansion of animal farming, especially pig-breeding, which continues until overproduction sets in (the so-called pig-breeding cycle).

In capitalist countries rents are usually stipulated in long-term agreements. A fall in the price of agricultural produce during the period the lease is valid may therefore bring losses to the lessee, without affecting the lessor.

Many more such examples could be given to illustrate the tremendous complexity of the agrarian crisis problem.

Under such conditions it is understandable that a number of our economists resort to known methods and draw an analogy between agrarian crises and industrial crises of overproduction, believing the former *to be a consequence of the latter*. In the second edition of the textbook on political economy we read: "Capitalist crises of overpro-

---

[1] Under present-day conditions any crop can be grown in any climate but it is often not economical to do so.

duction ... bring partial or general overproduction in agriculture. Crises of overproduction in agriculture are known as *agrarian crises*."[1]

True, agrarian crises and crises of overproduction have many features in common and are interrelated. The *common basis* of all agrarian crises—the same as that of the general crisis of capitalism and of industrial crises of overproduction—is the chief contradiction of social production and private capitalist appropriation. It is only commodity production that makes possible both agrarian and industrial crises. Where agriculture is aimed at satisfying the requirements of only the producers themselves, even though there may be surplus products, there can be no crises of overproduction, no agrarian crises.

There are close links between agrarian crises and industrial cycles. Agrarian crises exert an influence on the course of the industrial cycle, weaken the upward phase and deepen the crisis. Industrial crises of overproduction may become responsible for crises in those branches of agriculture supplying industry with flax, cotton, wool, jute, rubber, etc. *But industrial crises as such have never brought about an agrarian crisis*. Other causes are responsible for agrarian crises.

The interaction of agrarian and industrial crises has changed considerably in the course of capitalist development. In the 19th century when the share of agriculture in capitalist economy was still very high, agrarian crises exerted a major influence on the course of the industrial cycle. This can be clearly seen from the protracted industrial crisis of the 1870s. At present, when the share of agricultural production in the capitalist economy in general, and in the decisive capitalist countries—the U.S.A., Britain, West Germany—in particular, has decreased substantially, agrarian crises exercise a much smaller influence on the course of the industrial cycle. The presence of a deep agrarian crisis in the U.S.A. following the Second World War did not interfere with the boom in industry.

---

[1] *Politicheskaya ekonomiya* (Political Economy), Textbook, 2nd Russ. ed., 1955, p. 224. This point of view expressed earlier by I. D. Laptev and recently by E. L. Shifrin in *Selskoye khozyaistvo SShA posle vtoroi mirovoi voiny* (U.S. Agriculture Since the Second World War), published by the U.S.S.R. Academy of Sciences in 1956.

Contrariwise, the strong growth of the share of industry in capitalist economy and especially of the processing of agricultural raw materials, has strengthened the influence of industrial crises on the state of agriculture. *But they cannot cause a general agrarian crisis.* We shall show this by the example of the two agrarian crises of the 19th and 20th centuries.

THE 19th CENTURY AGRARIAN CRISIS

The agrarian crisis of the 19th century lasted roughly from 1870 to 1895.[1] Was this crisis a consequence of the industrial crisis? Of course not. This can be clearly seen from the following supplement to the manuscript of the third volume of *Capital*, written by Engels, a contemporary of that crisis, in the early 1890s.

To obviate unnecessary arguments, we are quoting the text in full:

"Transoceanic steamships and the railways of North and South America and India enabled some very singular tracts of land to compete in European grain markets. These were, on the one hand, the North American prairies and the Argentine pampas—plains cleared for the plough by Nature itself, and virgin soil which offered rich harvests for years to come even with primitive cultivation and without fertilisers. And, on the other hand, there were the land holdings of Russian and Indian communist communities which had to sell a portion of their produce, and a constantly increasing one at that, for the purpose of obtaining money for taxes wrung from them—frequently by means of torture—by a ruthless and despotic state. These products were sold without regard to price of production, they were sold at the price which the dealer offered, because the peasant perforce needed money without fail when taxes became due. And in face of this competition—coming from virgin plains

---

[1] It is difficult to find accurate data for the beginning and end of the agrarian crisis since only a yearly account is taken of the production of basic agricultural produce; and, unlike industry, no monthly figures are published. Price formation, too, may differ for various types of agricultural commodities, depending on the harvest, speculation and the nature of the commodity, i.e., whether it is a foodstuff or an industrial raw material, etc.

as well as from Russian and Indian peasants ground down by taxation—the European tenant farmer and peasant could not prevail at the old rents. A portion of the land in Europe fell decisively out of competition as regards grain cultivation, and rents fell everywhere; ... and therefore the lament of landlords from Scotland to Italy and from southern France to East Prussia."[1]

Engels does not mention industrial crises, but explains the agrarian crises by the rapid expansion of grain production in the newly raised lands in America, the improvement in the transportation of grain and lower freightage and Russia's and India's "hungry export", which filled the market with agricultural produce in excess of the effective demand of the food importing countries.

To dispel all possible doubts, we are quoting figures from a report by Professor Sering,[2] a competent bourgeois scholar, who, in 1883, by order of the Prussian Ministry of Agriculture made a detailed study of U.S. and Canadian agriculture (German agriculture was then seriously affected by the competition of North-American grain). His report contained the following points.

a) In the second half of the 19th century grain production expanded rapidly in the U.S.A. and in Canada.

Corn and Wheat Production in the U.S.A.[3]
(million bushels)

	1850	1860	1870	1880	1890	1891
Corn	592	839	1,125	1,707	1,650	2,336
Wheat	100	173	254	502	449	678

To exclude the influence of harvest fluctuations it would be necessary to compute averages for 5 to 10 years; the

---

[1] Karl Marx, *Capital*, Vol. III, p. 726.

[2] M. Sering, *Die Landwirtschaftliche Konkurrenz Nord Amerikas in Gegenwart und Zukunft*, Leipzig, 1887.

[3] M. Sering, op. cit., S. 730 et passim; *Historical Statistics of the United States*, 1st Edition, Washington, 1949, p. 106. Data for corn are for the preceding year (1 bushel of wheat=27.2 kg, 1 bushel of corn=25.4 kg).

1890 and 1891 figures show that these fluctuations are considerable. But even these figures clearly demonstrate that, over a period of 40 years, the output of wheat increased by 400 to 500 per cent and that of corn by 200 to 300 per cent.[1] The production of oats and barley grew at the same rate, that of linseed even quicker.

b) *Production grew predominantly through the expansion of areas under seed*, and not through intensification or higher yields. This is important for a comparison with the modern agrarian crisis.

Sown Areas in the U.S.A.[2]
(million acres)

	1866	1870	1880	1890	1891
Corn	30	38	63	75	79
Wheat	15	21	38	37	41

The acreage harvested is not an accurate measure since it does not include unharvested areas, which, in extensive farming, are often considerable.

Wheat; Acreage Harvested[3]
(bushels per acre)

1870-74	1875-79	1880-84	1885-89	1890-94
12.1	12.4	12.2	12.9	13.8

The above shows that the *average yield does not grow or grows exceedingly slowly*. The lagging behind of crop yields was even greater in Western Europe.

---

[1] Unfortunately we have no data for Canada, which was a major wheat producer and exporter.

[2] *Historical Statistics of the United States*, 1st Edition, p. 106.

[3] M. Sering, op. cit., S. 737; 1855-94.—Our calculation is based on *Historical Statistics of the United States*, 1st Edition, p. 106.

(bushels per acre)

Britain	Belgium	Germany	France	U.S.A.
29.9	27.9	19.5	17.1	12.25

In the U.S.A. wheat was produced by the extensive method and production costs were low. There were large strips of virgin land and, as Marx pointed out, rent was only nominal. New land was generally cultivated not by capitalist enterprises but by farmers who tilled it with the help of their families and who used railways owned by local monopolies.

Surplus wheat supplies were exported to the West European countries, notably to Britain, which was then experiencing a sharp crisis in grain products and an agricultural crisis in general.

U.S. Wheat and Flour Exports[2]
(in terms of '000,000 bushels of wheat)

1860	1870	1880
16	52	180

American wheat ousted other imported wheat from the British market and its share in British consumption grew from 12 per cent in 1851-55 to 54 per cent in 1876-80.[3] The imports of American wheat brought a sharp drop in prices on the British market, which in turn determined the price level of wheat on the world market. The prices of wheat in all countries were approximately equal to the British price minus transportation costs (from the country of production to Britain).

---

[1] M. Sering, op. cit., S. 472. Figures for France are probably underestimated.

[2] Ibid., S. 739.

[3] This was promoted by the building in America of transcontinental railways and the development of shipping.

Wheat Prices in Britain and Prussia[1]

(marks per ton)

	1871-75	1881-85
Prussia	235	190
Britain	246	180

According to a report of the Royal Commission charged with investigating the causes of the British farming crisis in nearly all counties of England and Scotland farmers had suffered unparalleled disaster, large areas of good arable land had been transformed into pastures. The unprecedentedly large import of grain, especially from the U.S.A., served merely to aggravate conditions for the farmers.

Let us summarise: the agrarian crisis of the 19th century was not brought about by an *industrial crisis*. Neither Engels nor Sering, nor any other student of the 19th century agrarian crisis, considered it the consequence of industrial crises.[2]

During the development of the agrarian crisis, three distinct industrial cycles, ending in the 1873, 1882 and 1890 crises respectively, hit the economy. If industrial crises produced agrarian crises, an upward phase in industry should, theoretically, have put an end to the crisis in agriculture.[3]

The 19th century agrarian crisis was an event unique in the history of capitalism. It was caused by the basic contradiction of capitalism, the limited purchasing power of society resulting from it, and by the rapid expansion of sown areas on fertile lands in the Americas.[4] This was

---

[1] M. Sering, op. cit., S. 555.

[2] True, Sering speaks of the influence exerted by the 1873 crisis but in a different sense. He wrote (p. 532) that the huge unemployment during the 1873 crisis favoured the expansion of grain production, since it freed many workers formerly employed in industry in the East for farming in the West.

[3] There are a number of factors—the fixed rent, the fact that the labour power of peasants cannot be used outside their own farms, etc.—which tend to protract agrarian crises.

[4] We must not exclude the possibility that this may recur somewhere else in the world. The well-known German geographer Humboldt

primarily a crisis of the *grain* economy[1] in Western Europe and the American East, and not a world agrarian crisis embracing all countries and all branches of agriculture (to the extent to which they produce marketable output), as is the case with the modern agrarian crisis.

Cattle Population in the U.S.A.
(million head)

	1867	1877	1887	1897
Cattle	29	37	57	50
Pigs	34	39	43	51

The 19th century agrarian crisis ended in the middle of the 1890s. How was it overcome?

1. Partly by the ruin of the economically weak peasants and landowners and the drop in ground rent and rents.

2. Partly by the introduction in continental Europe of duties on farm produce, notably on grain, in order to raise prices on the domestic market above world prices.

3. By stopping, after 1896, the expansion of areas sown to wheat in the U.S.A.; maize cultivation grew very slowly.[2]

4. And most important of all, *through the transition to more intensive farming in Europe*. This included a wider use of fertilisers and the expansion of branches other than grain production—intensive animal farming, the growing of fodder crops, vegetables, fruit and industrial crops. This was a *progressive development*, a fact that is very important in any analysis of the modern agrarian crisis.

---

said 100 years ago that the Amazon Valley could feed 500 million people if it were possible to destroy the weeds interfering with crop growth. The irrigation of the Sahara (present-day technology puts this within the bounds of possibility) could also play a major role. But these are only possibilities and it is unlikely that they will be realised under capitalism.

[1] Cattle farming developed in the U.S.A. much slower than crop farming.

[2] *Historical Statistics of the United States*, 1st Edition, p. 106.

What socio-historical conditions created additional markets for animal produce, vegetables, fruit and industrial crops at that time?

In the first place, the rapid development of industry and the steep growth of the urban population connected with it. This resulted in a large additional demand for these products. It was also the time of the final redivision of the world between the imperialist states and the resulting emergence of a wide layer of the labour aristocracy in the main imperialist countries of Europe, creating an additional demand for high quality foods. In short, the main factor in overcoming the agrarian crisis in Europe was the general acceleration of capitalist development, the trend for which was already obvious at the time when capitalism was entering the monopoly stage, and which was analysed by Lenin in his *Imperialism, the Highest Stage of Capitalism*.

These processes can be illustrated by the example of Germany. During the agrarian crisis animal farming developed as follows:

Cattle Population[1]
(million head)

Year	Horses	Cattle	Pigs	Sheep
1873	3.4	15.8	7.1	25
1892	4.0	17.5	12.2	13.6
1913	4.5	20.9	25.6	5.5

The large sheep population typical of this extensive farming was rapidly decreasing, while the cattle and especially the pig population was growing. At the same time the quality of the cattle improved and its average weight and milk yield increased.

Crop farming too became more intensive: the average wheat yield rose from 15.4^2 centners per square hectare

---

[1] *Statistisches Jahrbuch für das Deutsche Reich*, 1914, S. 51-53.
[2] M. Sering, op. cit., S. 472.

between 1878 and 1884 to 19.8[1] centners between 1903 and 1907. The yields of other crops rose in approximately the same proportion.

Naturally, it was not the peasants, but the German landowners, who were getting all possible help from the government and who gained from this intensification.

The problem of the 19th century agrarian crisis should be subjected to a detailed Marxist study based on documents of that period. It should be emphasised that the processes studied by Lenin in his famous writings on the agrarian problem—the formation of a capitalist domestic market by the differentiation of the peasantry, the concentration of the agricultural means of production in the hands of capitalist elements, etc.—take place irrespective of whether there is an agrarian crisis or not (Lenin wrote his works when the 19th century agrarian crisis had ended and before the 20th century crisis set in). The agrarian crisis accelerates these processes and results in even greater suffering for the peasants.

THE ABSENCE OF AN AGRARIAN CRISIS AT THE BEGINNING OF THE 20th CENTURY

In the beginning of the 20th century, up to the outbreak of the First World War, West European agriculture had adapted itself to American competition. The prices for agricultural commodities were no longer dipping, but had even tended to advance.

Exchange Quotation per Ton[2]

(German marks)

	Wheat		Rye		Corn	
	1904	1913	1904	1913	1904	1913
London	144	158	...	...	...	...
Amsterdam (American winter)	152	163	108	131	...	...
Chicago	...	...	...	...	83	103

[1] *Statistisches Jahrbuch für das Deutsche Reich*, 1914, S. 44.

[2] *Statistisches Jahrbuch für das Deutsche Reich*, 1914, Internationale Übersichten, S. 23x.

Exchange quotations for animal produce grew to an even greater extent between 1904 and 1913. In London, beef rose from 102 to 119 marks per 100 kg, Argentinian beef from 48 to 61; pork from 92 to 134 marks. A similar price movement could also be observed on other European markets.[1]

Of great importance in this connection was the fact that the area under wheat and maize in the U.S.A. stopped expanding, harvests stabilised and exports fell owing to the growing home demand. Prices in the U.S.A. picked up.

Sown Areas in the U.S.A.[2] *(average yearly in million acres)*			**Yields** *(million bushels)*		
	1896-1900	1909-13		1896-1900	1909-13
Wheat . .	47	48	Wheat . .	710	682
Corn . . .	92	101	Corn . . .	2,547	2,632

The farm price per bushel of wheat rose from 72 cents in 1896 to 99 cents in 1909 and 80 cents in 1913; maize rose correspondingly from 21 to 58 and 68 cents.

This shows that, by the early 20th century, the agrarian crisis had been overcome.

THE AGRARIAN CRISIS
FOLLOWING THE FIRST WORLD WAR

The first agrarian crisis of the 20th century began soon after the outbreak of the general crisis of capitalism. Wheat prices in the U.S.A., which had grown substantially during the war and had reached 2.13 dollars per bushel in 1919, dropped in 1921 to 90 cents, i.e., below the 1909 level. The same was also true of other grains.

---

[1] *Statistisches Jahrbuch für das Deutsche Reich*, 1914, Internationale Übersichten, S. 23x. The price advance was not of an inflationary nature, since the West European currencies were based on gold.

[2] *Historical Statistics of the United States*, 1st Edition, p. 106 (average yearly figures computed by the author).

What caused this sharp price drop? The main reason was the great expansion of sown areas in the Americas during and immediately following the world war. In this respect the 20th century crisis resembled that of the 19th. The area under wheat in the U.S.A. grew from 52 million acres in 1913 to 74 million acres in 1919. Sown areas expanded to an even greater extent in Canada—from an average 4 million hectares between 1909 and 1913, to an average 8.7 million hectares between 1920 and 1924.

But the growth of agricultural production in the 20th century was not due to the same causes that had been responsible for that growth in the 19th century. In the 1870s and 1880s sown areas expanded because American farmers cultivated virgin lands, in the 20th century the increase in sown areas was effected by capitalist entrepreneurs and capitalist farmers. Capitalists who had accumulated a comparatively small capital during the world war and who, because of monopoly control, could not elbow their way into industry and transport, were investing it in agriculture. *This situation is typical of the whole period of the general crisis of capitalism and is at the root of the 20th century agrarian crisis. During the 20th century agriculture in the highly developed capitalist countries gradually passed from the manufactory stage to the machine or factory stage of development.*

Proponents of the view that agrarian crises are a result of industrial crises of overproduction assert that the agrarian crisis was the outcome of the 1920-21 industrial crisis. A study of the facts does not endorse their view. The consumption of farm products should have dropped considerably if the industrial crisis really had engendered the agrarian crisis through a decline of prices on farm products. But the 1920-21 crisis was too short to have such far-reaching results. It embraced primarily the non-belligerent countries, notably the U.S.A., which had suffered from the war less than the other warring countries. Data on per capita consumption during the crisis prove convincingly that it was not the decrease in consumption that was at the root of the price drop. Even though the average yearly per capita consumption fell, it was far too small an amount to cause such a sharp fall in prices.

Average Yearly Per Capita Consumption
of the U.S. Population[1]

	1913	1920	1921	1922
Calories a day	3,480	3,350	3,260	3,460
Wheat flour (pounds per year)	206	186	177	181
Meat of all kinds " "	144	136	134	138
Fats of all kinds " "	37	36	36	40
Sugar . . . . . " "	81	86	87	104
Potatoes . . . . " "	185	146	154	154

Although we do not vouch for the accuracy of these data, they do show that the decrease in consumption (potatoes excepted) was very slight. The decrease in the consumption of bread was less than 10 per cent, while that of fats and sugar grew. The small drop in bread consumption certainly could not cause an agrarian crisis.[2]

Champions of the theory that industrial crises are the cause of agrarian crises will find it even more difficult to explain why the agrarian crisis deepened. In the above mentioned textbook on political economy we find: "Agriculture had not yet recovered from this crisis [1921—*Y.V.*] when at the end of 1928 there were clear indications that a new agrarian crisis was maturing in Canada, the U.S.A., Brazil and Australia."[3]

From the above it would appear that the 1921 agrarian crisis was over in three to four years, but this contradicts the correct statement by the authors that agrarian crises are of an enduring character.

We should be glad if K. V. Ostrovityanov, I. D. Laptev, E. L. Shifrin and other proponents of the above theory would explain how it was possible for the agrarian crisis

---

[1] *Historical Statistics of the United States*, 1st Edition, pp. 52-54.

[2] The class nature of consumption can be clearly seen from the fact that the drop was registered in flour (bread) and potatoes but not in the products predominating in the diet of the higher income bracket —meat, fats, sugar; consumption did not decrease as regards calory content.

[3] E. L. Shifrin quotes this paragraph verbatim in his book on page 8.

to set in "at the end of 1928", if at that time there was as yet no indication of an industrial crisis?

It is common knowledge that the 1929-33 crisis began in the U.S.A. with the stock exchange crash in the autumn of 1929, while industrial output, following a short drop, continued to expand even in the first months of 1930. The crisis really came into its own only in the second half of 1930, and in some capitalist countries, France, for example, it began only in 1931.[1]

How and with the help of what economic mechanism, could the 1929-33 crisis "produce" an agrarian crisis even before it emerged? It does not seem to make sense.

The allegation that agrarian crises are the outcome of industrial crises contradicts facts and also the views expressed by Marx. In his only remark on the agrarian crisis of the 19th century, Marx said: "As regards the agricultural crisis, it will gradually intensify, develop and eventually reach its peak, bringing with it a veritable revolution in land ownership, completely independent of the cycles of commercial-industrial crises."[2]

The contention that a *new* agrarian crisis began in the U.S.A. at the end of 1928 is not borne out by any concrete facts.

General Statistics on U.S. Agriculture
(million dollars)[3]

	Gross farm income	Cash receipts from farm marketings	Prices received by farmers	Prices paid by farmers
			(1910-14=100)	
1928	13,550	11,072	151	155
1929	13,824	11,296	149	154

The above data show no changes which could not be accounted for by statistical inaccuracies. The area sown to wheat in the U.S.A. even expanded from 59 million acres in 1928 to 63 million acres in 1929.

---

[1] *Miroviye ekonomicheskiye krizisy 1848-1935 gg* (World Economic Crises 1848-1935), Vol. I, Russ. ed., Sotsekgiz, 1937.

[2] Marx and Engels, *Collected Works*, Vol. XXVII, Russ. ed., p. 94.

[3] *Historical Statistics of the United States*, 1st Edition, p. 99.

Undoubtedly we could find some countries which showed a worsening of the situation in 1928. But a theory must not rely on individual cases. A Marxist theory must explain all, or at least the most important *general* phenomena.[1] It may be that the old agrarian crisis continued into 1928, but there certainly are no indications of a new crisis.

Admittedly, the 1929-33 industrial crisis, which was the deepest and most prolonged in history, deepened and intensified the agrarian crisis. The industrial crisis brought a sharp drop in prices of agricultural produce.

Wholesale (Exchange) Prices[2]

	1929	1932
Wheat (winter) (dollars per bushel) . .	1.16	0.47
Maize (dollars per bushel)	0.95	0.32
Pork (dollars per 112 British pounds) . .	10.42	3.89
Cotton (cents per British pound) . . .	18.50	6.36

The sharp drop in prices led to the system of state guaranteed prices which continues in the U.S.A. to this day.

The per capita consumption of the U.S. population dropped substantially,[3] as illustrated by the following figures:

	1929	1935
Calories per day	3,480	3,170
Wheat flour (pounds a year)	173	150
Potatoes	155	138 (1934)
Meat	131	116
Fats	45	42 (1932)

---

[1] How complex and contradictory these phenomena really are (especially in agriculture) can be seen from the following. In 1929 the price of a bushel of maize was 80 cents in the U.S.A.; in 1932 it dropped to 32 cents. Yet in spite of that, the area under maize rose from 97.8 million acres in 1929 to 106 million acres in 1933. In 1932, in spite of the industrial crisis, the area under maize was the largest ever, and a record harvest for those days was reaped.

[2] *The Morgan Guaranty Trust Survey*, December 1963, p. 10.

[3] *Historical Statistics of the United States*, 1st Edition, pp. 52-54.

The drop was substantial. It is particularly interesting to note that general consumption reached an all-time low in 1935, when continued mass unemployment had exhausted all the workers' means of subsistence and they could no longer obtain food on credit. This drop was also observed in other capitalist countries.

The decrease in consumption was accompanied by a sharp drop in the price of farm products. The monopolies, flour, dairy and meat factories which bought up farm products, cut their purchasing prices. In spite of the prostrating crisis, industrial monopolies maintained prices at a comparatively high level. The price gap spelled ruin to American farmers.

AGRARIAN CRISIS
OF THE 20th CENTURY COMPARED
WITH THAT OF THE 19th CENTURY

Although the agrarian crisis of the 20th century, like that of the 19th, was based on the contradiction between the social character of production and private capitalist appropriation, there were fundamental differences between the two. Let us emphasise that for our comparison we are examining the crisis at the peak of its development, i.e., the beginning of the 1960s, i.e., the same crisis that began before the Second World War and was only interrupted by the war.

The reason for the overproduction attending the 20th century agrarian crisis after the Second World War was not an expansion of sown areas[1] and a change in transportation techniques as in the case of the 19th century crisis, but the higher yields due to the intensification of production and utilisation of machinery and fertilisers on a mass scale, in other words, *the transformation of agriculture in the highly developed capitalist countries into one of the branches of capitalist machine production.*

The wheat yields in the principal capitalist countries provide an example of the above.

---

[1] Sown areas expanded in the U.S.A. and Canada only in the first years following the Second World War, when agriculture in West Europe was in a very bad state.

Wheat Yields[1]

(centners per hectare)

	Before the First World War (1912 or 1913)	Before the Second World War (1931-35)	1937	1960	1962
U.S.A.	10.2	8.8	9.2	17.4	16.1
Germany	23.6	21.2	21.7	35.6[2]	35.1[3]
France	13.8	16.0	13.3 (1936)	25.0	24.4
Britain	21.0	23.2	20.6	35.0	40.2
Argentine	7.8	9.4	8.2	13.3	...

The figures are accurate to ± 10 per cent (bearing in mind that all yields are influenced by climatic conditions). But, in spite of inaccuracies, two facts are obvious.

1. From just before the First World War and right up to the Second the average wheat yield in the leading capitalist countries remained at an approximately even level. This was due largely to the prostrating 1929-33 industrial crisis.

2. Between 1937 and 1960-62 the average wheat yield grew by 50 to 100 per cent. The yields of other agricultural crops grew similarly.

What is the reason for this unprecedented growth in yields, especially in the highly developed capitalist countries such as the U.S.A., Germany, France and Britain?

The reason is that fresh vast amounts of capital were invested in agriculture, it was supplied with machinery, artificial fertilisers, chemical weed-killers, etc., in other words, agriculture was becoming a branch of industry.

---

[1] *Statistisches Jahrbuch für das Deutsche Reich*, 1914, International-ale Übersichten; 1938, Internationale Übersichten; *Statistisches Jahrbuch für die Bundesrepublik Deutschland*, 1962; *Monthly Bulletin of Agricultural Economics and Statistics (FAO)*, 1962, various issues; 1963, No. 1.

Wheat as the main crop represents all grain production. This method was used by Marx in his analysis of ground rent.

[2] West Germany.

[3] *Wirtschaft und Statistik*, No. 10, 1962, S. 604-05.

Let us take U.S. agriculture for example.[1]

Year	Value of machinery and equipment (thousand million dollars)	Average per worker employed in agriculture (dollars)
1910	1.4	103
1958	17.4	2,020
1960	18.4	2,592

In addition to machinery and equipment, milch cows, pigs, meat cattle, hens, etc., are also fixed capital and their value should be added to the above. The capital invested per worker in means of production (machinery and equipment, without buildings) in U.S. manufacturing industry amounted to:

1,800 dollars in 1929
3,037 dollars in 1960

The increase in capital investments in U.S. industry was undoubtedly slower than in agriculture. In agriculture the capital investment per worker is now higher than in many branches of the manufacturing industry.[2] (We must, of course, take into account that part of the agricultural means of production—ploughs, combine harvesters, sowers—are not used all year round, as in the case of industrial machinery.)

Vast amounts of new capital investments in agriculture are also being made in the other highly developed countries, but these do not go to poor and medium peasant farms. The same applies to the less developed countries.

---

[1] Official data: *Agricultural Statistics of the United States*, 1959, pp. 443, 451; 1960, p. 448; *Statistical Abstract of the United States*, 1961, pp. 215, 628; *United States Income and Output*, Washington, 1958, p. 196.

[2] The well-known American capitalist farmer Roswell Garst gives other figures: 30,000 dollars capital per worker in U.S. agriculture and 15,000 dollars per worker in U.S. industry (*U.S. News and World Report*, April 2, 1962, p. 78). But he probably includes the price of land and the cost of housing, which is wrong.

The growth of the machine pool[1] on American farms in physical units (thousands) is given below:

Year	Tractors	Lorries	Combine harvesters	Maize harvesters	No. of farms possessing milking machines
1920	246	139	4	10	55
1940	1,545	1,047	190	110	175
1960	4,770	3,110	1,065	780	730

During the past 20 years the number of essential machines on U.S. farms has grown from 3 to 7 times. Similar conditions prevail in the other highly developed capitalist countries.

A major role in raising crop yields in the U.S.A. is the increased use of fertilisers. Their output has grown from 9.4 million tons in 1940 to 25 million tons in 1959[2]. The use of fertilisers has grown considerably since the Second World War also in the West European countries. The consumption of nitrogenous fertilisers in Western Europe increased as follows (per thousand tons of pure nitrogen)[3]:

1954/55	1960/61
2,167	3,060

The intensification of agriculture and the overproduction of agricultural products are observed only in the highly developed countries. In the less developed countries farming techniques have improved little if at all. According to the last census (1956) India had

Wooden ploughs . . . . 37 million
Metal ploughs . . . . 2 million
Tractors 18,000

[1] *Historical Statistics of the United States*, 2nd Edition, pp. 284-85; *Statistical Abstract of the United States*, 1961, p. 639.
[2] *Statistical Abstract of the United States*, 1961, p. 636.
[3] *Deutsches Wirtschaftsinstitut*, 1963, 8 Heft, S. 12.

With such means of production it is impossible to raise food production and thus satisfy the needs of the rapidly growing population. Similar conditions prevail in the other less developed countries.

The ever deepening disparity between the highly developed, rich capitalist countries and the less developed, poor countries lends the agrarian crisis a contradictory and dual nature: *in the highly developed countries (and on colonial plantations) there is an overproduction of foods; in the less developed countries—a shortage of food and hence, constant undernourishment.* This is the *second feature* distinguishing the agrarian crisis of the 20th century from that of the 19th century.

At present there is no "hungry export" of grain from the less developed countries, which Engels mentioned as one of the causes of the agrarian crisis. On the contrary, during the past few years the highly developed countries (the U.S.A., Canada, France) have been supplying the less developed countries—India, Pakistan and others—with foodstuffs. U. S. supplies often take the form of economic "aid". This shows that the old formula of regarding the less developed countries as "agrarian appendages" of the imperialist countries has to be reconsidered.

Whilst capitalism still exists, the dual nature of the agrarian crises is unlikely to change substantially.

The growing concentration of capital and strengthening of monopoly rule in the highly developed capitalist countries makes it more and more difficult for small capital to break into industry, except by the purchase at high Stock Exchange prices of shares yielding a low interest, or by using their available cash as loan capital. Small capitalists will, therefore, continue to invest their capital in agriculture, transforming it into one of the branches of capitalist production. Marx's analysis of ground rent in *Capital* predicted that agriculture would be conducted along purely capitalist lines—in the highly developed capitalist countries this has become a reality.

On the other hand, the less developed countries not only lack the capital necessary to raise yields, but in the presence of feudal and semi-feudal latifundias (in Turkey, Pakistan, Brazil, Argentina and even Spain and Southern Italy) capital could not be invested in agriculture, even if it were available. The present state of agriculture in the less developed countries cannot be improved without a radical land reform and large capital investments.

Marx wrote: "But the form of landed property with which the incipient capitalist mode of production is confronted does not suit it. It first creates for itself the form required by subordinating agriculture to capital."[1]

Owing to an agrarian system which fetters all possibilities of agricultural development, the less developed capitalist countries find it more and more difficult to provide food for their rapidly growing populations. In 1953, Norris Edward Dodd, Director-General of the Food and Agriculture Organisation of the United Nations said that the chasm between the badly fed and well fed was wider today than it had been before. Ten years later this organisation in its latest report correctly outlined the prospects for the period up to 1970 as a growing surplus of food in the highly developed countries and the continuing, even worsening, undernourishment and hunger in the less developed countries.

Speaking at the World Food Congress held in Washington in June 1963, President Kennedy solemnly declared: "The war against hunger is truly mankind's 'war of liberation'.... There is no battle on earth or in space more important, [for] peace and progress cannot be maintained in a world half-fed and half-hungry.... We have the capacity to eliminate hunger from the face of the earth," President Kennedy continued. "Victory will not come in the next year.... But it must in our lifetime."[2] But he gave no indication as to how this could be achieved. *Newsweek*, from which we are quoting, continues: "Behind this arresting declaration of war against hunger were some appalling facts.

"Every day of this week some 10,000 people will die of malnutrition or starvation—more than at any time in history. In India alone, 50 million children will die of malnutrition in the next ten years. More than half the world's 3 billion people live in perpetual hunger...."[3]

---

[1] Karl Marx, *Capital*, Vol. III, p. 617.

[2] *Newsweek*, June 17, 1963, p. 31.

[3] Ibid.

We believe that this will continue to apply not only up to 1970 but as long as capitalism continues to exist.

Feudal landowners in the less developed countries are stubbornly resisting even a bourgeois reconstruction of agriculture, which, with the help of capital investments, would lead to important agricultural advances. Below are a few interesting quotes, all taken from bourgeois sources.

"The classic case of the medieval Spanish hacienda system lingering into the twentieth century is Peru. One hundred and sixty thousand Peruvians (1.5 per cent of the population of 11 million) own 76.2 per cent of the arable land. In contrast, 6 million Peruvians own less than 1 per cent. . . .

"The big haciendas grow export crops like cotton, making fabulous profits for the owners, while the rural population lacks basic foods."[1]

Another magazine surveys the state of affairs in Latin America: "Less than 6 per cent is in tillage or tree crops. . . . Less than 5 per cent of the landowners own 70 per cent of all arable land. Barely a quarter of this land is under cultivation or in livestock use. One result is food shortages that force 17 governments of Latin America to import food, often at a heavy drain on foreign-exchange earnings. Another result: A big proportion of the population in many countries is living at a bare subsistence level under feudal conditions. . . . Average South American gets 1,200 calories a day. . . ."[2]

An increase in agricultural output is practically impossible under such agrarian relations.

The table on p. 264 shows that under existing agrarian relations, the developing countries, as distinct from the highly developed ones, are unable to increase harvest yields.

Since the Second World War only in the Argentine has a substantial growth in crop yields been observed. In India and in Algeria harvests are no higher now than they were before the First World War. Indeed in India the rice harvest is even lower now than it was before the First World

---

[1] *Newsweek*, May 28, 1962, p. 43.
[2] *U.S. News and World Report*, August 21, 1961, pp. 53-54.

War—it dropped from 16.5 centners between 1909 and 1914 to 15.2 centners in 1961.

Wheat Yields
(centner per hectare)[1]

Years	India	Algeria	Argentine
1909-1913	8.1	6.7	6.6
1923-1927	7.5	5.3	8.6
1925-1929	6.8	5.5	8.6
1929-1933	7.2	5.3	8.8
1934/1938	6.9	5.6	9.8
1948/1949-1952/1953	6.7	6.2	11.5
1958/1959	6.8	6.3	12.8
1959/1960	7.9	6.4	13.3
1960/1961	7.8	7.8	11.0

The much larger harvests gathered on the same, and sometimes even smaller, areas in the highly developed countries as a result of increasing capital investments *categorically repudiate* the theory of diminishing soil fertility,[2] a theory which dominated bourgeois political economy for the past 150 years, and which is still used to justify the poverty of the working people under capitalism. Post-war development fully endorses Marx's theory that additional capital investments in agriculture can, under certain conditions, increase yields and incomes over and above those of the preceding period.

The development of agriculture is not a linear process. In Britain, for example, the area of cultivated land grew during the Second World War and, immediately after, began to diminish.

---

[1] *Annuaire International de Statistique Agricole*, 1928/29, 1931/32, 1939/40; *International Yearbook of Agricultural Statistics*, 1933/34; *United Nations, FAO, Yearbook*, 1961.

[2] At that time I shared the then extremely popular view on the diminishing soil fertility.

Sown Areas and Meadows[1]
(million acres, average)

	1938	1944 max.	1948	1960
Total cultivated area	9.0	14.5	13.2	11.2
including under wheat .	1.9	3.2	2.3	2.1
Meadows (temporary and permanent)	22.7	16.4	17.9	19.6

Below we are giving data on three large wheat producers.[2]

	Area under wheat (million hectares)			Yield (centner per hectare)		
	1937	1960	1961	1937	1960	1961
Canada	10.4	9.4	9.6	4.8	14.2	7.4
Australia	5.7	4.9	5.7	9.0	11.1	10.4
Argentine	6.2	4.4 (1959)	4.6	8.1	13.3	...

The pattern of development imitates that of the advanced capitalist countries, namely, the area under wheat decreases, while total yields increase (in 1961 there was a bad harvest in Canada).

It is thus clear that *the reason for the overproduction in the capitalist countries was not due to an expansion of sown areas, as was the case during the 19th century agrarian crisis, but to an increase in yields over smaller areas.*

Livestock farming has also grown considerably in the highly developed capitalist countries. Not only has the cattle population[3] increased (except horses) but there has

---

[1] *United Kingdom Annual Abstract of Statistics*, 1938-48, p. 171; 1961, p. 169.

[2] *Statistisches Jahrbuch für das Deutsche Reich*, 1938. Internationale Übersichten, S. 44x; *Statistisches Jahrbuch für die Bundesrepublik Deutschland*, 1961, Internationale Übersichten, S. 46x; 1962, S. 46x.

[3] According to official data the growth in Britain between 1950 and 1960 (in millions) was as follows:

Cattle	from 10.6 to 11.8
Pigs	from 3.0 to 5.7
Sheep	from 20.4 to 27.9

been a marked increase in the *productivity* of livestock farming—the milk yield, the live weight of pigs and meat cattle, etc. This can be seen by the example of West Germany.

Average Yearly Milk Yield
(in kilograms)[1]

1937	1954-59	1960	1961
2,519	3,068	3,395	3,428

Capitalist development of agriculture has the same consequences as capitalist development of industry: small producers—small and medium farmers and peasants—are ruined and production is concentrated to an ever increasing extent in large capitalist enterprises.

Yet there is one essential difference. In capitalist industry the decrease in the number of workers resulting from higher labour productivity has, up to now, been compensated by an increase in the volume of industrial output. Only in the very recent past has there been a tendency in the U.S.A. towards a decrease in *productive* workers in industry. In agriculture, *the ousting of workers by capital*, as Marx foresaw almost 100 years ago, is, by its very nature, final and irrevocable. Marx wrote: "It is the nature of capitalist production to continually reduce the agricultural population as compared with the non-agricultural ... in agriculture the variable capital required for the exploitation of a certain plot of land decreases absolutely; it can thus only increase to the extent that new land is taken into cultivation...."[2] But cultivated areas are no longer increasing in the capitalist countries.

The absolute ousting of labour from agriculture can best be seen by the example of the U.S.A. Owing to the

---

[1] *Statistisches Jahrbuch für das Deutsche Reich*, 1938, S. 125; *Statistisches Jahrbuch für die Bundesrepublik Deutschland*, 1961, S. 183; 1962, S. 195.
[2] Karl Marx, *Capital*, Vol. III, p. 622.

growth in labour productivity, the number of those employed in U.S. agriculture is steadily decreasing.

Labour Force in U.S. Agriculture[1]

(million)

1929	1939	1949	1957	1961	1962[2]
10.5	9.6	8.0	6.2	5.5	5.2

Between 1949 and 1961 the number of people employed in U.S. agriculture decreased by 2.5 million, i.e., by 30 per cent. This was a result of the rapid growth in the productivity of agricultural labour. The hourly output grew (1947-49=100) from 54 per cent in 1929 to 210 per cent in 1961[3], i.e., by an average of 12 per cent a year.

The mighty progress of agriculture in the highly developed capitalist countries is accompanied by the usual consequences: mass ruin of the working peasantry[4] and the expulsion of many millions of workers from the production process. At the same time the overproduction of agricultural products brings no benefits to the urban workers since, due to the intervention of the government and the monopolies, food prices remain high.

* * *

[1] *Historical Statistics of the United States*, 2nd Edition, p. 70.

[2] *Federal Reserve Bulletin*, May 1963, p. 700; *Survey of Current Business*, December 1962, p. 27. Those ousted were mainly self-employed peasants; their number decreased between 1950 and 1962 from 4.3 to 2.6 million.

[3] *United States. Report of the President*, 1962, p. 293.

[4] Bourgeois statesmen of the U.S.A. and the Common Market countries consider the elimination of "non-viable" peasants, i.e., those not possessing sufficient capital, desirable. The final communiqué of the Meeting of Agricultural Ministers of the Common Market Countries held at the beginning of 1964 reads: "The Ministers admit the need to create viable agricultural enterprises.... The tendency to transform non-viable enterprises into a smaller number of economically healthy enterprises is considered a major step in raising agricultural incomes." (*Neue Zürcher Zeitung*, February 29, 1964).

The basic difference between the agrarian crisis of the 19th century and that of the 20th century lies in the following.

The agrarian crisis of the 19th century was a crisis *only in the grain economy* and involved *only Western Europe and the East of the United States*. It took place at a time when capitalism was still developing on an ascending line and was overcome (except for the drop in ground rent) by an intensified development of livestock farming. The rapid growth in the urban population created an additional demand for animal products.

The agrarian crisis of the 20th century is a crisis *involving all branches of agriculture*. The overproduction embraces both crop and animal farming in all highly developed capitalist countries and in capitalist plantations in the less developed countries. The universal character of the agrarian crisis was already evident in the 1930s; the Second World War interrupted the course of events, but in the 1960s the universal overproduction of all agricultural products reached its peak.

This is again best illustrated by the example of the U.S.A., the richest capitalist country in the world. To fight overproduction the U.S. government purchased and stored up the following agricultural products: wheat, barley, maize, oats, rice, cotton, butter, cheese, milk (powdered), four types of oil seeds, sugar and six other products. By June 30, 1960, the total value of stock in government stores amounted to 7,200 million dollars; wheat accounted for almost half of that amount. In 1960 storage costs alone amounted to 522 million dollars.[1]

Between 1950 and 1960 the United States used stocks to the tune of $13,800 million for loans and "aid", primarily to the less developed countries (i.e., not through the usual trade channels).[2] It is easy to imagine the disorganisation that would have resulted if American surplus agricultural products had been dumped on the world market at free prices.

The rapid development of capitalism in agriculture and the resultant overproduction of agricultural commodities

---

[1] *Statistical Abstract of the United States*, 1961, p. 633.
[2] Ibid., p. 632.

has also begun in the highly developed West European countries.

The Common Market member-countries, taken in corpore, will soon have food surpluses.

Extent to Which the Common Market Countries Are Supplied with Domestic Foods[1]
(per cent)

Fresh vegetables	104	Wheat	93
Pork	102	Beef	92
Butter	101	Eggs	90
Potatoes	100	All foods	87
Sugar	98		

The shortage occurs mainly in those products which for climatic reasons cannot be produced in these countries—citrus fruit, oil-bearing seeds and other tropical produce.

In France, where the share of agriculture in the national economy is comparatively high, there was already a large surplus of wheat in 1962: about 25-27 million centners of grain had to be exported. Higher crop yields, at present averaging 29 centners per hectare, are responsible for the surplus.

The processes at work in French agriculture are similar to those present in the United States. During the past 12 years the capital investments in French agriculture have doubled. The cow population has grown from 15 million to 20 million. Labour productivity has grown an average of 7 per cent a year and with every year some 100,000 workers leave agriculture for the towns.[2] Those remaining in the villages are mostly old people. The small peasant is vanishing and it is even doubtful whether the medium peasant will manage to survive. In France land is worth only one-third of what it is worth in neighbouring West Germany.[3]

These developments in agriculture fully confirm Marx's prediction: "...the more the capitalist mode of production

---

[1] *The Times*, February 3, 1963.
[2] According to "Etudes et Conjoncture", *Neue Zürcher Zeitung,* August 29, 1962.
[3] *The Economist*, September 1, 1962, p. 775.

develops, the more does the concentration of capital upon the same area of land develop...."[1]

In the U.S.A. and France, as distinct from Britain, capital investments in agriculture are facilitated by the fact that the land is mainly owned by rich farmers and peasants, themselves capitalists. Land ownership is no obstacle to capital investments. Marx wrote: "When the landlord is himself a capitalist, or the capitalist is himself a landlord ... for him landed property does not constitute an obstacle to the investment of capital."[2]

Owing to her climate and historical background, Britain concentrates mainly on animal-products. But in this field, too, there is overproduction. Britain's agrarian policy is in a critical state. *The Economist* comments: "...It was always assumed that if the subsidies were sensibly directed ...these gluts could be avoided.

"Last year it was proved that they could not; gluts appeared even in beef and mutton, and the Exchequer had to pay out £70 million more a year in deficiency payments than it had bargained for. This was the Rubicon; it meant that the million or so farmers and farmworkers of Britain were now sufficiently efficient to produce a glut in anything so long as the off-farm prices proffered to them remained at anything like their present level."[3]

Throughout the capitalist countries there is a growing overproduction of dairy products. In Britain in 1962, large amounts of skimmed milk were poured down wells and into rivers and French peasants poured milk out into the streets to maintain high prices, etc.

This is not a transient state of affairs. According to the evaluation made jointly by the Economic Commission for Europe and the Food and Agriculture Organisation Western Europe imported in 1958 some 97,000 tons of dairy products (in terms of butter). In 1965 Western Europe will have an export surplus of 235,000 tons and in 1970—of 424,000 tons.[4] In a number of developed capitalist countries there is also a surplus of meat, bacon, etc.

---

[1] Karl Marx, *Capital*, Vol. III, p. 692.
[2] Ibid., p. 751.
[3] *The Economist*, October 6, 1962, p. 20.
[4] *Neue Zürcher Zeitung*, December 11, 1962.

As regards plantation products, the crisis is deepest in coffee production. The price of Brazilian coffee dropped from 59 dollars a bag in 1957 to 40 dollars in 1962.[1] Coffee stocks now equal world requirements for the next two years.[2] The world agreement on coffee did not improve the situation.

Under existing conditions, Brazil, the main producer of coffee, has no alternative but to destroy vast numbers of coffee trees—under a government scheme about 1,000 million coffee trees are to be cut down.

* * *

The price of wheat and other grains dropped sharply during the 19th century agrarian crisis. During the 20th century agrarian crisis the governments of the West European countries and the U.S.A. made an all-out effort to prevent such a catastrophic price drop. This was done by raising customs duties,[3] establishing import quotas and fixing state prices for agricultural products, in fact, in the manner still being practised today. The result of these measures is that *prices lose touch with the value or cost of those commodities—a state of affairs determined by political factors*. This can be illustrated by the 1962 wheat prices for Western Europe.

State Wheat Prices[4]
(£ per ton)

West Germany	France	Britain
37	27	27

---

[1] Ibid., December 19, 1962.

[2] *The Times*, September 28, 1962.

[3] Between 1929 and 1934, when the agrarian crisis deepened under the influence of the industrial crisis, customs duties on wheat were raised: in Germany from 5 marks to 25 marks per ton, in Italy from 11 lira to 75 lira, in France from 35 francs to 80 francs.

[4] Data of the International Wheat Council. *The Economist*, March 31, 1962, p. 1214.

Neither the value nor the cost of wheat can be higher in West Germany than in neighbouring France, where the climatic conditions and soil are no better than in West Germany, while capital investments in agriculture are lower. The reasons for the fact that in West Germany the price of wheat is 36 per cent higher than in France or Britain, are purely political. Even in an agrarian country like Denmark there are minimum state prices on animal products.

Other agricultural products are also more expensive in West Germany.

Prices Paid to Producers[1]

(in 1961-62 in marks per 100 kg)

	West Germany	France	Italy	The Netherlands	Belgium
Fodder barley . .	37	25	30	29	33
Sugar beet	7	5	6	5	5
Pigs	235	226	228	187	210
Milk	35	31	29	31	27
Eggs	306	277	314	183	227

The price differences amount to as much as 30 per cent. Little wonder therefore that the German farmers and government are steadfastly resisting the plan to introduce equal prices for agricultural products in all Common Market countries by 1970.

At present, state prices have also been introduced in countries exporting agricultural products—in the U.S.A., Canada, Argentina, etc. In the U.S.A. in 1962 the state wheat price on the domestic market was $2.34 for 60 British pounds, while the export price was $1.63-1.73.[2] In the Argentine, too, the state fixes prices for wheat, maize, millet and all oil-bearing crops, and so on.[3]

These examples show that *at present the movement of prices gives no indication of the periodicity of agrarian*

---

[1] *Neue Zürcher Zeitung*, February 16, 1964.
[2] *Monthly Bulletin of Statistics*, June 1963, p. 132.
[3] *Neue Zürcher Zeitung*, September 11, 1962.

crises, or of the course taken by them in general. There are no longer free world prices for the bulk of agricultural products.

During the post-war period the formation of prices for agricultural products was distorted not only by government intervention but also by the unequal devaluation of various world currencies. We are using data only for the U.S.A., because the gold content of the dollar has not changed (at least officially).

Wholesale Price Index for Farm Products in the U.S.A.[1]

(1947-49=100)

1938	1945	1948	1951	1953	1957	1961[2]
38.3	71.6	107.3	113.4 (max.)	97	90.9	87.9

The 1945 prices do not take the black market into account; the high prices in 1951 are due to the war in Korea. After 1953 prices dropped little and were 150 per cent higher than in 1938, this in spite of huge overproduction and the fact that capitalist farm costs were undoubtedly much lower than in 1938.

The table below shows that similar conditions obtained in West Germany.

Retail Prices for Farm Products[3]

1938-39	1956-57	1959-60
100	211	228

From this we can see that prices more than doubled.

---

[1] *Historical Statistics of the United States*, 2nd Edition, p. 117.

[2] *Federal Reserve Bulletin*, November 1962, p. 1504 (recalculated by the author from the basis of 1957-59=100).

[3] *Statistisches Jahrbuch für die Bundesrepublik Deutschland*, 1961, S. 465.

(At present the mark is quoted in dollars at the pre-war rate; in fact even slightly higher.)

The relative stability of prices in the U.S.A. and Western Europe was achieved partly through the introduction of customs tariffs and partly through the very high expenditures incurred by the various governments in their attempts to maintain agricultural prices at a high level. In the last fiscal year government spending on agricultural subsidies amounted to:

6,036 million dollars in the U.S.A. (1962)[1]
399 million pounds=1,120 million dollars in Britain
6,600 million marks=1,650 million dollars in West Germany
(total for federal government and municipal administrations).

We see that the West German Government spends no less money on supporting agricultural production (in proportion to its share in the economy) than the U.S.A.

The state expenditure is profitable only for capitalist farmers and rich peasants (in Britain, ultimately, for the landowners). An official document of the U.S. Senate states that the policy of maintaining prices has benefited mainly two million of the larger highly mechanised farms. Production in the other 3.5 million farms is so small that the farmers gain very little from maintaining high prices.[2] In 1955, cotton producers received an average of 268 dollars in subsidies. The largest cotton producer gained 1,292,472 dollars.

The state incurs enormous expenditure in maintaining these artificially high prices—strictly for political and not for economic reasons. In the highly developed capitalist countries agriculture's share in the economy is insignificant. In the U.S.A. in 1961[3] total private incomes from sources other than agriculture comprised $399,000 million, from agriculture—17,000 million dollars. In other words, private incomes from agriculture accounted for only four per cent of the population's total private incomes. Out of this sum one-third is accounted for by state subsidies. A

---

[1] *Federal Reserve Bulletin*, November 1962, p. 1479.
[2] United States, 83rd Congress, 2nd Session, Document No. 292.
[3] *Federal Reserve Bulletin*, November 1962, p. 1507.

similar situation prevails in other highly developed capitalist countries (except Canada, and partly France).

In Britain particularly, state subsidies account for a large share of farmers' incomes. This is explained by the great political influence exerted by the landowners. The London *Times* wrote: "In 1961-62 the sum paid in direct price support to British farmers represented over half of their whole estimated net income for the year. If other forms of subsidy are included, the total came to 83 per cent. These are the hard figures which have called in question the present system of agricultural supports and deficiency payments, first established under the 1947 Act."[1]

The political cause underlying such extensive subsidies is obvious. In the highly developed capitalist countries where 80 to 95 per cent of the gainfully employed population are factory and office workers, i.e., a class which (except for the upper echelons of office workers) is not in the least interested in the continued existence of capitalism, the well-to-do peasantry (capitalist farmers) remain the only large layer of the population defending the system of private property, the only ally of the bourgeoisie. It is for this reason that the governments of the leading capitalist countries spend huge funds on supporting them.[2]

The system of maintaining agricultural prices with the help of large government subsidies harms the working class in three respects:

1. The subsidies paid out to capitalist farmers and peasants are, to a large extent, derived from the wages of workers by means of direct and indirect taxation.

2. The maintenance of artificially high prices means that in spite of the overproduction of foodstuffs, workers are compelled to pay high prices for food. Look at the figures for the U.S.A., for example:

---

[1] *The Times*, February 27, 1963.

[2] The political importance of that problem was clearly illustrated during the negotiations on Britain's entry into the Common Market. British monopoly capital did not obstruct the entry, but Britain could not come to terms on agricultural questions, even though agriculture carries little weight in Britain's economy. The ground rent of the British lords naturally played an important role in that question.

Consumer Price Indexes for All Foods[1]

(1947-49=100)

1938	1948	1957	1961	1962
48.4	104.1	115.4	121	122

In spite of overproduction, consumer prices are constantly growing and are now double their pre-war level.[2] To a great extent this is due to monopoly practices.

3. The system of subsidising capitalist farmers and peasants increases mechanisation in agriculture and every year hundreds of thousands of workers become "surplus" in that branch of the economy and have to seek employment in industry, thereby exerting pressure on the labour markets.

* * *

Let us now summarise.

1. Agrarian crises are not cyclical, periodically repeating processes. Industrial crises in themselves do not produce agrarian crises. The 19th century agrarian crisis lasted throughout three industrial cycles. The 20th century agrarian crisis reached its peak after the Second World War at a time when there was no *world* crisis of overproduction. But, *ceteris paribus*, industrial crises deepen agrarian crises and vice versa.

2. The 20th century agrarian crisis was caused not by an extensive expansion of sown areas, but by a growth in crop yields and the productivity of livestock farming owing to large capital investments in the agriculture of the developed capitalist countries and capitalist plantations.

3. In the 1960s, the 20th century agrarian crisis reached a contradictory stage in its development: the overproduc-

---

[1] *Historical Statistics of the United States*, 2nd Edition, p. 125. *Federal Reserve Bulletin*, November 1962, p. 1504; May 1963, p. 704 (recalculated by the author for 1957-59=100).

[2] In Britain the official retail price index for foods grew from 100 in January 1956 to 111.4 in June 1961 (*United Kingdom Annual Abstract of Statistics*, 1961, p. 303).

tion of agricultural products in the highly developed capitalist countries co-exists with a shortage of food in the less
developed capitalist countries, which is due to a general
lack of means and the retarding influence of the semi-
feudal agrarian system. The developed capitalist countries
supply the less developed countries with food, and not vice
versa as was the case during the 19th century.[1]

4. The movement of prices for agricultural commodities
(in countries with a temperate climate) has ceased to be
an indicator of the development of the agrarian crisis,
since market prices are determined not by competition on
the world market but by politically inspired government
subsidies to support a comparatively wide layer of small
capitalists who uphold the capitalist system in agriculture.

It follows that the glut of agricultural commodities in
the highly developed capitalist countries cannot be eliminated, since small capital is trying to find application in
agriculture and will continue to do so; at the same time
there will be an intensification in the policy of high state
prices serving to support the capitalist layer in agriculture
and in the inevitable polarisation of society in the advanced
capitalist countries into a handful of monopolists and
an enormous mass of manual and white-collar workers.

In the highly developed capitalist countries there is room
for a further growth in food consumption since broad
sections of the population still eat unsatisfactorily. But the
average consumption of calories, especially of fats and
meat, is higher than is considered healthy by modern
science.[2] The consumption of some foods—fresh vegetables
and fruit—which are of secondary importance to the
agrarian crisis, will continue to grow.

Theoretically there is the possibility of increasing
agricultural production in the poor, less developed capitalist countries, which would make it unnecessary for them

---

[1] Britain is the only highly developed capitalist country which is
still a major food importer.

[2] The absolutely reliable statistical data collected by large American
insurance companies, which are interested in extending the lives of
their clients, prove that people above normal weight live an average
five or six years less than people of a normal or slightly sub-normal
weight. The insurance companies periodically send doctors to their
richer clients to persuade them to eat less.

to import foodstuffs. But in practice this is no easy matter: it would require a radical land reform, a veritable agrarian revolution, and a major influx of foreign capital for agricultural investments.[1] Obviously, such development would aggravate the overproduction in the highly developed capitalist countries.[2] According to a Ministry of Agriculture Report, the U.S.A. exported in 1961 one-sixth of its annual harvest, accounting for 6,000 million dollars. In that year the United States was the largest exporter of agricultural commodities in the world. At the same time agricultural produce accounts for one-quarter of U.S. exports.[3]

An analysis of the development of the agrarian crisis since the Second World War confirms the view I expressed 30 years ago, namely, that the *20th century agrarian crisis is not a periodical and transient phenomenon, but part of the general crisis of capitalism.*

Critics of my views referred to Marx's remark that "there are no permanent crises". This objection is based on a primitive logical error. The critics wrongly declared that agrarian crises repeat periodically in the same way as industrial crises and, in an attempt to justify themselves, quote Marx's remark on *cyclical* crises.

Nobody denies the permanent character of the general crisis of capitalism, which will end only when the capitalist system as such ceases to exist. Nor does anyone deny the permanent underemployment of enterprises or the permanent mass unemployment arising from the general crisis of capitalism.

What does the constant underemployment of factories involve? It involves potential permanent overproduction in the industries of the highly developed countries. In agriculture permanent overproduction is a fact, while in industry, with the exception of crisis periods, it is potential—this is the only difference between the two.

The reason for this difference is explained by the following:

---

[1] The *socialist* countries are able to redistribute investments and thus allocate funds for the development of agriculture when they consider it necessary.

[2] During the past decade the U.S.A. has been exporting foods almost exclusively to the less developed countries.

[3] *Neue Zürcher Zeitung*, February 1, 1963.

In industry the production period is short and becomes even shorter as a result of technical advance. (This excludes large building projects: factories, ships, special purpose machine-tools which are built according to order and, therefore, rarely give rise to overproduction.) This means that production can be adapted to demand, it can be decreased by 10, 20 or even 50 per cent. Overproduction is therefore only potential. At a certain stage in the curtailment of production profit disappears, but even if production ceases completely, the capital invested in the enterprise remains intact.

The production period is much longer in crop farming: for winter crops it lasts almost a year, for spring crops— up to six months. It is very difficult to limit production, the only thing that can be done is to destroy part of the crops. In livestock farming the curtailment of production involves great losses. You cannot feed cows on half rations or milk only half their milk. Besides, the size of the ground rent is often stipulated in rent agreements and this also makes it difficult to cut down production. For peasants who till the land themselves or are helped only by their families, such a lowering of production would mean that they could not apply their labour and the farm would run to rack and ruin. In other words, large industrial enterprises can limit production without great loss, but to most agricultural producers a curtailment of production spells disaster. This explains why during the general crisis of capitalism in the industries of the highly developed capitalist countries there is permanent potential overproduction in the form of a constant underemployment of enterprises, while in agriculture there is constant actual overproduction, a chronic agrarian crisis.

The coal industry proves that there can be a chronic crisis even in industry. The causes of this chronic crisis in the coal industry are similar to those of the agrarian crisis in the highly developed capitalist countries. They are—the improvement of technology through large capital investments; the growth in labour productivity; the decrease in the number of employed workers; the growth of stocks. The only difference is that it is easier to cope with overproduction in industry by decreasing output, than it is in agriculture.

	Production (million tons)	Average number of workers (thousand people)	Stocks at end of year (million tons)	Output per manshift (tons)[2]
1929	535	503	40	5.06
1939	395	422	45	5.19
1956	501	228	78	9.84
1959	412	179	—	12.22

The above table shows that between 1929 and 1959 the output of coal dropped by 21 per cent, while coal stocks doubled; and the number of workers decreased by two-thirds, the output per shift grew by 140 per cent. At the same time the price of coal rose from $1.88 per ton in 1936-40 to $4.73 in 1960.[3]

An identical process is at work in the British, West German and Belgian coal industries. A similar chronic crisis is expected to develop in iron and steel, the motor industry, etc.

The development therefore resembles that of the agrarian crisis in the highly developed capitalist countries, except that output does not grow, as in agriculture, but decreases.

We must not approach the chronic nature of the agrarian or coal industry crises dogmatically. A chronic crisis does not exclude improvements over short periods. "Chronic" implies that there can be no improvement *over a long period of time*, that *the crisis cannot be overcome within the framework of capitalism*.

It is interesting to note that L. I. Lyuboshits, even though he theoretically denies the chronic nature of the 20th century agrarian crisis, remains unbiased and disagrees

---

[1] *Historical Statistics of the United States*, 2nd Edition, p. 356 et passim; *Statistical Abstract of the United States*, 1961, p. 725.
We are excluding the war years so as not to distort the picture of the main course of development, and for the sake of simplicity exclude also anthracite, since it accounts for only six per cent of total coal output.
[2] *Statistical Abstract of the United States*, 1961, p. 725.
[3] Ibid., p. 713.

with the view often expressed by Soviet economists that the agrarian crisis was overcome in 1929. Actually the crisis continued, and later, during the Second World War, became deeper than it had been before the war.

L. A. Mendelson correctly separates temporary critical phenomena arising in agriculture under the influence of industrial crises from independent enduring agrarian crises.[1] But his analysis is abstract and theoretical, lacks a concrete historical approach and contains little facts and figures. Nor does his analysis cover the modern agrarian crisis.

L. A. Mendelson speaks in detail about the price drop. "Agrarian crises . . . are expressed primarily through a long-term drop in prices,"[2] he says. But *at present there is no price drop*[3] in the countries which overproduce agricultural commodities since all prices are fixed by the government. All the author's arguments about the influence of price drops on production, on the non-utilisation of inferior lands, on rent decreases, on ways to overcome the agrarian crisis, are therefore pointless.

L. A. Mendelson makes these mistakes because in his works economics have lost touch with politics. He does not take into account that in conditions of an acute struggle between the two systems the big bourgeoisie in the developed capitalist countries cannot tolerate a sharp drop in the price of agricultural commodities because this would ruin the only wide layer still supporting capitalism, namely

---

[1] *Mirovaya ekonomika i mezhdunarodniye otnosheniya* (World Economy and International Relations), Russ. ed., 1958, No. 7, p. 45.

[2] This was correct before the Second World War. Between 1929 and 1933 the price index for agricultural products fell: in the U.S.A. from 138 to 63 (1909-14=100), in Germany from 137 to 93 (1913=100). But this drop was due primarily to the exceptionally deep industrial crisis of 1929-33.

[3] In the U.S.A., the centre of agrarian overproduction, the index for all agricultural produce was (1910-14=100):

1946	1951 maximum	1957
236	302	235

(*Historical Statistics of the United States*, 2nd Edition, p. 283.) The price advance in 1951 was due to the war in Korea.

the well-to-do farmers, and leave agriculture with only a narrow layer of large capitalist producers. Mendelson did not realise the dual character of the modern *world* agrarian crisis, namely, the overproduction of agricultural commodities in the highly developed capitalist countries on the one hand, and the hunger in the less developed countries on the other; he also did not recognise one of the most important manifestations of the split in the modern capitalist world—the division of countries into rich and poor.

In modern conditions there is also no point in arguing about the role of fixed rent in prolonging agrarian crises. Even though stable prices tend to stabilise and raise the ground rent, the share of all rents (rent per se, indebtedness on mortgages) in the total expenditure of agricultural producers falls as agriculture intensifies.

Bourgeois statistics do not enable us to compute the net ground rent, but the following figures do give us a rough picture[1]:

Agricultural Income and Expenditure in the U.S.A.

(1960)

Gross Income[2]	Gross expenditure on agricultural production	Of which				
		Taxes	Interest on mortgages	Pure rent paid to non-agriculturists	Including pure rent to farm owners[3]	Total of enumerated expenses
Thousand million dollars		million dollars				
38	16	1,548	640	1,031	1,500	4,719

The table shows that fixed expenditure—taxes, interest on mortgages and rent—accounted for 4,700 million dollars in 1960, i.e., for less than one-third of the total expenditure of U.S. farmers. Obviously this fixed expenditure cannot play a major role in protracting the agrarian crisis,

---

[1] *Statistical Abstract of the United States*, 1961, p. 629.

[2] Including state subventions (over 3,000 million dollars).

[3] *United States Agricultural Statistics*, 1960, p. 492.

the more so since one-third of it is redistributed between these same farmers. Naturally, for many poor farmers this fixed expenditure can become ruinous. But it is unimportant as far as the agrarian crisis is concerned.

Lyuboshits writes: "The agrarian crisis ... should be analysed on the basis of the general crisis of capitalism, but not as one of its component parts...."[1] This statement is of little help in understanding the essence of the modern agrarian crisis, since *all* economic and political processes unfolding in our time must be analysed on the basis of the general crisis of capitalism. It is not a question of whether we should consider agrarian crises as a "part" or on the "basis" of the general crisis of capitalism. The question is whether the agrarian crisis as we see it today is *cyclic and transient* or, as we believe, a *non-cyclic* and *permanent process* (ceasing only with the downfall of capitalism).[2]

We must also avoid a dogmatic approach to this question. Just as there is no "pure" mode of production, no "pure" imperialism, there is no "pure" agrarian crisis in the sense that all branches of agriculture in all countries are never simultaneously in the throes of an acute crisis of overproduction. Long world wars put a temporary halt to agrarian crises of overproduction. The harvest failures of specific crops on large territories can also temporarily mitigate it. (Thus, for example, the large wheat purchases on the capitalist market by China in 1961-62 and the Soviet Union in 1963 decreased the glut. But this is a transient phenomenon, the result of a bad harvest, and does not affect the chronic character of the overproduction of wheat and of the agrarian crisis in general.) A change in agrarian policy can exert a certain effect on the course of agrarian crises. That is why the agrarian crisis for some products

---

[1] L. I. Lyuboshits, *Voprosy marksistsko-leninskoi teorii agrarnykh krizisov* (Marxist-Leninist Theoretical Problems of Agrarian Crises), Russ. ed., p. 228.

[2] Lyuboshits, a conscientious researcher, speaks of a "mitigation" of the agrarian crisis (between 1924 and 1926 and between 1935 and 1937) and not of its end (p. 327) but of its renewed intensification in 1937 (p. 329).

in some countries becomes increasingly acute at one time and hardly noticeable at another.[1] But these fluctuations do not alter the fact that the overproduction of agricultural commodities will intensify in the major capitalist countries, the concentration of production and land in the hands of capitalist farmers and the ruin of the working peasantry[2] will continue and monopoly oppression grow. At the same time the underproduction of agricultural commodities in the less developed capitalist countries will apparently continue until the overthrow of capitalism as a whole.[3]

The agrarian overproduction in the highly developed capitalist countries and the shortage of food in the less developed countries intensify because of the different population growth rates in these two groups of countries.

Population in the Five Principal Highly Developed Capitalist Countries—the U.S.A., Britain, France, West Germany and Italy
(*million people*)[4]

1953	1962	Increment
350	392	42

[1] As we understand it, the new Programme of the C.P.S.U. speaks of agrarian crises in this sense, and not of their cyclic nature.

[2] Beginning with 1955, in spite of the rapid growth of agricultural output in France, some 100,000 people left the countryside yearly. According to the 1955 census 380,000 peasants owned plots of an area below two hectares. Two-thirds of all peasant households were worked by people above the age of 55. Young people left to work in industry (*The Economist*, September 1, 1962, p. 775).

[3] The interpretation of the agrarian crisis in the *Textbook of Political Economy* edited by N. A. Tsagolov, published in 1963 has the same shortcomings as the writings of L. A. Mendelson—it ignores the radical contradiction between the overproduction in the rich countries and the chronic food shortage in the less developed countries, i.e., the most important and insuperable obstacle of the modern agrarian crisis (see *Textbook of Political Economy*, Russ. ed., p. 508-10).

[4] *Statistical Yearbook of the United Nations*, 1957, p. 23 et passim; *Monthly Bulletin of Statistics*, January 1964, p. 1 et passim.

Population in the Five Principal Less Developed Countries—India, Pakistan, Indonesia, Brazil, Mexico
(million people)[1]

1953	1962	Increment
616	760	144

For ten years the percentage increment of the population comprised: in the highly developed countries—12, in the less developed countries—22! The growth in agricultural production in the latter hardly keeps pace with the population growth rate.

---

[1] Ibid.

THEORETICAL PROBLEMS
OF THE COMMON MARKET ECONOMY

The Common Market and the plan of capitalist integration is the handiwork of the giant West European monopolies. Their aims are many and varied. By expanding their market, they want to raise sales and profits at the expense of weaker competitors and to consolidate the forces of capitalism in the struggle against the socialist system and the working class of the member-countries. They are also making efforts to perpetuate and strengthen the economic exploitation of the former African colonies through various forms of neo-colonialism, and to unite the forces of West European monopoly capital against the economic supremacy of the United States. Monopoly capital uses state power to solve these tasks. The Common Market and the attempts to integrate Western Europe, as we remarked above, are but a new stage in the development of state-monopoly capitalism.

It goes without saying that all the contradictions of capitalism are preserved within the framework of the Common Market—direct tendencies clash with counter-tendencies, for every participant in the Common Market defends not only the general interests of monopoly capital but also his own particular interests, everyone holds different views on the course further integration should take, etc.

A concise but fitting description of this divergence was given by G. Dell, an economist with the U.N., who said that the champion of free trade dreamed of abolishing barriers to foreign trade. The protectionist hoped that Western Europe would be walled in by new customs barriers. The Right wing wanted to ensure the business interests and to resist the demands for wage increases more effectively. The

Left wing dreamed of the international alliance of workers and the approach of the ideal of universal fraternity. The federalists hoped for a supranational power and the gradual setting up of a federal government. The confederationists saw the prospects of a "Europe of States"—a Europe of national states. The "Europeists" dreamed of an emergence of the European spirit and self-consciousness. The champions of the Atlantic Alliance believed that there would be a far wider union.

Obviously, all these hopes cannot be realised at once.

The whole range of problems connected with the Common Market and West European integration has been investigated by the Institute of World Economy and International Affairs of the U.S.S.R. Academy of Sciences and has been thoroughly discussed at the International Conference of Marxist theoreticians, held between August 27 and September 3, 1962 in Moscow.[1]

We shall examine only one question: is the Common Market able to expand the West European capitalist market at all, or to any considerable extent, over and above the expansion brought about in all capitalist countries as a result of population growth and technical development?

The advocates of the Common Market claim that it opens up a new era of economic advance for capitalism in Western Europe. They believe that a common market embracing the West European countries with a population equal to that of the United States, will automatically raise Western Europe to the level of the U.S., both economically and politically. The theoretical basis for this assertion is that the volume of the domestic market and economic power are dependent on the population of the countries joining the market.

Let us quote a few facts to prove that this view is entirely unfounded. India has twice as large a population as the United States but the volume of her domestic market and her economic power are incomparably smaller. In 1959 India's national income was evaluated at 128,000 million rupees (27,000 million dollars).[2] The U.S. national income

---

[1] See *Problems of Modern Capitalism and the Working Class*, Peace and Socialism Publishers, Prague, 1963.

[2] *Monthly Bulletin of Statistics*, May 1962, pp. 150, 151.

for that year was 397,000 million dollars, or 15 times as high. The relation between the volumes of the domestic markets of those countries is approximately equal to the above.

It is common knowledge that evaluations of the national income level are extremely inaccurate. But the enormous difference makes these inaccuracies unimportant. One might argue that it is wrong to compare developing India with the U.S.A., one of the most developed capitalist countries. Like the U.S.A., the Common Market countries have already reached a high level of development. In one sense this is true, and yet, in others, completely false. As compared with the less developed Asian, African and Latin American countries the Common Market countries are highly developed, but as compared with the United States they are relatively backward.[1] In the Common Market countries labour productivity is $\frac{1}{3}$ to $\frac{1}{2}$ and the per capita national income $\frac{1}{2}$ of that in the U.S.A. Their domestic markets lag behind the U.S.A. in approximately the same proportion.

The advantages of the U.S.A. in the development of labour productivity are in part explainable by the historical factors described in Lenin's works. These factors may vary. But there are also factors of a permanent nature which cannot be eliminated by the creation of a Common Market. The U.S.A. has a better climate, is far richer in natural resources and has greater stocks of minerals (oil, coal, copper and other non-ferrous metals). In addition the agricultural area of the U.S.A. is four times the size of all the West European Common Market countries taken together.

Owing to the uneven development of capitalism, the economic supremacy of the U.S.A. over Western Europe has decreased substantially in comparison with the years immediately following the Second World War. Even so, the difference is still considerable. The association of a number of West European countries into a common market cannot remove the natural and historical reasons responsible for this supremacy (the enormous national wealth, technical equipment, etc.).

---

[1] If we base the comparison on the labour productivity level, which Lenin considered decisive for determining the degree to which a social system is progressive.

The population figure is also unable to determine production growth *rates*. Let us take Japan, for example. As a result of the Second World War the country lost a large share of its pre-war "domestic" market of more than a 100 million people, more than live in Japan itself. Yet the production growth rate in Japan between 1951 and 1961 was higher than in any other capitalist country.

Industrial Production Index

(1953=100)

	1951	1961		1951	1961
Japan	74	317	Italy	90	200
West Germany . .	85	191	Britain	97	128
France	99	184	U.S.A.	89	120

In spite of the loss of most of her market, Japan managed to increase her industrial production by 300 per cent between 1951 and 1961. During the same period the principal West European countries raised their industrial output by about 100 per cent, the U.S.A. by only 33 per cent. In the agricultural field Japan succeeded in harvesting an average of 48.6 centners of rice per hectare on an area of 3.3 million hectares, as compared with 39 centners before the Second World War.

Thus, the contention that the merging of a number of West European countries into a single market with a population as large as the U.S.A. will, in future, "economically equalise" Western Europe and the U.S.A., is completely unscientific.

If the proponents of the Common Market approach the analysis of the problem scientifically, they should be able to explain how the merger of a number of European countries into a single market can expand that market by 100 to 200 per cent. This they have failed to do. Let us attempt to make a theoretical analysis of the economic changes that would result from a complete economic integration of Western Europe.[1] Can it improve the economic position of the countries in the Common Market? Marxists should formulate the question as follows: *can such an association lead to a constant, or enduring non-cyclic expansion of the population's consumption capacity?* Thus it is more a question of an expansion of the demand for Department II (consumer) goods than that of an expansion of the market as such. An expansion of the market for Department I goods cannot ensure an enduring upswing of production as a whole. If the demand for goods produced by Department II is not high enough, the production of Department I goods is bound to decrease. Only adherents of Tugan-Baranovsky's theory can believe that a constant expansion of fixed capital can ensure a steady crisis-free upswing of capitalist production.

It is common knowledge that capitalist reproduction follows a cyclic course. During the revival and boom phases the fixed capital expands (new factories are built, new equipment replaces old) and the market for producer goods widens. This in turn temporarily expands the market for consumer goods, since more workers are drawn into production, the wage fund increases, and the demand for consumer goods grows. But we are not interested in this cyclical and transient expansion of the capitalist market. Our aim is to discover whether a merger of the domestic markets of a number of countries can generate a steady high demand for consumer goods. We shall attempt to study this problem in a pure form, excluding from our analysis all secondary and irrelevant issues. We shall therefore adopt the method of scientific abstraction and analyse the following:

1. The consequences resulting from the union of two highly developed imperialist countries.

2. The consequences resulting from the union of a highly developed and a less developed country.

We shall proceed from the assumption that this union will take place not over a decade, as is planned in the case of the Common Market, but immediately, without any tran-

---

[1] This assumption is naturally unrealistic. The Common Market is by no means a full economic union and it is even doubtful whether such a union will ever be achieved. But for the sake of an abstract analysis, we can make this assumption.

sition period.[1] We shall further assume that complete economic union has already been effected and that the united countries enjoy absolutely equal conditions as regards competition. These conditions presuppose the abolition of customs tariffs between them, a complete freedom of movement for all commodities, capital and labour force; full equality in taxes, social security, economic legislation, etc.; the abolition or equalisation of all state economic measures—subsidies, export credit guarantees, etc.

* * *

Proceeding from the above assumption, what will be the economic consequences of the union of two highly developed capitalist countries? It can be said with certainty that the changes will be insignificant because there will be no change in the operation of the objective economic laws of capitalism (imperialism).

Therefore, no constant or even protracted expansion of the market for consumer goods should be expected, at least not in excess of that usual for more or less enduring periods. There will also be no enduring rise in the production level of the united countries. This, however, does not mean that there will be no changes at all, but that these changes will lead to the strengthening of some tendencies and the weakening of others.

The monopolies will continue to remain the decisive factor in economic development but their effect on that development will be a contradictory one. The largest monopolies in the various industries of both countries will attempt to corner the newly acquired market for their own goods. With this aim in view they will expand production capacities and invest more capital,[2] thereby intensifying

---

[1] In the presence of a transition period of ten years, it is difficult to determine what is a consequence of the union and what is brought about by other factors, such as the cyclical development of reproduction, a stock exchange crash, political events, etc. The Common Market is given credit for the production growth in West Germany in recent years. But opponents of the Common Market could equally attribute to it the deterioration of West Germany's economic position in 1962.

[2] The length of the period during which considerable new capital investments will be made and their size will depend (all other conditions being equal) on the phase of the cycle during which the union

the competitive struggle. In fact, the development will resemble that characteristic of revival and boom phases: the
market capacity for goods of Departments I and II will
temporarily expand. But the very same processes responsible for the expansion will ultimately create the prerequisites for a crisis of overproduction and lead to a shrinking
of the market. Other monopolies will abstain from open
competitive struggle. They will create cartels and trusts
on the basis of the coalescence of capital and the economic
links that existed between them prior to the union of the
two countries, and this will consolidate the might of the
monopolies.

The intensification of the competitive struggle in the
united countries will bring certain structural changes. These
in turn will affect primarily the weaker branches of the
economy and individual enterprises, which, for historical
reasons or due to an unsuccessful economico-geographic
location, are producing commodities at a cost exceeding
world market prices. These branches and enterprises
would exist only with the help of high protective customs
tariffs. Any "common market" merger will abolish this protection. Rival enterprises producing goods of the same quality at a lower cost will then push aside and ruin their
weaker competitors, forcing them to close down their factories and sell out for a song. The centralisation of capital
will thus intensify.

The merger will also bring changes in the geographic
distribution of factories. One of the consequences of the
union (granted completely free competition) will be the
gradual concentration of production in the most profitable
locations, i.e., in places where production outlay is lowest.
This process will take a long time, since the transfer of
factories (if the share of fixed capital is high, and large
sums have been spent on buildings, underground installations, access roads and on bulky and complicated machinery) usually involves great losses, and is therefore unprofitable. But new factories will gradually be built in the

---

is effected. If it coincides with the boom phase, the shortage of material and manpower resources will hamper the investment of large
sums. If it is effected in the crisis phase, the capitalists will be in no
hurry to invest new capital. The most profitable time for new capital
investments is the revival phase.

most suitable places. Enterprises less profitably located will slowly be forced to close down[1] and production will shift to more profitable areas.

How will these changes affect the domestic market? Social labour productivity will grow: the socially necessary labour time embodied in a commodity unit will decrease, and, all other conditions being equal, less workers will be needed to produce the same amount of goods. This will result in a decrease of total wages, even if the size of real wages of every individual worker remains unchanged, and will flatten the market for commodities produced by Department II. The result will therefore be diametrically opposed to that predicted by the advocates of the Common Market.

The outcome will depend greatly on the gains made in the class struggle. The most pressing question in all highly developed capitalist countries at present is who should reap the fruits of technological progress and the growth of labour productivity and how these fruits should be divided between capital and labour. This problem will be none the less acute after the merger of the two highly developed countries. The market capacity will depend on how this question is solved. Factory and office workers comprise the bulk of the population in the highly developed capitalist countries and the size of their wages decides the market for consumer goods, and thus the market capacity in general.

In recent years capitalist economists in a number of countries, and especially in the U.S.A., have declared that the national income *as a whole* should be considered the yardstick of a country's economic progress. They completely ignore the importance of the distribution of the national income and even demand that the share received by capital be increased because, they assert, only a constant growth of investments can ensure the steady expansion of production and wider employment, save the capitalist world from crises of overproduction and ensure victory in the competition with the socialist countries.

---

[1] The closure of factories may be brought about not only by their unfavourable location, but also by other factors, such as the obsolescence of equipment, financial machinations, etc.

Their arguments hold no water. The market capacity depends largely on the distribution of the national income between the capitalists and the workers, because the latter generally spend their total earnings on the purchase of consumer articles; their savings (life insurance and savings account deposits) form only a small part of their income and are ultimately also spent on articles of consumption. With the spread of the hire-purchase system for consumer durables (cars, TV sets, housing, etc.) they are even buying things on account of future earnings. The capitalists, on the other hand, do not spend a large share of their income on articles of consumption, but accumulate their profits. The higher their income, the larger the savings, which can ultimately be spent on means of production. But as the market capacity in the final analysis depends on the market for consumer goods, so the distribution of the national income exercises a substantial effect on the development of capitalist reproduction.

Constant expansion of fixed capital without a corresponding increase in the demand for consumer goods cannot produce a stable prosperity, as is affirmed by the spokesmen of the monopolies, but only constant underemployment of enterprises, chronic mass unemployment and an aggravation of the market problem. Neither continuous, large capital investments, nor a dearth of them (which would lead to stagnation) can ensure the permanent welfare of capitalism. This is even more true in the present epoch of the general crisis of capitalism than it was when Karl Marx discovered and formulated the laws governing the movement of capitalist society towards its inevitable doom.

Thus, the amalgamation of two highly developed capitalist countries is able to give an impetus to the temporary expansion of production, the resultant changes will resemble the revival phase of the cycle. But it cannot ensure an enduring expansion of the market capacity in the amalgamated countries, nor can it improve their economic position for any length of time. On the contrary, the intensified competitive struggle, the ousting of weaker competitors, the more rapid centralisation of capital, the concentration of industrial production in the most favourable locations— all tend to decrease labour requirements and real wages, with a resulting drop in the demand for consumer goods, and hence an aggravation of the market problem. Whether this tendency will gain the upper hand depends on the progress of the class struggle, an analysis of which is beyond the scope of this essay.[1]

A. G. Mileikovsky doubts the correctness of our views.[2] That is his privilege. But he attempts to refute them with faulty arguments.

Our abstract theoretical arguments could be refuted: a) if it were shown that they contradict Marxism-Leninism or are based on a faulty premise; b) if an investigation based on Marxist methodology uncovered an economic mechanism by means of which a merger of the markets of two or more highly developed capitalist countries could lead to an enduring expansion of the market (longer than is usual for capitalism). Mileikovsky chose a different approach. He attempted to contradict this theoretical discourse by referring to the practical historical example furnished by the advance of German capitalism after the merger of industrialised Alsace-Lorraine with the highly developed Ruhr region. We would have no objections if the concrete historical conditions prevailing in Germany at that time corresponded to the conditions postulated in our abstract theoretical discourse his example claims to refute. However they do not.

In Germany in 1871 there was no union of two highly developed regions, but a union of these regions with other,

---

[1] The reactionary trade union functionaries of the Western countries invariably stress their hostility towards communism and their loyalty to capitalism. George Meany, head of the AFL-CIO, for example, is the most rabid maligner of socialism and calls ceaselessly for a crusade against the socialist countries. He, and other trade union functionaries of his ilk, do not or will not see that the trade unions in capitalist countries have gained some measure of success not only because of the intensification of the working class movement and the increasing determination of the workers to stand up for their interests, but also because of the existence of the socialist community. It is this fear of socialism, this fear that communist ideas may gain a firmer hold on the minds of workers, that sometimes made U.S. statesmen—the Republican Nixon and the Democrat Kennedy—intervene in labour conflicts in the interests of capitalism as a whole and contain, at least to a certain extent, the more militant monopolies. The socialist world is a staunch defender of the interests of the working people in capitalist countries.

[2] *Problemy sovremennogo kapitalizma i rabochy klass*, p. 155.

much larger parts of Germany which were far less developed (Bavaria, East Prussia, etc.), where the bulk of the peasants conducted subsistence farming. Marx, an eye-witness, wrote of Germany at that time: "We, like all the rest of Continental Western Europe, suffer not only from the development of capitalist production, but also from the incompleteness of that development."[1]

The expansion of the market in Germany, after all regions had been merged into a single economic territory, cannot be used to refute our theory because the concrete historical relations obtaining at that time in no way correspond with our contentions.

* * *

The situation will be entirely different in the case of a union of a highly developed with a less developed country. Under certain conditions such a union will facilitate a temporary, though relatively protracted, expansion of the capitalist market.

By "less developed" we mean a country in which a high proportion of the population is engaged in agriculture and in which the productive forces are at a low level of development, the national income is low and the population lives in poverty.[2] The volume of domestic trade in such countries is insignificant since the marketable percentage of the total output is low. The peasants are mainly engaged in subsistence farming.

This last point is of overriding importance as regards the possibility of extending the market. Karl Marx demonstrated that the historical basis for the creation of the capitalist market is the transformation of producers for their own needs into commodity producers and consumers. In his *Development of Capitalism in Russia*, Lenin

---

[1] Karl Marx, *Capital*, Vol. I, p. 9.

[2] This, of course, does not mean that there are no rich in those countries. In poor countries like Iran, Turkey, Pakistan, Brazil, etc., there are huge feudal possessions. In the less developed countries there is also large capital, often amassed through plain robbery. The Chiang-Kai-shek clique's "bureaucratic capital" in Kuomintang China, for example, and the wealth of Latin American dictators, carefully salted away in foreign bank deposits, etc., were gained in precisely that way.

analysed the process of the creation of the capitalist market by the transition from subsistence farming to commodity production. He also explained the stratification of the peasantry in connection with this transition, their division into rural capitalists (kulaks) on the one hand, and farm-hands, who are compelled to sell their labour power, on the other. On the basis of Lenin's analysis it is clear that the union of a highly developed and a less developed country will accelerate the formation of a capitalist market in the latter in precisely that way.

The abolition of such obstacles as customs tariffs, the shortage of foreign currency, etc., will result in a vast influx of industrial commodities from the highly developed to the less developed country. These commodities will do away with many of the products previously produced by peasants. At the same time capitalists will buy more of other peasant-produced commodities. Capital investments will be encouraged by the fact that profits will remain in the country, there will be less danger of nationalisation, and so on. The development of capitalist industry will also be accelerated by the disintegration of the peasantry and the growth of agrarian overpopulation, which will create an abundant and cheap labour force, as yet not organised into trade unions or badly organised.

Thus there will be a prolonged expansion of the capitalist market in both parts of the merger. But the process will not be continuous. It will stop as soon as all subsistence producers become commodity producers.

Not every union of a highly developed with an agrarian country expands the market. Let us presume that New Zealand enters into a union with some highly developed industrial country. New Zealand has an advanced, purely capitalist agriculture[1] producing commodities for the capitalist world market. In spite of its agrarian economy, New Zealand is very rich. Her per capita national income (about 1,200 dollars a year) exceeds that of the highly developed West European industrial countries. Quite obviously a union of New Zealand with a highly developed

---

[1] In 1960 farm produce accounted for 95 per cent of New Zealand's exports. Wool, meat, butter and cheese accounted for 85 per cent of her exports.

industrial country would not expand her market. The only result would be that the industrial country merging with New Zealand would seize most of the market for industrial goods, which would bring a redistribution of the positions already existing on the capitalist market, but no actual expansion.

The scale by which the market of the new union will expand depends also on the area and population of the merging countries. If, for example, a highly industrialised country with a population of say 50 million unites with a less developed country with a population of only 5 million, the market in the small country may rapidly expand. For the union as a whole, however, this expansion will be of no consequence.

Following this line of reasoning it is easy to predict that no great expansion in the size of the market is to be expected from an "association" of the Common Market with former colonies which have recently gained political sovereignty but are still economically dependent on their former metropolitan countries. The population of the Six is over 170 million, that of the "associated" African countries—about 70 million.[1] Besides, the per capita market capacity is much greater in the E.E.C. countries than in Africa. This can be seen from a comparison of the national incomes of the Common Market and the "associated" countries. The total national income of the Six is evaluated at 44,500 million pounds sterling.[2] We do not know the exact size of the national income of the African countries joining the Common Market, but by analogy with other less developed countries, their national income will hardly exceed 20 to 25 pounds sterling per capita a year, i.e., not more than 2,000 million pounds sterling a year. It should be emphasised that market capacity and the national income do not correspond.[3] However, the size of the national income does give a rough indication of the market

---

[1] *Deutsches Wirtschaftsinstitut,* Bericht N. 13, 1963, S. 238.

[2] *Barclay's Bank Letter,* March 16, 1962, p. 1.

[3] The market capacity is greater than the national income because commodities are resold. In the U.S.A. in 1961, sales (industry and trade) accounted for $738,000 million, while the gross national product was $449,000 million (*Survey of Current Business,* May 1962, p. 7, S-4). In West Germany the figures were: sales (together with the export

capacity. One thing is obvious. Even if the development of capitalist relations expands the market capacity of the "associated" African countries threefold,[1] there will be hardly any noticeable expansion in the E.E.C. countries. As regards the large countries in which capitalist relations are as yet weakly developed (India, Pakistan, Indonesia, the Latin American countries), they would not be accepted into the Common Market even if Britain joins.

From this we may conclude that the economic integration of the E.E.C. member-countries with some of the emergent African countries will not result in a considerable expansion of the capitalist market. In view of the universal striving of the African peoples for economic liberation from imperialism, it is unlikely that they will be willing to remain economic appendages of the Common Market for any length of time. The Congo with its 13 million population is becoming more and more dependent on the U.S.A.

* * *

What does the future hold in store for the E.E.C.? The answer to this question hinges on whether the capitalist market will expand or shrink. But, far from stressing this aspect of the problem, the proponents of West European integration harp on the prospects for greater exports. Reading their "works" it reminds one of the days of Mercantilism. What other assessment could be made of the basic theory of the Common Market advocates who insist that the economic development of modern capitalism depends on the size of exports. This renascence of mercantile ideology is not accidental. It is explained by the following:

a) production and production capacities grow faster

---

and sales of farm products)—675,000 million marks (1960), and the gross national product (1959)—281,000 million marks (*Statistisches Jahrbuch für die Bundesrepublik Deutschland*, 1961).

[1] Such growth is highly improbable since capitalist plantations play an important role in the agriculture in some of these countries. What is more, an expansion of the domestic market would involve great expenditure on road-building, transport, etc. Considering the sparsity of the population in the "associated" countries, it would be extremely difficult to recoup this outlay.

than consumer demand, a state of affairs typical of modern capitalism. The bourgeoisie and bourgeois scholars, who can see only what goes on upon the surface, think that export is the universal remedy for the narrowness of the domestic market. They either cannot or will not see that today the narrowness of market is characteristic of all capitalist countries (disregarding, of course, the rare boom phases of the trade cycle);

b) the currencies and finances of capitalist countries are unstable. Prior to the advent of the general crisis, "hard" currencies were a feature of capitalism, i.e., the money unit was convertible into the stipulated amount of gold. This stability was based on the unrestricted circulation of gold coins in the country and gold bars on the world market. At present currencies are only relatively hard. The bulk of the less developed, and even many highly developed countries, such as the U.S.A., Canada and Britain, are constantly worried about the state of their balance of payments and are forced to resort to various measures to avoid devaluation.

Incomes from exports are the main factor contributing to a favourable (active) balance of payments. It is therefore easy to see why the U.S.A., Britain and almost all other capitalist countries consider the increase in exports the key to a stable economic policy. Exports are important not only for modern bourgeois states, but also for many large capitalist enterprises. They often deliberately provide these enterprises (even if exports take the form of dumping) with additional activity, without which they would have to operate at a loss. Export subsidies, state credit guarantees, etc., are a source of additional monopoly profits.

But important as exports are, their increase is not the universal cure-all that some bourgeois economists and statesmen imagine. This can be seen by analysing the role of exports in the economy of some of the leading capitalist countries. In West Germany, for example, the market capacity (excluding resales) was approximately the following[1]:

---

[1] *Statistisches Jahrbuch für die Bundesrepublik Deutschland*, 1961, S. 168, 243, 252.

Gross industrial product (according to the 1954 census)	154,000 million marks
Sales of artisan produced commodities (1955)	37,000 million marks
Sales of farm produce (1957-58)	17,000 million marks
Market capacity	208,000 million marks

In 1956,[1] 31,000 million marks worth of commodities were exported. This means that exports accounted for 15 per cent of West Germany's total market capacity. It can be reasonably assumed that the share of exports in the other Common Market countries, for which we have no data, is approximately the same.

It is very difficult to give a concrete appraisal of the E.E.C.'s export prospects. They depend on a multitude of factors, as yet unknown. But one thing is clear, even if the export of the E.E.C. countries grows by 50 per cent, this would expand the aggregate market capacity by only 7.5 per cent, which will solve neither the problem of realisation nor the other ills of modern capitalism.

In fact, an increase in exports by 50 per cent would expand the general market capacity by even less than 7.5 per cent. First of all, a country exporting commodities receives reimbursements for their value from abroad.[2] These reimbursements predominantly take the form of other commodities, since no country is able to pay for all its imports in gold. Moreover the imports often consist of commodities which are also produced in the country in question. This naturally results in a narrowing of the market for domestic goods. To illustrate our point let us look at the 1960 trade figures between West Germany and the U.S.A. for machinery of identical categories.[3]

---

[1] We are operating with sales figures for 1956 because they are the only ones available. In recent years exports have grown considerably: in 1961 they rose to 51,000 million marks. But the volume of industrial output has also grown: from 129 in 1955 to 191 in 1961 (1953=100). Thus, the ratio between the realisation of commodities on the domestic and foreign markets has hardly changed.

[2] Except in those cases when goods are exported for the purpose of capital investments abroad.

[3] *Statistisches Jahrbuch für die Bundesrepublik Deutschland*, 1961, S. 310-11.

	West German Imports from the U.S.A.	West German Exports to the U.S.A.
	(million marks)	
Machine tools	129	74
Machinery for the textile and tanning industries	53	78
Office machines	78	63
Machinery for the paper industry and printing plants . . . .˚.	21	68
Cars and aeroplanes	259	1,183
Electric equipment	200	214

Most of the imported machinery could have been produced at home, albeit at a higher cost. Imports tend to decrease the market for domestic machinery of the same type.

We assumed that the exports of the Common Market countries would grow by 50 per cent over a period of five years. But production within the E.E.C. country itself will also grow by about 15 per cent (an average of 3 per cent a year). A growth in exports of 50 per cent would therefore expand the aggregate domestic and foreign markets not by 7.5 per cent but only by about 6 per cent.

* * *

In conclusion we would like to remind the reader that our analysis is abstract and theoretical. It does not touch on the concrete historical conditions in which the Common Market has been created and functions. The theoretical assumption that full economic integration will be achieved has been postulated in order to show that even this would not solve the insuperable problems facing capitalism. But such a complete economic union is entirely unrealistic. Equal conditions for all competitors within the Common Market are to be created only by 1970. Even when they are, there will be no complete union.

A complete economic union would mean a single currency, a single budget, a single state, i.e., complete political integration, the rejection of all individual sovereignty by the countries in question. The chances of this happening are so slight as to be negligible. How could countries such as Britain and France, which have a long history as independent nations, voluntarily reject their sovereignty and submit to the decisions of a body in which they will be in the minority? It is therefore quite logical that de Gaulle speaks only of a federation which would preserve the sovereignty of each individual participant, and not of complete political integration.

Proponents of political integration have not thought out their plan to its logical conclusion. It is easy enough to set up a West European Parliament that would decide on the common affairs of the Common Market member-countries. One can even imagine a European Government that would exercise complete control over all mutual West European interests. A joint military command, like that of NATO, could be created. But this is still a far cry from full political integration. Who, for instance, would command the armed forces of the member-countries? The existence of NATO did not stop de Gaulle from withdrawing his fleet from the joint command and from creating his own nuclear weapons. As long as each capitalist country has its own armed forces, all political integration is conditional and temporary.

The advocates and propagandists of political integration will have us believe that after 1970 the Rome Treaty will be eternal and that no member-country will have the right to leave the community. This is nonsense. The decisions of an international court cannot force a sovereign state, possessing its own armed forces, to observe a treaty it considers no longer advantageous, let alone harmful. In such a case war would be the only means to make a sovereign country fulfil the agreement. But a war of the Common Market countries against a member who has decided to withdraw or who is sabotaging the Rome Treaty, is extremely unlikely.

Irrespective of all these concrete historical conditions, it is still highly debatable whether a union of highly developed capitalist countries is able to effect any appreciable expansion of their markets over and above the normal. Marxists who answer this question in the affirmative have yet to demonstrate the economic mechanism producing this expansion.

THE REASON FOR THE POPULARITY
OF KEYNESIAN THEORIES

This essay is not aimed at subjecting Keynes's theories to a barrage of criticism; that has been done by other economists.[1] We are only interested in explaining why Keynes's theories have become so dominant in capitalist economic thought. What can explain the fact that statesmen who embody the interests of monopoly capital, university professors in the capitalist countries, and reformist leaders of the working-class movement have all become adherents of Keynesian theories?

A multitude of facts show that this is so. When the U.S. budget showed a deficit of 10,000 million dollars, President Kennedy attempted to "whip up" U.S. economic development according to Keynesian precepts. Both monopoly capital and U.S. trade union leaders insisted on tax cuts in spite of the budget deficit and their demands were met. At the beginning of the sixties "deficit financing" became a general rule, while a balanced budget was an exception. West Germany, France, Mexico and the U.A.R. are the only capitalist countries where state expenditure does not exceed revenue.

The Democratic and Republican parties in the U.S.A., the British Conservatives, John Strachey, the Labour Party theoretician, and even Hjalmar Schachat, the former chief nazi economist, are all guided by Keynes's theories.

It may be argued that it is not surprising that capitalists and reformist labour leaders and also professors of bourgeois political economy consider that the capitalist system

---

[1] See the writings of W. Foster, I. Blyumin, A. Trakhtenberg et al.

304

is eternal. In their attempts to preserve it and to adjust it to changing conditions in order to avert a proletarian revolution, it is therefore quite natural that they all adhere to one economic theory.

But this is an oversimplification. During the past fifty years hundreds of bourgeois economic theories have emerged, all of which are based on the assumption that the capitalist system can be preserved and improved. Why has Keynes's theory become the most popular of all?

Maybe, because it gives a deeper and more rational analysis of capitalism than other theories? No, this is not so.

Keynes dealt only with the superficial phenomena of capitalist economy. Paraphrasing Marx's words, we could call him the surface genius of bourgeois society.[1] He does not pay the slightest attention to the *basic categories* of capitalist economy, the explanation of which takes up so much space in the writing of the classics of bourgeois political economy (and which were later exhaustively explained by Marx). He does not analyse categories such as commodity and money, value and surplus value, interest and entrepreneur's profit; he draws no distinction between the law of the movement of individual capital and that of the aggregate social capital, etc. Everything is clear to him, nothing poses a problem.

Capital per se brings in interest, like land brings in rent, for both are "scarce": "The owner of capital can obtain interest because capital is scarce, just as the owner of land can obtain rent because land is scarce."[2] But Keynes neither shows the economic sources of interest and rent, nor does he indicate their place in capitalist economy.

What is more, an explanation of interest and rent by

---

[1] "Classical economy," Marx said, "never arrived at a consciousness of the results of its own analysis; it ... was thus led, as will be seen later, into inextricable confusion and contradiction, while it offered to the vulgar economists a secure basis of operations for their shallowness, which on principle worships appearances only." (Karl Marx, *Capital*, Vol. I, p. 538.)

[2] J. M. Keynes, *The General Theory of Employment, Interest and Money*, London, 1936, p. 376. We shall refer to Keynes's main work repeatedly since he himself rejected many propositions he had advanced in his former "theoretical" work—*A Treatise on Money*.

the "scarcity" of capital and land is wrong even in a superficial analysis. During depressions large sums of money lie idle, yet no one ever loans them out to others free of charge. In Brazil, Argentina, Peru, etc., large landowners block the cultivation of vast areas in order to make land "scarce" and thus force the peasants to pay high rents. This "scarcity" of land is completely unnatural; the artificial creation of bourgeois land monopolists.

Keynes's explanations of other economic categories are no less superficial. Profit is a reward for the entrepreneur's work and business risks. Price, he continues, is the amount of money offered for a commodity in accordance with the prevailing supply and demand situation.

Keynes has not created an economic theory of his own: he is a typical eclectic. Marx's description of Macleod suits him remarkably well: "Macleod, who has taken upon himself to dress up the confused ideas of Lombard Street in the most learned finery, is a successful cross between the superstitious mercantilists, and the enlightened Free-trade bagmen."[1]

Keynes openly refutes the teaching of the founders of bourgeois political economy. The reason for it is not hard to see. Their teachings logically lead to Marxism and the admission that the capitalist mode of production is historically transient—a truth unacceptable to those who represent the interests of monopoly capital. He draws his "theoretical" views from a multitude of sources: he explains prices, profit and interest by the theory of marginal utility advanced by the Austrian school, poverty—according to Malthus and attempts to justify profit by the "refusal theory". In many cases Keynes reverts to the mercantilists; he praises the entirely unknown Silvio Gesell and places him on an equal footing with Malthus and Marx(!).

Keynes's eclecticism is one of the reasons for his popularity: in his confused rag-tag of economics, everyone can choose what he likes best.

Keynes's "analysis" has nothing in common with genuine political economy in the classical and Marxist sense. His is an invented psychology hopefully applied to economics.

Keynes openly declares that: "Thus we can sometimes

---

[1] Karl Marx, *Capital*, Vol. I, p. 61.

regard our ultimate independent variables as consisting of
(1) the three fundamental psychological factors, namely,
the psychological propensity to consume, the psychological
attitude to liquidity and the psychological expectation of
future yield from capital-assets, (2) the wage-unit as determined by the bargains reached between employers and
employed, and (3) the quantity of money as determined
by the action of the central bank; so that, if we take as
given the factors specified above, these variables determine
the national income (or dividend) and the quantity of
employment."[1]

We see that profit, the deus ex machina of the capitalist
mode of production, is not even mentioned.[2] He attempts
to depict the everlasting capitalist search for profits as a
secondary consideration. "If human nature felt no tempta-
tion to take a chance, no satisfaction (profit apart) in
constructing a factory, a railway, a mine or a farm, there
might not be much investment merely as a result of cold
calculation."[3]

In his pseudo-psychology Keynes borders on the absurd.
He says: "In estimating the prospects of investment, we
must have regard, therefore, to the nerves and hysteria and
even the digestions and reactions to the weather of those
upon whose spontaneous activity it largely depends."[4]

He completely forgets that competition forces the individual capitalist to make a profit or perish.

Since Keynes does not recognise a class analysis, does
not mention classes[5] at all, his psychological analysis
applies to abstract economic man and his psychological
"laws" have no validity in the real capitalist world. Let us
illustrate this by an example.

Keynes advances a "law"[6] according to which an increase in a person's income is attended by an increase in his

---

[1] J. M. Keynes, op. cit., Bk. IV, Ch. 18, pp. 246-47.
[2] He later introduced profit into his theory in the form of entrepreneur profit.
[3] J. M. Keynes, op. cit., Bk. IV, Ch. 12, p. 150.
[4] Ibid., p. 162.
[5] He mentions classes only once, referring to them as the "saving
classes", an expression one cannot read without a smile. (Ibid., Bk.
III, Ch. 10, p. 123.)
[6] J. M. Keynes, op. cit., p. 28.

consumption, but to a lesser degree than that of his income, since part of it is saved.

An investigation of this would-be law as applied to the various classes of society, would show that its operation is far from universal.

In the capitalist world there are at least a thousand million people whose incomes are so low that they are forced to live in perpetual hunger. Even in the U.S.A., the richest capitalist country, there are millions of people whose income cannot provide them with even normal daily nourishment.[1] Obviously, any addition to the incomes of that poorest bracket of the population will be fully spent on increased consumption and, with a few exceptions, nothing will be left to save. What sense is there in the "propensity to save" if nothing is left to be saved?

Conversely, in the highly developed countries, especially in the U.S.A. and Britain, there is a wide layer of civil servants, office workers and skilled workers whose consumption would expand if their incomes were to increase. These are the layers which usually buy durables on the instalment system (houses, cars, furniture, TV sets, etc.) and spend more than they earn.

As soon as their income rises, they buy more things on credit for sums which exceed by far the actual increment in their income. This process can be clearly seen from U.S. statistics, comparing the sum of wages with the sum of credit sales.[2]

Year	Factory and Office Workers' Wages	Personal Savings	Consumer Credit
	(thousand million dollars)		
1958	249	24.4	40.8
1959	268	23.4	49.0

---

[1] The third report of the FAO states "a quarter of American households had a calorie intake below the FAO national requirement scale" (*The Economist*, June 29, 1963, p. 1348).

[2] *United States. Economic Report of the President*, 1961, pp. 141, 145, 180. The figures are not very accurate, but are good enough to prove our argument.

Thus, Keynes's assertion is at variance with facts.

And finally, in the highly developed capitalist countries there is a layer, admittedly a narrow one, which includes those at the top of the monopoly bourgeoisie, whose incomes are so large that it would be simply impossible to spend them on consumer goods. How could one spend an income amounting to millions of dollars a year on consumer goods?

An advertisement hung up outside a large American department store at Christmas speaks volumes: *"What can you give for Christmas to one who has everything?"* The husband can present his wife with a new elegant four-seater aeroplane costing $45,000. Or the wife can give her husband a new plane for $60,000. Or even better—the husband can give his wife a coffee-pot (!) made of pure gold and studded with diamonds, worth $150,000.

Naturally, a further increase in the incomes of such people will not promote consumer spending.

Keynes's would-be universal psychological "law" applies only to people in a certain income bracket: that is, to rentiers with a moderate income.

All this would seem to indicate that Keynes's wondrous panacea for overcoming the narrowness of the capitalist market, namely an increase of unproductive consumption among the non-working classes, advanced in his time by Malthus, is ridiculous in present concrete historical conditions.[1]

Keynes's other psychological "laws" are no less schematic and senseless when applied to modern capitalism but his proposal to expand unproductive consumption is not as absurd as it would seem at first glance, but has a very definite class sense: it is intended to justify the expenditure on arms and wars, so profitable for monopoly capital. "Pyramid-building, earthquakes, even wars may serve to increase wealth. . . ."[2]

---

[1] Keynes quotes Malthus's letter to Ricardo and expresses his agreement with it. In that letter Malthus says: "How can it be said ... that an increase of unproductive consumption among landlords and capitalists may not sometimes be the proper remedy for a state of things in which the motives to production fail?" (J. M. Keynes, *The General Theory...*, Bk. VI, Ch. 23, p. 363.)

[2] Ibid., Bk. III, Ch. 10, p. 129.

The third, and perhaps greatest shortcoming of Keynes's "theory" is the absence of any historical approach to the problems of capitalism. He completely ignores the *development* of capitalism from one historical stage to the other.

He does not mention one of the most important laws of capitalist development—the concentration of capital as a result of its accumulation and centralisation, every year transforming millions of "small people", peasants, artisans, merchants, small capitalists into propertyless proletarians. He makes no mention of the transformation of the capitalism of the free competition era into modern monopoly capitalism, and completely ignores the existence of the Soviet Union and the struggle between the two systems.

The absence of any historical analysis of necessity leads to a false and impractical approach to the problems of modern capitalism,[1] reducing its special features to mere tenets which, though theoretically correct, are untenable in prevailing conditions. Let us give a few examples.

Keynes repeatedly speaks with irony about the fact that under capitalism hundreds of thousands of workers are busy transferring gold from the bowels of the earth to the vaults of the central banks. Looking at it from an abstract point of view this is absurd. We also know what role Lenin assigned to gold in a communist society. Yet Lenin never once spoke of the absurdity of gold mining under capitalism. Since there are independent states in the capitalist system, which are based on commodity production and world trade, *world money* is absolutely essential. Attempts are being made at present to limit the role of gold as world money. The International Monetary Fund and the numerous agreements on mutual currency assistance between the central banks of the highly developed capitalist countries all serve this aim. To this day a deficit in a country's balance of payments (albeit an accidental and temporary deficit) can be settled only by paying out world currency, in other words, gold.

Throughout the capitalist world, the state of the gold reserves is being given constant attention. The threat of

---

[1] It is typical that Keynes completely ignores the monopoly character of modern capitalism. Even the word "monopoly" appears in his main work only once, when he speaks of "monopoly price".

a "gold drain" from the U.S.A. is the greatest worry of the U.S. economic administration. No matter how senseless it may seem, the mining and accumulation of gold is unavoidable under capitalism, and only someone who utterly disregards the historical development of the capitalist system and the concrete conditions prevailing at the modern stage, and who resorts to inventing hypothetical laws, can doubt the need for mining gold under modern capitalism.

* * *

How is it to be explained that in spite of all these shortcomings, Keynes is recognised as the leading authority on bourgeois economic science and economic policy in the capitalist world?

Keynes's main work was written in the first half of the thirties, when the impact of the greatest economic crisis in the history of capitalism and the resulting protracted depression and mass unemployment were being felt throughout the capitalist world.

It was no longer possible to deny the existence of the general crisis of capitalism, which Marxists had diagnosed immediately after the First World War. The theory, advanced by the unworthy successors of classical bourgeois political economy about the harmonious development of capitalism, about the internal force of capitalism automatically overcoming all emerging difficulties, had broken down.[1] The diseased state of capitalism could no longer be denied. Keynes wrote: "The outstanding faults of the economic society in which we live are its failure to provide for full employment and its arbitrary and inequitable distribution of wealth and incomes."[2]

Keynes was out to achieve the following: a) to prove that the faults of capitalism, in particular that of chronic mass unemployment, are not products of the capitalist system per se but are an effect of general psychological

---

[1] Keynes unfoundedly attempts to pass off a number of vulgar economists, including the "vulgar" J. Say, as Marx called him, as classics of political economy and criticising the teachings of the former about the harmonious nature of capitalism discredits the classics, in particular, Ricardo, who discovered many truths about capitalism.

[2] J. M. Keynes, op. cit., Bk. VI, Ch. 24, p. 372.

laws, and that the responsibility for them therefore falls not upon the ruling big bourgeoisie (monopoly capital) but upon permanent factors independent of the social system; b) to recommend measures which in reality would serve the interests of the monopoly bourgeoisie, but would, on the face of it, be acceptable to the reformists.

William Foster formulated this as follows: "Keynesianism is essentially a product of the general crisis of capitalism."[1]

How does Keynes manage to whitewash capital and the bourgeoisie in general of all responsibility for the faults of capitalism?

First of all he justifies all unearned incomes in the spirit of the marginal utility theory, declaring that they are based not on the appropriation of surplus value, not on exploitation, but on the scarcity of the factors of production. The bourgeoisie, he says, has a natural right to profit, since capital is scarce; the landowner has a natural right to rent, since land too is scarce; the owner of loan capital has a natural right to interest, as a reward for his willingness to temporarily part with the "liquidity" of his capital (here we have the old "refusal theory"); capitalists who direct companies are entitled to profits because their work calls for a high qualification and at the same time they risk the capital invested in the enterprise. Indeed, to understand all is to pardon all!

But how does he explain and justify mass unemployment and the resulting privations of the working class?

On the basis of his high-sounding but meaningless arguments we can draw the following conclusions.

The number of employed workers depends on the "effective demand", i.e., on consumer spending and new capital investments. "If the propensity to consume and the rate of new investment result in a deficient effective demand, the actual level of employment will fall short of the supply of labour, potentially available at the existing real wage. . . ."[2]

This is quite true but it does not explain unemployment.

According to Keynes, unemployment emerges because the more workers an entrepreneur hires, the less profit

---

[1] *Political Affairs*, No. 1, January 1948, p. 27.
[2] J. M. Keynes, *The General Theory...*, Ch. 3, p. 30.

each worker brings in (the law of "diminishing returns").[1] Thus the greater the number of employed workers the larger the wage expenditure in comparison with work produced, a process which continues until profits disappear completely.

The second reason for unemployment is that not all people spend all their income on personal consumption or on investments, preferring to keep some of it in the form of cash and demanding and receiving a certain interest for it. The interest on loan capital stops the utilisation of workers by capital when the profit this capital yields to the capitalist becomes smaller than the interest he has to pay for it.

The rate of interest is a "highly psychological phenomenon".[2] But "the costs of bringing borrowers and leaders together and uncertainty as to the future of the rate of interest ... set a lower limit, which in present circumstances may perhaps be as high as 2 or 2.5 per cent on long term".[3]

As an incorrigible eclectic, Keynes combines the theory of marginal utility with Knapp's quantitative theory of money.

Backed only by verbose and meaningless arguments, Keynes declares that loan capital and rates of interest determine the marginal profitability of capital and thus lead to a decrease in employment. This whitewashes industrial capital of all blame for the resulting unemployment.

Both his arguments are absolutely fallacious.

In the boom phase preceding a crisis, when employment is almost maximal and much overtime is worked, the expenditure on wages may increase somewhat. But this is attended by a decrease in general expenditure per unit of output and, the decisive factor, a price rise. It is not the drop in profits resulting from higher expenditure on wages and interest that is responsible for the drop in production and employment but the overproduction of commodities.

---

[1] Ibid., p. 17.
[2] Ibid., Ch. 15, p. 202.
[3] Ibid., Ch. 16, p. 219.

As regards the role of interest, every Marxist knows that interest is a special part of profit, that the rate of interest is regulated by supply and demand and more or less depends on the rate of profit, and not vice versa, as declared by Keynes. The exceptions are monetary and credit crises of short duration, when money is at a premium and entrepreneurs are willing to pay virtually any price for it.

The error of Keynes's theories can even be proved from statistics. If we analyse a detailed balance of any large capitalist company it will show that the expenditure on interest accounts for a small share of the total production expenditure. The summary balances of the largest British companies, published quarterly in *The Economist*, show that even directors' salaries exceed the interest paid for long-term credits.[1]

The "return on invested capital" of the 500 largest U.S. companies was 10.3 per cent.[2] How can the rate of interest being paid for a relatively small sum of credits determine the rate of employment?

The same applies to American capital (excluding banks and insurance companies) in general.

Below are data for 1962[3]:

	(thousand million dollars)
Money funds of companies	57.6
including those deriving from	
bonds	5.0
other debt	2.5
bank loans	3.0
Total	10.5

We do not know the rate of interest paid on these credits but assume that it was 6 per cent (which would be very high). In that case the sum total of interest would

---

[1] These items do not show the expenditure on interest for short-term bank credits but these, too, cannot amount to much.

[2] *Statistical Abstract of the United States*, 1961, p. 482.

[3] *Survey of Current Business*, May 1963, p. 10. We do not take into account current, interest-free credits.

amount to some 600 million dollars. In 1962 the total profits of American corporations (excluding banks and insurance companies) amounted to about 40,000 million dollars. This shows that the interest hardly affected their profits. But Keynes dedicates a large proportion of his book to proving the decisive influence of the rate of interest.

Every Marxist realises that the principal cause of unemployment is the capitalist system itself—the contradiction between the social character of production and private capitalist appropriation, or to be more concrete, the contradiction between the striving of capital for unlimited expansion of production and limited consumption,[1] the so-called "enduring narrowness of the capitalist market".

Under capitalism there is permanent unemployment in the form of agrarian overpopulation and periodic unemployment during crises of industrial overproduction. During the period of the general crisis it gradually assumes a chronic mass character. It is aggravated by the rationalisation, mechanisation and automatisation of production. Following the Second World War, chronic mass unemployment temporarily decreased as a result of the enormous losses in human resources during the war, the decline in the birth rate and the mobilisation of millions of people for the armed forces and war production. But in the coming decades chronic mass unemployment is bound to become capitalism's thorniest problem. The explanation invented by Keynes has no connection with the real causes of unemployment.

Keynes puts the cart before the horse when he explains overproduction by the achievement of full employment and the cut in profits which is supposed to be caused by it. Marx wrote: "It is these absolute movements of the accumulation of capital which are reflected as relative movements of the mass of exploitable labour-power, and therefore seem produced by the latter's own independent movement."[2] The reasons why the big bourgeoisie, and

---

[1] This contradiction is so obvious that even Keynes noticed it. His vague explanation reads: "Each time we secure today's equilibrium by increased investment we are aggravating the difficulty of securing equilibrium tomorrow." (J. M. Keynes, *The General Theory...*, Ch. 8, p. 105.)

[2] Karl Marx, *Capital*, Vol. I, p. 620.

especially the industrial bourgeoisie, have made Keynes their prophet is not hard to see.

Keynes declares that the bourgeois system can be preserved with the help of state-capitalist measures. He recommends state intervention in the economy "as the only practicable means of avoiding the destruction of existing economic forms in their entirety and as the condition of the successful functioning of individual initiative."[1]

As mentioned above, he maintains that the principal evils of capitalism—crises of overproduction and mass unemployment—are not the fault of the bourgeoisie but a result of "high wages".

We shall give only one example (although we could give thousands) of how the bourgeoisie makes use of Keynesian theories. William F. Butler, Vice-President of the Chase Manhattan Bank, the largest concern in the Rockefeller financial empire, declared that the following causes were responsible for the crisis that broke out in the U.S.A. in 1960.

"Wages have continued to increase more rapidly than output per man-hour, raising unit labour costs about 2 per cent per annum. . . .

"Thus, profits have been squeezed. . . . A decline in the rate of profit invariably leads to a cutback in expenditures for new plant and equipment. Business must reduce the rate of growth of capital assets in an attempt to maximise the rate of return. This means that only those investment projects which offer a good return can go ahead."[2]

This is quoted almost verbatim from Keynes's book.

The remedies Keynes offers the big bourgeoisie for decreasing unemployment are in complete harmony with the interests of the monopolies. To lower wages he recommends a gradual advance of prices with the help of a controlled inflation. He constantly reiterates that the capitalists should not lower the nominal wages, for this would encounter far stiffer resistance from the workers than an indirect lowering of wages resulting from an increase in the prices of those commodities bought mainly by workers. "In fact, a movement by employers to revise money-wage

[1] J. M. Keynes, *The General Theory. . .*, Ch. 24, p. 380.
[2] *U.S. News and World Report*. September 19, 1960, p. 68.

bargains downward will be much more strongly resisted than a gradual and automatic lowering of real wages as a result of rising prices."[1]

During the post-war years the bourgeoisie of most countries resorted to this policy.

Index of Consumer Goods Prices[2]
(1953=100)

Year	U.S.A.	Britain	Italy	France	West Germany	India	Canada	Japan
1948 . .	90	77	86	70	99	91	87	63
1960 . .	111	121	115	134	111	116	111	114

The scale of the price advance differs from country to country, but a universal tendency can be clearly discerned amongst them.

Keynes also recommends deficit financing of public works (and incidentally the chance of securing profitable state orders) as a measure for improving the economy.

He urges entrepreneurs not to expand productive capacities excessively: ". . . Capital has to be kept scarce enough in the long-period to have a marginal efficiency which is at least equal to the rate of interest for a period equal to the life of the capital, as determined by psychological and institutional conditions."[3]

How is the surplus capital to be used?

Keynes recommends that surplus capital in the production sphere be spent unproductively on the private and public consumption of luxury goods. In this he supports Malthus. Moreover, he also backs Silvio Gesell's recommendation that money should be periodically changed, to force people to spend it and not to keep it in a liquid form; this would raise the interest rate on loan capital and limit the possibilities of profitable new investments for produc-

---

[1] J. M. Keynes, *The General Theory. . .* , Ch. 19, p. 264.

[2] *Statistical Yearbook of the United Nations*, 1961, p. 480 et passim; *Monthly Bulletin of Statistics*, June 1963, p. 144 et passim. We do not give data for countries with a strong inflation.

[3] J. M. Keynes, *The General Theory. . .* , Ch. 16, p. 217.

tion capital. In addition to high wages, Keynes lays the blame for all capitalist evils on the "striving to increase liquidity", loan capital and a high rate of interest. This leads straight to Hitler's division of capital into "creative" and "predatory" capital.

What is the class connotation of Keynes's never ending talk about the decisive influence of the rate of interest on capitalist economy and unemployment?

As mentioned above the question of the rate of interest is unimportant to industrial monopoly capital—the big monopolies use comparatively small sums of loan capital, financing new capital investment mainly out of their own reserves. There are many factors which exert a much greater influence on cost and profit than the rate of interest. These are the prices of raw materials and fuel, railway and freightage tariffs, import duties, the extent to which productive capacities are employed, etc., etc.

Nor should we forget that, as a result of the increasing coalescence of industrial and banking capital (including insurance companies), the finance oligarchy, which rules over both, stops to worry how the total profits appropriated by it are distributed between the various companies under its control.

Both in the highly developed and in the poor capitalist countries there are hundreds of thousands of medium and small "unviable" capitalist enterprises which are doomed to ruin by the centralisation of capital. They are always up to their ears in debt and have to pay usurers and bankers high rates of interest. The reason for their bankruptcy is often their inability to pay off credits and accrued interests by the appointed date. The class connotation of Keynes's teaching about the decisive role of the rate of interest is best expressed in his attempts to exonerate capitalism in general, and monopoly capital in particular, from the responsibility for the mass ruin of small capitalists, peasants and artisans.

All this proves that it was no accident that monopoly capital preferred Keynes to hundreds of other vulgar economists and made him its standard bearer.

To obviate any idealistic or other such interpretation of the views expressed above, we would like to emphasise that monopoly capital develops state-monopoly capitalism, deficit financing, indirect wage cuts through a steady raise of retail prices, etc., not simply because these measures were recommended by Keynes. Monopoly capital would conduct this policy even if Keynes had never been born. Keynes only gave the policy conducted by monopoly capitalism a pseudo-scientific foundation cloaked by demagogy to make it acceptable to the other classes of capitalist society.

* * *

All this leads to a new question: why is it that not only monopoly capital but also the reformist parties and the trade union bureaucracy champion Keynesian ideas?

The union between reformism and Keynesian theories is based on the fact that reformists and revisionists consider Marxism obsolete. They are unable to create their own theory of modern monopoly capitalism and are therefore in need of a sound bourgeois theory, which on the one hand criticises capitalism and declares that it must be re-organised (this is intended to pacify unsatisfied workers), but, on the other hand, nullifies this criticism by leaving the door open for co-operation with the bourgeoisie. Keynes's theories suit the requirements of these reformists to a tee.

The reformist leaders value Keynes particularly highly because he, as distinct from hundreds of other vulgar bourgeois economists, does not attempt to refute Marx or argue with him, but simply ignores him.[1]

To argue against Marxian theories would undermine the position of the reformist leaders, and attract workers' attention to Marx's revolutionary teaching, and discredit the reformists with the intelligentsia. They know from their own experience that all attempts to refute Marxist theory have failed. Now, when a third of mankind has rid itself of capitalist oppression and is building socialism under the banner of Marxism-Leninism, it would be absurd to declare

---

[1] In his main work Keynes mentions Marx in passing three times: he compares him with Gesell, that scientific fraud, saying: "I believe that the future will learn more from the spirit of Gesell than from that of Marx." (J. M. Keynes, *The General Theory...*, Ch. 23, p. 355.)

In one of his books he declares Marx "boring". Keynes neither understood nor wished to understand anything of Marx's teaching.

Marx's teaching "Utopian" and impracticable. The reformists are now compelled to defend themselves by a far simpler method: they declare that Marxism may be good enough for the poor underdeveloped countries, but is inapplicable to the rich, highly developed capitalist countries. This throws them into Keynes's camp, with whom they have much in common, and saves them from fruitless attempts to prove Marx wrong.

We shall enumerate only a few of the views shared by Keynes and the reformists:

a) both believe that capitalism is the best social system;

b) both agree that capitalism needs reorganising and that this can be effected through reforms by a supra-class state, by-passing a revolution.

In his characteristically vague style, Keynes predicts the future of capitalism resulting from state intervention as follows: "Thus we might aim in practice (there being nothing in this which is unattainable) at an increase in the volume of capital until it ceases to be scarce, so that the functionless investor will no longer receive a bonus; and at a scheme of direct taxation which allows the intelligence and determination and executive skill of the financier, the entrepreneur *et hoc genus omne* (who are certainly so fond of their craft that their labour could be obtained much cheaper than at present), to be harnessed to the service of the community on reasonable terms of reward."[1]

This is irrefutable proof of Keynes's muddled thinking. First he declares that capital brings profit because it is "scarce", then he describes a capitalism in which capital is no longer scarce and therefore does not bring in any profit, i.e., there emerges a capitalism without profits, where capitalist entrepreneurs are only receiving high "wages" according to merit.

But this nonsense suits the reformists ideally as a means for deceiving the workers;

c) both advocate the development of state capitalism. Keynes says: "I conclude that the duty of ordering the current volume of investment cannot safely be left in private hands."[2]

---

[1] J. M. Keynes, *The General Theory...*, Ch. 24, p. 376-77.
[2] Ibid., Ch. 22, p. 320.

For this reason he is for "peaceful", i.e., for bourgeois socialisation of a part of the means of production. Keynes declares that in his opinion "the necessary measures of socialisation can be introduced gradually and without a break in the general traditions of society".[1] In present-day conditions this position falls in perfectly with the interests of the big bourgeoisie and the propaganda needs of the reformist leaders;

d) Keynes "analyses" capitalism, as was pointed out above, without paying any attention to the class stratification of capitalist society. This, too, harmonises with the wishes of the reformist leaders, who attempt to gloss over the class struggle and thus purge it from the minds of the workers;

e) at present the main worry of the reformist leaders in the highly developed capitalist countries is not the wage problem but the ever growing mass unemployment, the concomitant of technological development, which threatens to affect also office workers and civil servants. The rapid increase in labour productivity and the relatively insignificant shortening of the working-day during the post-war years has greatly enlarged the mass of surplus value being appropriated by the bourgeoisie, both in value and in physical terms. This enabled the bourgeoisie to raise the wages of workers organised in trade unions without cutting back profits when this was necessary to avoid an intensification of the class struggle. However these wage rises are more or less neutralised by inflated prices.

But neither the capitalists nor the reformists knew how to fight growing unemployment. It was at this point that Keynes produced his universal cure-all. He declared that government measures, such as public works financed at the expense of a large deficit in the state budget, the maintenance of low-interest rates, etc., would abolish unemployment. The reformists regard these conclusions as Keynes's greatest "contribution".

Thirty years have passed since Keynes made these promises and although bourgeois statesmen, reformist leaders and bourgeois professors have all become active supporters of Keynesian ideas, they have not succeeded in

---

[1] Ibid., Ch. 24, p. 378.

eliminating unemployment. An analysis of the genuine causes of unemployment under modern capitalism shows that in future, too, *unemployment* (apart from cyclical fluctuations) *will not decrease but rise considerably above the present level.*

Let us now take a closer look at the measures suggested by Keynes. We have already shown above that the rate of interest has but little influence on the volume of production and employment. As regards the influence exerted on employment by public works and state orders the following can be said.

If a capitalist country has underemployed productive capacities and man power resources, new state orders (public works) may indeed give an impetus to greater employment. Additional workers will be hired and will spend their wages on consumer goods, which, in turn, *may* expand the production of such goods and thus promote an expansion in the production of producer goods. The growth in production will call for a further increase in employment and the result would be a decrease in unemployment. Every Marxist understands this.

But whether there will be a reduction in unemployment and how important that reduction will be depends on several factors—the size of consumer article stocks at the time when the "revival" begins, the extent of capacity underemployment, i.e., by how much the market must be extended to offer the capitalists incentives for additional capital investments. In assessing the needs for a long period, it is important to specify who will pay for the state expenditure: the working people (through taxes on their incomes and higher prices) or the capitalists and rentiers out of their profits. These are but a few of the factors that need to be taken into consideration. It is only by evaluating all these particulars that a scientific appraisal can be made of the effect a "revival" of the economic conditions would have.

There is no doubt, however, that any revival through state orders and the resultant growth in employment can be only temporary, since the volume of the capitalist market depends on the laws operating permanently in capitalist society.

All these concrete factors have been ignored by Keynes. He invented the notorious "multiplier" (he designates it as coefficient K), which is now universally applied by his followers. The coefficient K "tells us that, when there is an increment of aggregate investment, income will increase by an amount which is K times the increment of investment".[1] A growth in incomes increases employment and unemployment disappears.

Theoretically this is quite correct. The difficulties only appear in practice. Keynes's followers have not the slightest idea (in spite of Keynes's strictly "scientific" mathematical formulas) what the size of coefficient K is in the various countries. In 1963 some considered the "multiplier" as 2.5, others as 3.8. In keeping with Keynes's theory they say that with the progress of technology, increasing sums of new capital investments are needed to create more jobs for workers. According to the computations of Nat Goldfinger, Research Director of the AFL-CIO every new job demands the following capital investments:

"The actual figures are $39,667 per job in the 1961-62 period, $20,567 in 1958-60, $10, 725 in 1954-56."[2]

Keynes himself gives only one concrete numerical example. He asserts: "If, at a time when employment has fallen to 5,200,000, an additional 100,000 men are employed on public works, total employment will rise to 6,400,000. But if employment is already 9,000,000 when the additional 100,000 men are taken on for public works, total employment will only rise to 9,200,000. Thus public works even of doubtful utility may pay for themselves over and over again at a time of severe unemployment. . . ."[3]

The reformists consider this an excellent basis for their demand to extend public works during times of heavy unemployment. But Keynes does not mention *when* this fantastic rise in employment is expected to set in—in six months or ten years!

An elementary analysis shows the absurdity of Keynes's statement that the employment of 100,000 people for public works will increase the total employment by 1,200,000 people when the total number employed in the country (he evidently refers to Britain) has fallen to 5,200,000 and

---

[1] J. M. Keynes, *The General Theory...*, Ch. 10, p. 115.

[2] *The New Republic*, May 25, 1963, p. 14.

[3] J. M. Keynes, *The General Theory...*, Ch. 10, p. 127.

unemployment exceeds 1,200,000. In his example the number of unemployed comprises over 20 per cent of all employed, which is a state of affairs that could only be the result of a long crisis of overproduction.

Let us consider two different cases:

1. 100,000 workers are hired for road building. They work with manual instruments and receive a pay of £15 a month, which, for 1936, was a very high pay. That means that 100,000 newly employed workers will draw £1.5 million a month in new income. We maintain that in that case coefficient K, the "multiplier", will most probably not exceed *one*, i.e., there will be virtually no further increase in employment.

What makes us believe that?

During the protracted crisis and mass unemployment period the workers were half-starving, wore out their clothes and ran into debt with their landlords and shop-keepers. The newly earned million and a half pounds will be almost completely exhausted on buying food, clothes, shoes and on repaying debts. The small increase in demand for foodstuffs can easily be satisfied from available commodity stocks. Many months will pass before these branches will have to engage additional labour, and an even longer time will pass (if there is a chronic underemployment of capacities) before there will be an increase in employment in the sphere producing capital goods.

A different situation would arise if the 100,000 workers were engaged in building factories, large power stations, submarines, etc. Within a very short time there would be a growth of employment in engineering and instrument-building and a little later in the iron and steel and coal-mining industries. But even in that case, an original increase in employment of 100,000 will not result in a total increase of 1,200,000.

Both Keynes and the reformist leaders, who are deceiving the workers by promising them the abolition of unemployment under capitalism, are avoiding concrete analyses.[1]

The astonishing thing is that Keynes himself never really

----

[1] It is clear to every Marxist that the growth of production does not depend on the number of newly employed workers, or the extent of unemployment but on the amount of newly invested capital.

believed that full employment could be achieved. He wrote: "Full, or even approximately full, employment is of rare and short-lived occurrence."[1]

Speaking of full employment Keynes is concerned not with the interests of the workers but with the application of capital. He says: "We have full employment when output has risen to a level at which the marginal return from a representative unit of the factors of production has fallen to the minimum figure at which a quantity of the factors sufficient to produce this output is available."[2]

The extent to which Keynes's ideas have taken root in the reformist workers' movement can be seen from the following. In Sweden, where the most extreme of all reformist Social-Democratic parties has been continuously in office since 1930 (alone or in coalition with other bourgeois parties), there is a law adopted in 1938 which gives joint-stock companies the right to set aside 40 per cent of their profits. This part of the profits is exempt from tax. About half of it must be deposited in the state Riksbank and receives no interest. During crises these funds may be spent, with the permission of the Ministry of Labour, on measures to fight unemployment.[3]

The Swedish reformists are proud of their adherence to Keynesian theories. In his *Industrial Relations, Sweden Shows the Way*, a Fabian pamphlet published in 1963, Jack Cooper, the General Secretary of the National Union of General and Municipal Workers, wrote that the Swedish Social-Democratic Party "was following a policy on Keynesian lines before Keynes's *General Theory of Employment, Interest and Money*".[4]

* * *

There is no point in discussing at length why Keynes's views are so prominent in the universities of the capitalist countries. Quite apart from the fact that he pursues the interests of monopoly capital, Keynes is popular with bourgeois professors because he deals only with superficial

---

[1] J. M. Keynes, *The General Theory...*, Ch. 18, p. 250.
[2] Ibid., Ch. 21, p. 303.
[3] *The Economist*, June 15, 1963, p. 1175.
[4] *Labour Monthly*, July 1963, p. 321.

matters, which frees them from the labour involved in studying the *essence* of capitalism, as demanded by the founders of classical bourgeois political economy and by Marx. They also like Keynes because he has succeeded in cloaking his senseless statements with vague, pseudo-scientific formulas. Blatant tautology is disguised by a veneer of mathematics, his confused theories are termed "scientific" discoveries and his ambiguity furnishes the professors with endless material for various "scientific" interpretations and discussions. *The dominance of Keynesian ideas in modern bourgeois economic science illustrates the final degradation of bourgeois ideology.*

We shall give only a few examples of Keynes's "scientific" approach.

It would seem that it is simple enough to decide what an unemployed worker is. An unemployed worker is one who cannot find work at the wage normal for the given country.

Keynes formulates this "scientifically" in the following manner: "Men are involuntarily unemployed if, in the event of a small rise in the price of wage-goods relatively to the money-wage, both the aggregate supply of labour willing to work for the current money-wage and the aggregate demand for it at that wage would be greater than the existing volume of employment."[1]

Or take another example: it is common knowledge that the volume of personal consumption under capitalism depends first and foremost on the total wages and profits. Keynes's "scientific" formulation of this reads: "For whilst the other factors are capable of varying (and this must not be forgotten), the aggregate income measured in terms of the wage-unit is, as a rule, the principal variable upon which the consumption-constituent of the aggregate demand function will depend."[2]

The simple and well-known fact that a capitalist will hire more labour only if this gives him additional profit, is formulated by him as follows:

"The aggregate demand function relates various hypothetical quantities of employment to the proceeds which

---

[1] J. M. Keynes, *The General Theory...*, Ch. 2, p. 15.
[2] Ibid., Ch. 8, p. 96.

their outputs are expected to yield; and the effective demand is the point on the aggregate demand function which becomes effective because, taken in conjunction with the conditions of supply, it corresponds to the level of employment which maximises the entrepreneur's expectation of profit."[1]

This scientific "intricacy" and obscurity gives the professors a chance to demonstrate their own "scientific" methods. Keynes's pseudo-scientific chatter about the "wheat-rate of interest", "copper-rate of interest", etc., is typical "oversubtlety".

His elaborate and long-winded way of expressing himself is usually an attempt at disguising the class-biased nature of his teaching. He maintains that full employment is the cause of inflation, i.e., that the workers are responsible for inflation. But Keynes does not say it as straight-forwardly as the capitalists of today, who constantly blame wage increases for the inflation. Keynes is much subtler. He writes: "When a further increase in the quantity of effective demand produces no further increase in output and entirely spends itself on an increase in the cost-unit fully proportionate to the increase in effective demand, we have reached a condition which might be appropriately designated as one of a true inflation."[2]

Keynes's eclecticism is also a godsend for the professors. They find in it some of the old theories and can thus interpret the historical roots of Keynesian theories in any way they choose.

With Keynes's help they are able to defend capitalism more subtly, going so far as to criticise it. They can express deep regret that the working people are still living in poverty under capitalism. But, also with Keynes, they can declare that it is not exploitation, not the extremely uneven distribution of the national income that is at the root of the evil; that it is, in fact, not capitalism at all! There are other reasons, they say, such as:

"That the world after several millennia of steady individual saving, is so poor as it is in accumulated capital-assets, is to be explained ... by the high liquidity-premi-

---

[1] J. M. Keynes, *The General Theory...*, Ch. 6, p. 55.
[2] Ibid., Ch. 21, p. 303.

ums formerly attaching to the ownership of land and now attaching to money."[1]

On the other hand Keynes justifies the unevenness of incomes and property. He writes: "I believe that there is social and psychological justification for significant inequalities of incomes and wealth. . . ."[2]

In another place he declares that the unevenness in the distribution of incomes is too large. This enables the learned professors to interpret Keynes as a "radical" petty bourgeois.

In conclusion we should like to point out that the varied and often extremely complicated mathematical formulas Keynes uses to create the impression of a "scientific" approach are of not the slightest help in understanding the economics of capitalism. All he does is to reiterate truths we have known for decades in mathematical terms. Let us analyse, for example, his first formula, the one he calls the "supply function".

The capitalist hopes to make a profit (Keynes designates this Z). To these ends he hires several workers who produce a certain amount of output or of value and surplus value (depending on whether we consider the process in physical or money form). The output he designates O_r. All other conditions being equal, the hiring of additional labour force brings with it a corresponding extension of production. This very simple ratio Keynes expresses mathematically as follows: P(the supply curve) is equal to:

$$\frac{Z_r}{O_r} = \frac{\Phi_r(N_r)}{\Phi_r(N_r)}.$$

All this means is that the mass of the output (a definite profit being assured) depends on the number of employed workers, a fact obvious even to the layman.

His other mathematical formulas are similarly useless in widening our knowledge of capitalism, being merely an outward show of "scientificalness".

* * *

---

[1] J. M. Keynes, *The General Theory...*, Ch. 17, p. 242.
[2] Ibid., Ch. 24, p. 374.

Let us summarise.

Keynes's popularity is explained not by his defence of capitalism but by the fact that he cloaks this defence by an aura of pseudo-scientificalness and a sterile criticism of capitalism. Keynes's popularity is explained not by his depth of knowledge, not by new ideas, but by eclecticism.

His popularity shows that monopoly capital cannot find a better answer to the insoluble contradictions of capitalism, the prelude to its historically inevitable doom. *The dominance of Keynesian ideas is proof of the ideological bankruptcy of monopoly capitalism.*

THE ASIATIC MODE
OF PRODUCTION

In his Preface to *A Contribution to the Critique of Political Economy*, a short outline of world history, Marx wrote: "In broad outlines Asiatic, ancient, feudal, and modern bourgeois modes of production can be designated as progressive epochs in the economic formation of society."[1]

This shows that Marx attached no less importance to the Asiatic mode of production than to the later modes of production.

Nevertheless, the term "Asiatic mode of production" has disappeared from Soviet Marxist literature. It is mentioned neither in textbooks on political economy, nor in textbooks on Marxism-Leninism. Throughout the 51 volumes of the Great Soviet Encyclopaedia there is no mention of an "Asiatic Mode of Production". All attempts to find out why so important a tenet of Marxist theory has been omitted will be in vain. It is simply passed by in silence, condemned and forgotten.

A rejection of this postulate would be justified in one of two cases:

a) If this postulate were merely a chance remark made in passing, to which Marx never referred again, having thus by implication rejected it himself. However, we shall prove that this was not the case.

b) If Marx's concept were at fault. Marx was not infallible. He himself would be the first to indignantly deny any statement to this effect. Over a hundred years ago this genius foresaw the historically transient nature of capital-

---

[1] Marx and Engels, *Selected Works*, Vol. I, Moscow, 1958, p. 363.

ism, at a time when capitalism was still facing a period of progressive development, while the workers' movement was only making its first hesitant steps. On the other hand, his prediction of the simultaneous downfall of capitalism in all the industrially developed European countries, and the time he set for this collapse, did not materialise.

But he was rarely wrong: the above mentioned cases refer to particulars of future development and not to an analysis of past events. The vital role played by Marx's teaching in the formation of modern scientific thought and our world outlook and the infrequency of his mistakes, demand that a rejection of one of his postulates be preceded by a thorough analysis by competent Marxists. As will be shown later such an analysis was not made.

As is usual in such cases, young students should be given an explanation of why Marx's teaching on the Asiatic mode of production was so completely ignored. We do not know what our professors of Marxism-Leninism tell their students and audiences when they are asked why the Asiatic mode of production has fallen into such neglect. Maybe they repeat the words of the Orientalist from the Communist International who, some thirty years ago, told me: "By the Asiatic mode of production Marx understood the Asiatic variety of feudalism." I replied with conviction that Marx was a past master at expressing his thoughts, and that if he had considered the Asiatic mode of production a variety of feudalism, he would have said so.

Besides, Marx, enumerating the succession of "historical epochs" of mankind, spoke of the Asiatic, ancient, feudal and modern bourgeois epochs. If he had regarded the Asiatic mode of production a "variety" of feudalism, the order would have been: ancient, feudal, Asiatic modes of production. His remarks in other places also warrant the conclusion that he placed the Asiatic mode of production before the slave-owning period.

Let us now look at the essence of the problem.

Marx repeatedly stressed that the Asiatic mode of production differed fundamentally from all other modes of production. The problem of the specific features of Asiatic society had interested him (and also Engels) ever since he began his scientific activities and his interest in the problem did not flag right up to his death. We shall not quote all the places in his works relating to this problem—it would take up too much space. Besides, excerpts taken out of context often give a false picture of Marx's train of thought. We shall give only excerpts from works written at different periods of his life in order to show that the term "Asiatic mode of production" is a component part of his economic teachings.

1857. In the Preface to *A Contribution to the Critique of Political Economy* he says: "Thus, only with the advent of self-criticism, could bourgeois political economy begin to understand feudal, ancient and Oriental society."[1]

Marx alternates the terms "Asiatic" and "Oriental", depending on the context.

In 1853 Marx wrote: "Climate and territorial conditions, especially the vast tracts of desert, extending from the Sahara, through Arabia, Persia, India and Tartary, to the most elevated Asiatic highlands, constituted artificial irrigation by canals and waterworks the basis of Oriental agriculture.... This prime necessity of an economical and common use of water ... necessitated ... the interference of the centralising power of Government. Hence an economical function devolved upon all Asiatic Governments, the function of providing public works."[2] He goes on to say that vast areas of Egypt, the Yemen, Persia and Hindustan, which once were flourishing, have now deteriorated into desert because the governments failed to organise public irrigation.

From Marx's above remarks it clearly follows that:

1) the term "Asiatic mode of production" *should not be interpreted in a geographic sense*, since he includes vast areas of Africa. For this reason he sometimes uses not only the term "Asiatic society" but also "Oriental society";

2) *Marx did not extend the concept "Asiatic mode of production" to the whole of Asia*, but only to those regions where the rainfall was insufficient for agricultural production. It follows that it would be useless to attempt to solve the problem of the Asiatic mode of production on the basis

---

[1] K. Marx, *Grundrisse der Kritik der Politischen Ökonomie (Rohentwurf). 1857-1858*, S. 26.

[2] K. Marx, *The British Rule in India* (see Marx and Engels, *On Britain*, Moscow, 1953, pp. 479-80).

of conditions in China, as was done by our sinologists. In most regions of China there was enough rainfall to carry on agriculture without irrigation, especially in former times when the country was less densely populated and there was no need to raise fertility by irrigation.

During the years Marx was working on *Capital*, and Engels on *Anti-Dühring*, they gradually returned to problems of the specific features of Asiatic economy. Let us give a few examples.

"In Asia, on the other hand, the fact that state taxes are chiefly composed of rents payable in kind depends on conditions of production that are reproduced with the regularity of natural phenomena. And this mode of payment tends in its turn to maintain the ancient form of production."[1]

Marx repeats this view in the third volume of *Capital*. "The direct producer ... is to be found here in possession of his own means of production.... He conducts his agricultural activity and the rural home industries connected with it independently.... Under such conditions the surplus-labour for the nominal owner of the land can only be extorted from them by other than economic pressure, whatever the form assumed may be.... Should the direct producers not be confronted by a private landowner, but rather, as in Asia, under direct subordination to a state which stands over them as their landlord and simultaneously as sovereign, then rent and taxes coincide, or rather, there exists no tax which differs from this form of ground-rent.... The state is then the supreme lord. Sovereignty here consists in the ownership of land concentrated on a national scale. But, on the other hand, no private ownership of land exists, although there is both private and common possession and use of land."[2]

He makes a detailed study of conditions in Asia analysing labour rent and laying special emphasis on non-economic coercion in India.

This gives a clear picture of the specifics of the Asiatic mode of production.

In their writings, both Marx and Engels repeatedly

---

[1] Karl Marx, *Capital*, Vol. I, pp. 140-41.
[2] Ibid., Vol. III, pp. 790-91.

touch on the Asiatic mode of production. Engels writes in *Anti-Dühring*: "However great the number of despotisms which rose and fell in Persia and India, each was fully aware that above all it was the entrepreneur responsible for the collective maintenance of irrigation throughout the river valleys, without which no agriculture was possible there."[1]

Engels categorically denies the existence of the feudal mode of production in ancient Asia: "It was the Turks who first introduced a sort of feudal ownership...."[2] To substantiate his view he cites the following fact: "In the whole of the Orient, where the village community or the state owns the land, the very term landlord is not to be found in the various languages, a point on which Herr Dühring can consult the English jurists, whose efforts in India to solve the question: who is the owner of the land?—were... vain...."[3]

There is no need to quote any more extracts from Marx's and Engels's writings: their correspondence right up to Marx's death shows how interested they were in the question of various pre-capitalist forms of development and modes of production. Nowhere do we find an indication that they doubted the existence of a special Asiatic mode of production.[4]

Did Lenin ever refute the term Asiatic mode of production? No, he did not. Nowhere in his writings do we find anything to that effect. On the contrary, he recognised the Asiatic mode of production.

In one of his first works—*What the "Friends of the People" Are and How They Fight the Social-Democrats*—

---

[1] Engels, *Anti-Dühring*, p. 248.

[2] Ibid., p. 244.

[3] Ibid., pp. 243-44. Academician N. N. Konrad, a great authority on oriental languages told me that he endorsed Engels's statement.

[4] One opponent of the view that in the past there had been a special Asiatic mode of production, declared that Marx and Engels had revised their point of view because the term is used only in the Preface to *A Contribution to the Critique of Political Economy*. This is pure pedantry. Marx often used different terms for the same phenomenon depending on the aspect he wanted to stress. In *Capital* we meet the terms "capitalist mode of production", "capitalism", "capitalist society", "capitalist social system", etc., all of which mean the same thing.

he quotes the above excerpt from Marx's Preface to *A Contribution to the Critique of Political Economy* in full and expresses his agreement with it. The same applies to a later article entitled "Karl Marx". Moreover, Lenin did not even exclude the possibility of the Asiatic mode of production having also existed in Russia. In his polemics with Plekhanov, who considered the nationalisation of land regressive because it had existed in *Muscovy*, Lenin wrote: "Insofar as (or if) the land was nationalised in Muscovy, the economic basis of this nationalisation was the *Asiatic mode of production*. But it is the *capitalist mode of production* that became established in Russia in the second half of the nineteenth century, and is absolutely predominant in the twentieth century.... He confused nationalisation based on the Asiatic mode of production with nationalisation based on the capitalist mode of production.... The logical deduction from his premises is the restoration of Muscovy, i.e., the restoration of the Asiatic mode of production—which is a sheer absurdity in the epoch of capitalism."[1]

Opponents of the Asiatic mode of production attempted to interpret these words of Lenin as a refutal of Marx's thesis. This is wrong. Lenin does not deny the existence of the Asiatic mode of production per se: he only doubts that this mode of production existed in Muscovy (and he is right in so doing, since one of the main elements—wide-scale irrigation organised by the state—was absent).

Finally we have Lenin's notes on the margin of his recently published conspectus of the correspondence between Marx and Engels. One of these remarks reads: " 'The *key*' to Oriental *customs is the absence of private ownership of land*." "All land is the property of the head of state."[2]

"Asiatic villages are self-contained, self-sufficient (natural economy), constitute the *basis* of Asiatic customs +public works of the central government."[3]

* * *

[1] V. I. Lenin, *Collected Works*, Vol. 10, p. 332.
[2] V. I. Lenin, *Conspectus of Correspondence of K. Marx and F. Engels, 1844-1883*, Russ. ed., Gospolitizdat, 1959, p. 260.
[3] Ibid., p. 263.

At the discussions held in Tbilisi and Leningrad in 1930-31, the existence of the Asiatic mode of production was denied and it was transformed into an "Asiatic variety of feudalism". The editors' note to the Tbilisi discussions reads: "The development of the Asian countries has, throughout history, been highly individualistic. In a certain sense this peculiarity has created a special structure of feudalism which may be called the Asiatic mode of production."[1]

An identical formulation can be found in M. Godes's concluding remarks at the Leningrad discussion: "We prefer to speak of a peculiar feudalism in the Orient, and not of an Asiatic mode of production."[2]

The extensive and lively discussion did nothing to further science. If it were only a question of whether we should call a definite mode of production "Asiatic mode of production" or "Asiatic variety of feudalism" this would mean that from a scientific point of view the discussion was nothing but a storm in a teacup. What's in a name?

We shall try to throw light on the maze of ideas expressed during these discussions. But first let us once more emphasise that true Marxists, no matter how highly they esteem Marx, never regarded his works as set dogma. If new facts demanded that changes be made in Marx's propositions, this would be in full keeping with the spirit of Marxism. The only qualification is that such changes be well-founded.

Is the denial of the existence of an Asiatic mode of production as an independent mode, differing from all other modes of production, well-founded? In our opinion it is not.

A denial of the Asiatic mode of production would be justified a) *from a theoretical point of view*: if the features peculiar to society in a number of Oriental countries, on the basis of which Marx singled out the Asiatic mode as one independent of and differing from all other pre-capital-

---

[1] *Ob aziatskom sposobe proizvodstva* (On the Asiatic Mode of Production), Russ. ed., Zakkniga Publishers, 1930, p. 14.

[2] *Obshchestvo marksistov vostokovedov. Diskussiya ob aziatskom sposobe proizvodstva* (Society of Marxist Orientologists. Discussion About the Asiatic Mode of Production), Moscow-Leningrad, Russ. ed., Sotsekgiz, 1931, p. 170.

ist modes of production including feudalism, were insufficient, and hence such a singling out would be unjustified;

b) *from a concrete-historical point of view*: if it were proved that in the history of human society no people lived in the conditions Marx characterised as the Asiatic mode of production.

The assertion, or even the implication, that Marx (and Engels) in saying one thing meant another, that Marx and Engels themselves did not understand their own teachings sufficiently well, as was often implied at the discussion, is *obviously intolerable*.

In our opinion the participants in the discussion, a narrow circle of Orientologists, sinologists and historians, were not competent to solve this theoretical problem. Not a single well-known and competent Marxist philosopher or Marxist economist attended. We cannot say for certain whether the Orientologists there were sufficiently competent to solve this concrete historical question, but we doubt it.[1]

In our opinion, the main reason for the confusion was that many of the participants, although frequently quoting Marx, did not understand his dialectical method.

Let us glance at the book written by G. Dubrovsky,[2] one of the main opponents of the Asiatic mode of production.

Dubrovsky is a very "bold" person. He radically revises Marx's teaching on modes of production. Of the modes of production Marx described as "progressive epochs in the economic formation of society", he leaves only two: the ancient (slave-owning) and the capitalist. He completely denies the Asiatic mode of production, splits the feudal into two modes of production: the feudal and "serfdom", introduces "the economy of small commodity producers" as a special mode of production and discerns three specific modes of production within socialism: "the economy of the transition period—the epoch of the dictatorship of

---

[1] The discussion centred mainly on the question whether an Asiatic mode of production existed in China or not, and, if so, what aspects of it had been preserved or had disappeared. Yet many of the principal opponents of the Asiatic mode of production did not understand the Chinese language and were unable to read Chinese characters.

[2] See G. Dubrovsky, *K voprosu o sushchnosti "aziatskogo" sposoba proizvodstva*, etc. (Concerning the Essence of the "Asiatic" Mode of Production, etc.), Russ. ed., Moscow, 1929.

the proletariat", "socialist economy" and "the economy of the epoch of world communism".[1] In all, he enumerates ten types of economy and modes of production. Having wrongly understood or interpreted Lenin's remarks, he declares that Marx understood capitalist, but not precapitalist modes of production.

All this nonsense has been rightly refuted by our historians. Anyone who has an inkling of history knows that feudalism and "serfdom" in Europe were closely interlinked and often alternated.

Marx writes: "To whatever extent rent in kind is the prevailing and dominant form of ground-rent, it is furthermore always more or less accompanied by survivals of the earlier form, i.e., of rent paid directly in labour, corvée-labour, no matter whether the landlord be a private person or the state."[2]

As regards the "economy of small commodity producers", Dubrovsky quotes Marx, and the quote itself proves that it can be found in the most widely differing epochs of world history. Thus, if it can be found both in the ancient epoch and under capitalism, i.e., *within* various modes of production, it follows that it cannot be a special mode of production.

Dubrovsky's tenets were refuted but the actual foundations on which his faulty concept rests have never been criticised. It is based on a complete ignorance of dialectics. To him A is always A, and B is always B. He cannot understand that a phenomenon seen from one angle may be A, but becomes B when seen from another. Lenin's famous example with a glass by which he attempted to explain dialectics to Bukharin does not seem to have convinced Dubrovsky. Or to take another example. Gold is always gold. But in the mining industry gold is an ore, in metallurgy—a metal, in chemistry—an element, to a goldsmith—a raw material, to a Shylock—the embodiment of wealth, to a commodity producing economy—a measure of value, under capitalism—world money, to an emission bank—the backing of the banknotes issued. In each case it is the same gold and yet it is far from being the same thing.

[1] G. Dubrovsky, op. cit., pp. 17-19.
[2] Karl Marx, *Capital*, Vol. III, p. 794.

Dubrovsky's mistake is rooted in a false, undialectic understanding of the famous place in the Preface to *A Contribution to the Critique of Political Economy*, where Marx says: "At a certain stage of their development, the material productive forces of society come in conflict with the existing relations of production, or—what is but a legal expression for the same thing—with the property relations within which they have been at work hitherto."[1]

Any Marxist realises that production and property relations are one and the same thing even when regarded from different viewpoints.

This remark by Marx is interpreted by Dubrovsky and also by E. Iolk and some other opponents of the Asiatic mode of production without any regard for the principles of dialectics. The "legal" is part of the ideological superstructure: for this reason, they say, property relations are not a component part of the economic basis and have nothing in common with production relations. "It is quite obvious," Dubrovsky declares, "that property relations, and land relations, in particular, are not a basic but a superstructural phenomenon. . . ."[2]

He repeats this over and over again in his book. Being unable to understand that two different things can create an entity, that property relations and production relations are one and the same thing, he writes: "The quoted excerpts do not change Marx's and Engels's basic proposition that it is not the forms of property that determine the mode of production, but vice versa—that they are determined by the mode of production and production relations."[3] Moreover he says: "It would not enter a Marxist's head to explain the mode of production by property forms. . . ."[4]

It would be difficult to make a more serious blunder. First he splits up an entity, then declares that the two resulting parts have nothing in common.

Marx writes: "It is always the direct relationship of the owners of the conditions of production to the direct producers—a relation always naturally corresponding to a

---

[1] Marx and Engels, *Selected Works*, Vol. I, p. 368.
[2] G. Dubrovsky, op. cit., p. 27.
[3] Ibid., p. 142.
[4] Ibid., p. 143.

definite stage in the development of the methods of labour and thereby its social productivity—which reveals the innermost secret, the hidden basis of the entire social structure...."[1]

This means that the development of the productive forces determines the mode of production and the property relation, forming an entity with the former. In pre-capitalist social formations property relations determined the relations of lordship and servitude.

Marx also wrote: "In all forms in which the direct labourer remains the 'possessor' of the means of production and labour conditions necessary for the production of his own means of subsistence, the property relationship must simultaneously appear as a direct relation of lordship and servitude."[2]

This shows that Marx unites the productive forces, property relations and relation of lordship and servitude into the mode of production.

Let us attempt to explain this in the simplest way possible. Every normally thinking person will realise that:

if the land and water were not *state property* but belonged to the direct producer of material wealth, there could not have been an Asiatic mode of production.

If, in addition to the means of production, the producers of material wealth had not been the *property of the slave-owners*, there could have been no ancient mode of production.

If the land had not been the *property of the feudal lord* but had been owned directly by the producer of material wealth, the peasant would not have been dependent on him (serfs) and there could have been no feudal mode of production.

If the means of production were not the *property of the capitalist*, and the workers were not deprived of them, there could not be a capitalist mode of production.

The mistake of Dubrovsky, Iolk and many others is all the more remarkable since they themselves witnessed the birth of the socialist mode of production. They should have seen that it was insufficient merely to overthrow the

---

[1] Karl Marx, *Capital*, Vol. III, p. 791.
[2] Ibid., p. 790.

political power of the bourgeoisie, that it was also necessary to confiscate their property in the form of means of
production, to transform them from private to public
ownership in order to lay the foundation for a socialist
mode of production. To assert that the property form has
nothing in common with the mode of production is sheer
stupidity.

For the sake of clarity we should like to elucidate some
of the principal propositions explaining the category "mode
of production".

1) The expression "mode of production" is a *scientific
abstraction*, a singling out and summing up of the decisive
properties of social production. It never existed in a pure
form. "We are only concerned here with striking and general characteristics; for epochs in the history of society are
no more separated from each other by hard and fast lines
of demarcation, than are geological epochs."[1]

2) *Modes of production are not immutable. They are in
a state of constant change.* The main reason for this is the
development of the productive forces which, at a certain
historical stage, undermines the existing mode of production and creates[2] the shoots of the new mode of production.
It is precisely to these constant changes that Marx coun-
terposed the permanency—naturally not absolute—of the
Asiatic, and particularly the Indian, form of economy.

In addition to the development of the productive forces,
several other factors play an important role in changing
the mode of production, one of the most important being
that of force. The invasion of the Roman Empire by the
Germanic tribes accelerated the transition from a slave-
owning to a feudal mode of production; in America, European colonialists created a new capitalist economy based
on slave labour; the conquest of India by Britain destroyed
or at least accelerated the downfall of India's economic
system, etc.

In connection with the division of society into the
owners of money and commodities on the one hand, and

---

[1] Karl Marx, *Capital*, Vol. I, p. 371.

[2] The socialist mode of production is an exception: only the prerequisites for the transition to socialist relations mature under capitalism; there can be no socialist production within the capitalist framework.

workers on the other, a condition typical of the capitalist system, Marx wrote: "It is clearly the result of a past historical development, the product of many economic revolutions, *of the extinction of a whole series of older forms of social* production."[1]

But this chain of historical changes is dialectically interlinked with historical unity, for it is only logical that every new mode of production, once it has become dominant, must begin with the productive forces it inherits from its precursor.

In the final analysis, it is not only on a world scale, but also on a national scale that remnants of the past and shoots of the future mode of production live side by side.

Marx declares: "Bourgeois society is the most developed and most diversified historical organisation of production. The categories expressing its relations, and understanding of its organisation, enable also us to penetrate into the organisation and production relations of all the extinct social forms, of the bits and elements of which it is built, partly dragging along remnants not yet overcome, partly developing to the full what formerly was no more than an indication."[2]

This is also true of the present epoch of monopoly capitalism. After the liberation of a large number of the peoples in Central Africa from colonial dependence, it was found that in a number of cases the ancient tribal system had been preserved almost unchanged. In South Germany, Austria and Switzerland there still are remnants of the former Germanic communal property of land in the form of communal pastures and forests, which are used jointly by the local peasants. Almost open slavery continues to exist in the Portuguese colonies, where the state forcibly "enlists" workers for work in the Rhodesian mines, etc. In Saudi Arabia slavery was officially abolished only on November 6, 1962; in practice it continues to exist to this day. In Eastern Turkey there exists an almost classical feudalism, and some landlords own up to 500 villages. Strong remnants of feudalism have also been preserved in

---

[1] Karl Marx, *Capital*, Vol. I, p. 169 (italics mine.—*Y. V.*).
[2] K. Marx, *Grundrisse der Kritik der Politischen Ökonomie* (*Rohentwurf*). *1857-1858*, S. 25-26.

the south of Italy, while, at the same time, monopoly capital has fully developed in the north—this in spite of the fact that Italy is a comparatively small country.

There is not and never were "pure" modes of production; they all undergo constant changes. In addition to the dominating one there are always survivals of past and shoots of future modes of production (socialism being the sole exception).

3) *All class-antagonistic societies*, irrespective of their mode of production, *are based on the exploitation of the direct producer of material wealth.* Marx says that wherever a part of society has a monopoly over the means of production, the direct toiler must voluntarily or involuntarily produce means of subsistence for the owners of the means of production.

This refers also to the Asiatic mode of production, although in that instance the state was the owner of the land, the decisive means of production. "We must not forget," Marx said, "that these idyllic village communities, inoffensive though they may appear, had always been the solid foundation of Oriental despotism.... We must not forget that these little communities were contaminated by distinctions of caste and by slavery...."[1]

4) In all class-antagonistic societies there is a constant class struggle.

5) All pre-capitalist modes of production are based on (a) the production by the direct producer for his own needs and (b) the needs of the exploiter, the owner of the means of production; only a small share of the output assumes a commodity form. In addition to the generally low level of development of the productive forces a vital role was played in this respect by the absence of transport facilities capable of conveying bulk cargoes over land. Draught animals were the only means of transportation. Bulk cargoes could be shipped only by water, but here too the volume of shipments was limited by the small capacity of the vessels and the absence of mechanical movers. Vessels had to be hauled upstream by men or animals.

In summing up we can say the following: historical modes of production never existed in a pure form, they are

---

[1] Marx and Engels, *On Britain*, p. 397.

variable and constantly changing—the dominant mode of production lives side by side with remnants of the former and shoots of the coming mode of production; different modes of production have some features in common. For example, every class-antagonistic society is based on exploitation and is the scene of constant class struggle; all pre-capitalist modes of production are based on production for the satisfaction of personal needs; at present the Asiatic mode of production is not dominant anywhere in the world. It was on these points that Orientologists based their assertion that the Asiatic mode of production is a type of feudalism. In our opinion this is both an unnecessary and unwarranted correction of Marx's original concept.

* * *

If we were to examine the Asiatic (Oriental) mode of production as it was depicted by Marx, and classical feudalism as it existed in Western Europe, as scientific abstractions, and then compared the two, it would become quite clear that we are dealing with *two entirely different modes of production*, having different superstructures.

Under the Asiatic mode of production the land—the most important means of production—was *state property*. Under classical feudalism it was the *property of the feudal lords*. "Nulle terre sans seigneur" says the law of feudalism. The land was inherited en masse by the eldest son (that the land was considered a fief from the king, which he put at the disposal of the feudal lord, and which, in the absence of heirs, was supposed to return to the royal house, was of little practical significance).

According to Marx the Asiatic mode of production existed in desert areas, where rainfall was scarce and the population concentrated on small irrigated strips of land. There was no shortage of labour. Irrigated land was very expensive. Typical in this respect is that the measure for land in China, the *mu,* is $^1/_{16}$ of a hectare. For this reason land censuses were made even in ancient times and the ownership of cultivated land was registered.

Under classical feudalism there was plenty of land but not enough labour to work it.

For this reason feudal lords attacked neighbouring

regions, captured peasants and cattle and moved them to their own lands.

Documents from the Middle Ages clearly show the difference in value attached to land and to labour force. When feudal possessions passed to a new owner, boundaries were only roughly delineated: from such and such a river to such and such a mountain, from the highway to the forest, etc.

In contrast, any transfer of labour force was described in detail; not only was its number shown but also its particular skills, e.g., two blacksmiths, two carriage makers, three coopers, etc. In Russia, right up to the first half of the 19th century not only the dessiatins of land but also the number of serfs was mentioned.

Under the *Asiatic mode of production* the state is the only primary owner of the surplus product created by the direct producer—of the ground rent in the form of taxes. All the exploiting layers receive their unearned incomes through the state.

Under *feudalism* the landowner is the direct exploiter, appropriating both the labour rent and the rent in kind. The state has nothing, or very little, to do with it.

Under the *Asiatic mode of production* the state fulfils a function vitally important for the population: it builds and controls irrigation systems. They can be built only on large areas and without them there can be no agricultural production in these arid regions (they also serve as protection against floods). This gives rise to a strong centralisation of state power which often assumes the form of an "Asiatic tyranny", in which officials are appointed for definite periods. The state takes measures to see that food reserves are laid in against possible bad harvests. The well-known biblical story, according to which Joseph advised the Pharaoh to lay in stocks of grain during seven fertile years to provide for the succeeding seven years of draught, reflects the existence in Egypt of the Asiatic mode of production at the time the Bible was written.

Under classical feudalism the feudal lord himself fulfilled most state functions, and the state had no economic role to play. The feudal lord was the concentrated embodiment of all forms of exploitation: he ruled the peasants with the help of his armed soldiers, presided over them in court, could fine them, imprison them, condemn them to death and execute them. Every feudal lord was supreme master of his possessions. The king was the *primus unter pares*. In some countries, such as Germany, Poland, Hungary, the king or emperor (during some periods) was elected by the feudal lords. His power extended only to his own possessions, and no further. If a powerful feudal lord became king, he sometimes subjected the weaker lords to his power. But this was the exception rather than the rule.[1]

The feudal state—if it can be considered a single state at all—did not have any economic, administrative or legislative functions. These were fulfilled by individual feudal lords. Even the waging of wars was essentially their domain. The state troops were actually the sum total of the troops of the feudal lords, and fought under their own banners. The king could declare war but the feudals could refuse to send their troops. If they arrived, the war began, if not, there was no war.

The above shows that the *nature of the Asiatic mode of production differs fundamentally from that of the feudal mode of production* and that there is no reason to reject Marx's classification and to characterise the Asiatic mode as a variety of feudalism.

* * *

There is no need for detailed historical studies to decide whether an Asiatic mode of production really existed or not; it was never a question of whether such a mode historically existed, but whether it should be regarded as an independent mode of production or as an Asiatic variety of feudalism.

Yet, to convince those who may still doubt its existence we shall point out to two important facts.

a) In both African and Asian deserts, towns have been found buried by sand; indeed archaeologists are constantly discovering more. How could towns with large temples,

---

[1] It was only when feudalism was disintegrating, when the "third estate" that gave birth to the bourgeoisie had already emerged, when the infantry began to take the upper hand in battles with the cavalry of the feudal lords, that "absolute monarchies" based on these forces could emerge.

pyramids, etc., grow up in the middle of the desert? Considering the low level of development of the productive forces, how could the large population inhabiting those towns live without irrigation systems, i.e., without a strong central power building and controlling the water system; or, in other words, without an Asiatic mode of production?

b) In Oriental languages, as we noted above, there is no word for "landowner". Language is a product of history. How can we explain the absence of this word in the Orient, if there was no Asiatic mode of production but feudalism and landownership?

It is far more difficult to find documentary evidence to prove the existence of the Asiatic mode of production. The lack of sources relating to these ancient times is responsible for vacillations in the views of scholars. We shall quote Academician V. Struve.

In 1928 he denied the existence of an Asiatic mode of production.

In 1931 he declared that the Asiatic mode of production had existed in ancient Egypt: "After studying all ... facts, I...have come to the conclusion that there really was in Egypt some sort of a special formation which cannot be called feudal.... Work on irrigation systems preserved this primeval community ... even after the exploiting ruling clique had separated from it.... Only by preserving this community could the public works necessary to irrigate the land be carried out.... Typical of the Asiatic mode of production was that owing to the institution of public works for irrigation the community did not disintegrate, was artificially preserved. It is also noteworthy that it continued to exist until comparatively recent times, right up to the Ptolomean epoch."[1]

Speaking of the vital importance of water in Egypt he said: "The Egyptian peasant ... in many cases owned land but did not own the water, and was only granted the use of it. To show that he is subordinated to someone, the Egyptian says: I am on his water, or, I am on his canal."[2]

Academician Struve gives his conclusion in the following

---

[1] *Diskussiya ob aziatskom sposobe proizvodstva* (Discussion on the Asiatic Mode of Production), p. 96.
[2] Ibid., p. 97.

sentence: *If I should be asked how long the Asiatic mode of production existed in Egypt, I should say that it existed up to the Roman epoch, when Roman rule introduced a different formation.*"[1]

Later Struve again declared that there was no Asiatic mode of production in Egypt, that it was a slave-owning society.

An identical state of affairs is said to have obtained in China. I shall abstain from offering an opinion on the then widely discussed question of whether or not there really existed an Asiatic mode of production in China, since I, like the majority of the participants in the discussion, do not possess sufficient qualifications to give an expert opinion.

China is a very large country; it was inhabited not only by the Chinese but also by other peoples who were at a lower stage of development. Her history is many thousands of years old, and has witnessed class battles, coup d'états, foreign invasions, etc. It is therefore even more difficult to study the constantly changing, distintegrating and intertwining modes of production in China.

Another major difficulty lies in interpreting Chinese writings dating back four thousand years, since the characters then used were far more complicated than those used at present. Among Chinese scholars there are wide differences of opinion on how these ancient characters should be deciphered.

The differences in the interpretation of a single character could give rise to differences of opinion as to whether somewhere, at some period or other there existed a feudal or some other social system in China.

We maintain that the Asiatic and feudal modes of production are two different modes and that the former also existed.

* * *

Today, thirty years after the discussion on whether the Asiatic mode of production was a variation of feudalism. it is difficult to see why the existence of this mode of pro-

---

[1] *Diskussiya ob aziatskom sposobe proizvodstva,* p. 99 (italics mine—Y. V.).

duction was denied with such stubbornness and why Marx's proposition was misinterpreted. This is all the more surprising if we remember that the Comintern Programme accepted by all Communist Parties three years before the discussion, spoke of countries in which there were still remnants of that mode of production.[1]

This problem was of both scientific, political and strategic interest to China. The opponents of the Asiatic mode of production declared that everybody (including the author of this book) who did not recognise the social order in China of the twenties as ordinary feudalism was a political enemy. Such an attitude barred the way to a solution of these important questions.

It would be a waste of time to go into a detailed analysis of the arguments advanced by the opponents of the Asiatic mode of production. Since they did not understand Marx's dialectical method, did not heed his repeated warnings that every generalisation must be based on a detailed study and analysis of concrete facts, their arguments, based on quotations taken out of context and misinterpreted, boil down to a statement that Marx was a bad Marxist, and did not understand Marxism!

Iolk, one of the participants, declared that "the theory of the 'Asiatic' mode of production" contradicts ... the basic principles of the Marxist-Leninist teaching on society..."[2], this in spite of the fact that in his Preface to *A Contribution to the Critique of Political Economy* Marx attaches equal significance to the Asiatic, ancient, feudal and capitalist modes of production as epochs in the historical development of humanity.

This was not just a statement made in the heat of the discussion. He repeats his view in the magazine *Pod znamenem marksizma* (Under the Banner of Marxism). "... The conception of a special 'Asiatic' mode of production is es-

---

[1] The most rabid opponents of the existence of the Asiatic mode of production tried to justify their stand by saying that in the Programme the term "Asiatic mode of production" was given in inverted commas. In their opinion this should be interpreted as a denial of that mode. But why should the Programme mention the Asiatic mode of production at all if it was of absolutely no importance? The inverted commas were a concession to the doubtful.

[2] *Diskussiya ob aziatskom sposobe proizvodstva*, p. 68.

sentially an anti-Marxist system...."[1] In his speech at the discussion he said: "The Asiatic mode of production ... is theoretically unfounded, because it contradicts the foundations of the Marxist-Leninist teaching on classes and the state."

This statement is tantamount to saying that Marx did not understand his own teaching.

To mitigate this flagrant mockery of Marx, Iolk said that by the term Asiatic mode of production Marx meant something entirely different. This is merely adding insult to injury.

M. Godes, the main speaker for the opponents of the Asiatic mode of production at the discussion acted with greater circumspection. Speaking of Marx's statement in the Preface to *A Contribution to the Critique of Political Economy* he stated: "The whole context, just like the Preface as a whole, makes it impossible to say that this is an accidental formulation. Every one of the modes of production enumerated in it represents a specific social formation and holds a definite place in the succession of formations, that, in which they were placed by Marx....

"...It is about time to stop discussions on whether Marx recognised the Asiatic mode of production as a specific social formation. We must not close our eyes to Marx's indisputable statements, even if we do not share his view on the Asiatic mode of production."[2]

Any Marxist could agree to this. How then did Godes, proceeding from a correct premise, arrive at a denial of the Asiatic mode of production? He declared that in Marx's time many facts about the Oriental countries were unknown and that Marx, who was not familiar with Lewis H. Morgan's research, therefore advanced the existence of the Asiatic mode of production as a working hypothesis. "Marx ... had, on the one hand an idea of primeval relations, on the other—of the system of ancient society with its sharp class differentiation, the gap in Marx's understanding of the historical process compelled him to look for the missing link."[3]

---

[1] *Pod znamenem marksizma,* 1931, Russ. ed., No. 3, p. 133.
[2] *Diskussiya ob aziatskom sposobe proizvodstva,* pp. 21-22.
[3] Ibid., p. 24.

Godes's other arguments differ but little from those of the other opponents of the Asiatic mode of production. He, too, reaches the conclusion that "the Asiatic mode of production is nothing but feudalism". Like Dubrovsky, he advances the identical conditions for the exploited and the exploiters as his main argument. The reply to this, we think, has been given above, when we compared the Asiatic mode of production with feudalism.

We thus see that all the opponents of the Asiatic mode of production are agreed that Marx himself was wrong. Godes explains this by Marx's poor knowledge of facts; Dubrovsky says that Marx understood the capitalist mode of production but not the feudal; and Iolk declares bluntly that Marx did not understand his own teachings. All this is backed up by quotes from Marx's writings.

The denial of the former existence of the Asiatic mode of production was silently sanctioned by Stalin when he failed to mention it in his *Dialectical and Historical Materialism*.

The problem can be reduced to the following: did recent research prove Marx's "hypothesis" wrong or not? Did an Asiatic mode of production exist at any time in history? I do not consider myself competent enough to give a *categorical* answer to these questions.

I think that the time has come when competent Marxist scholars—philosophers, economists and historians—should re-open this discussion and rehabilitate Marx's and Engels's correct (in my opinion) teaching on modes of production.